POLITICAL STRUCTURES
AND DEMOCRACY IN URUGUAY

Political Structures and Democracy in Uruguay

Luis E. González

Published for the Helen Kellogg Institute
for International Studies by
UNIVERSITY OF NOTRE DAME PRESS
NOTRE DAME, INDIANA 46556

Library of Congress Cataloging-in-Publication Data

González, Luis E.
    Political structures and democracy in Uruguay /
    Luis E. González.
        p. cm.
    Includes bibliographical references.
    ISBN 0-268-01589-9
    1. Uruguay—Politics and government. 2. Political
participation—Uruguay. 3. Democracy—Uruguay.
4. Political parties—Uruguay.
I. Title.
JL3681.G66 1991
320.9895—dc20   90-70850
                                                      CIP

Manufactured in the United States of America

To Luis Javier González and Margarita Ferrer

Contents

Acknowledgments

Since I was born in Montevideo in 1945 I had a first-hand experience of life in a democratic order, and I also witnessed the whole process which led to the breakdown of democracy in Uruguay in 1973. Many young students of my generation, including some friends, became involved in the radical, revolutionary left. I felt that the whole enterprise was crazy, but I was not able to sustain those feelings in a reasoned way. Therefore, I became a student of the social sciences, beginning studies in a systematic mode in 1974 in Bariloche, Argentina, just in time to witness the debacle of Peronism, the birth of another military regime, and the reiteration of some histories I already knew so well. Because of that, too, when I had to plan my Ph.D. dissertation—of which this book is a revised version—I wanted to study the 1973 breakdown. Juan Linz convinced me that I could do that later if I so wished, but that the present involved more urgent problems that somebody had to study. He proved right; I could reflect about that bitter past looking towards the future, which helped me, I think, to work in a more dispassionate way. This is only the first of the many debts I owe to him.

Margaret Keck read the whole text, suggested many useful ideas, and provided critical help when I was working in New Haven and Juan Linz was busy in Spain; besides, she greatly improved my rather poor English. In Montevideo I am particularly indebted for sharing insights, work, and innumerable discussions to César Aguiar, Carlos Filgueira, Jorge Notaro, and Diego Piñeiro. Agustín Canzani, Andrés Rius, and Mónica Vives shared generously with me their experience in the intricacies of the work of pollsters—they already were six-month veterans of an intense campaign when I began to work with them. Margarita Huber and Rosario Peyrou coordinated a difficult work with legislators. Scott Mainwaring and a reviewer from the University of Notre Dame Press also read the whole manuscript and suggested many improvements. Chances are that I did not wholly follow their advice wherever this book looks more like a dissertation than like a book. My friend Charlie Gillespie, whose untimely death we still mourn, helped me in many ways both in Montevideo and New Haven. Adriana Raga was the first editor of most of the text; she helped me to clarify my ideas and was a permanent stimulus throughout the whole work. The responsibility for the final product is of course mine.

The field work for this research was possible thanks to a doctoral fellowship from Inter-American Foundation. I was able to finish the writing thanks to a grant from the Ford Foundation. Equipos Consultores Asociados allowed me to use and reprocess the results of a post-electoral survey conducted in February, 1985, and to quote some results of two surveys conducted in November and December of 1989, most of them already published in the Montevidean weekly *Búsqueda*. I must thank collectively the Uruguayan legislators who were willing to share their time and ideas and to answer a not-so-brief questionnaire. I know that perhaps few of them will agree with all my conclusions, but I hope they will think I did a honest Job and that their time was not wasted.

I am grateful to all the persons and institutions mentioned above, and I also have some deep personal debts which will remain private except for two of them: to Carmen and Inés my apologies for my absences during their first years.

1. Introduction:
Political Structures and
Democracy in Uruguay

1. Democracy

This study is concerned with the prospects for democracy in Uruguay, which I think is both possible and desirable. At least in part because of personal experience, I believe Dahl is right in saying that those "who have actually experienced life under severely repressive hegemonic regimes rarely argue that differences in regime are trivial" (Dahl 1971, p. 7). Nevertheless, I hope that this definite normative bias in my approach to these themes will not affect the analysis presented in the following pages. The *desirability* of democracy is not the subject of this study; instead it discusses several issues regarding its *stability*.

The theoretical point of departure is thus a definition of democracy. For the present purpose, this definitional problem is solved best by Dahl's *polyarchy* (Dahl 1971). His general discussion of the main dimensions of polyarchy—participation and opposition—seems to me a difficult but successful synthesis of history, normative concerns, and analytical rigor. Though for most of us democracy is a multidimensional concept, it makes sense to consider a purely political dimension of democracy—polyarchy— which, according to Dahl, consists of (a) meaningful political *participation* and (b) the possibility of organizing public *opposition* towards those who govern and their policies.

Dahl *operationalizes* these two main concepts as multiparty systems (opposition) and regular elections (participation) plus the usual legal guarantees that protect them. This operationalization involves some difficult theoretical problems concerning its applicability in the so-called third world or "developing" countries which do not fulfill certain minimum levels of modernization and material well-being—often referred to as "threshold conditions" or "prerequisites" for democracy, though Dahl himself chose more nuanced terms.

Leaving aside these situations, however, Dahl's case looks very strong. Among societies which have surpassed those minimum threshold conditions it seems true that: (i) the institutional arrangements involved in Dahl's operationalization of democracy have allowed a consistent development of individual and collective rights and liberties which in turn reinforced the possibilities and opportunities for meaningful political participation and opposition; and it also seems true that (ii) no other set of institutional arrangements has led to those results—in fact, all other paths have led to significant restrictions of political participation and opposition. With regard to affluent societies with market-oriented economies—the "first" world—these statements have not been seriously disputed since World War II. Eastern European citizens have just vigorously affirmed that in their view they are true for the now revolutionized "second" world as well.

Thus, the most difficult theoretical problems concern essentially the question of democracy in the "third" world. In order to discuss Uruguayan democracy, however, it is not necessary to tackle those problems. For it is clear that Uruguay—as well as Argentina and Chile—already satisfied several decades ago any reasonable, empirically based characterization of the threshold conditions for democracy. It is useful to keep in mind these considerations, though, for it is equally clear that at least some Latin American countries—e.g., Haiti—have never fulfilled those prerequisites. It follows that there is no single common theoretical perspective within which to study the prospects for democracy in Latin America. Although this is an unpleasant conclusion, I do not see how can we avoid it. At any rate, to acknowledge this seems better than to maintain a rather vague terminology according to which the questions of democracy in Argentina and Haiti, for example, may be discussed as if they shared the same theoretical grounds.

It may be added that polyarchy, as Dahl understands it, is not a synonym for democracy in either empirical or normative terms—though in the rest of this book I will use *democracy* meaning *polyarchy* to avoid a somewhat pedantic departure from established practice. Even after a polyarchy has been consolidated the pursuit of democracy remains open. At least within the contextual limits mentioned above, however, that pursuit *requires* polyarchy. This is, in my view, the basic rule as to which should be the political priorities of the region. Polyarchy has been an elusive possibility in some parts of Latin America for many years; today its range of possibility—in spite of the so-called "lost decade" for development—has expanded considerably. But it still is a mere possibility. What is needed in a large part of Latin America is the building and consolidation of polyarchies.

2. The Oldest Latin American Democracy

The Uruguayan polity was uncommon in the Latin American context. For many years it was unanimously seen as one of the few real democracies in the region.[1] For this and other reasons—including the small size of the country and some atypical institutional innovations—it was often called "the Switzerland of Latin America."

This polity was built upon other peculiarities. The country was colonized very late, in the first half of the eighteenth century. Before then it was only sparsely populated by tribal societies that did not practice agriculture, so that the present population is mostly Spanish, with a strong Italian component, and completely homogeneous, with no socio-ethnic cleavages. At the beginning of this century the per-capita income was comparable to that of Canada. The country has lost that position in the past eighty years, but its former relative affluence is still reflected in social and economic indicators. The distinctiveness of the Southern Cone countries in the Latin American context is a well known fact, but Uruguay fares well even by comparison with this special subset. According to a recent source, Uruguay's GNP per capita (US\$ 2,820 in 1981) was higher than those of Argentina, Brazil, and Chile. The adult literacy rate (94 percent) and the number enrolled in secondary school as a percentage of the age group (60 percent) were also higher in Uruguay than in the other three countries. Life expectancy at birth (seventy-one years) was equal to Argentina's, and higher than in Brazil and Chile; the Uruguayan infant mortality rate (thirty-nine per thousand) was the lowest of the four countries. Urban population as percentage of total population (84 percent) was the highest. The Uruguayan income distribution probably is still the most egalitarian among the four nations.[2]

Uruguayan democracy also fares well in relation to the rest of the Southern Cone. Comparing democratic performance is not as simple as comparing, say, per capita GNP. Nevertheless, the distance between the Uruguayan and the Argentinian and Brazilian historical records is large enough to make detailed examination unnecessary, This is not so with regard to Chile. For the present purpose, however, it may suffice to note that (i) during the present century the Uruguayan military was effectively subordinated to civilian rule until 1973 (even during the de facto regime in the 1930s), which was not the case in Chile; (ii) both in Chile and Uruguay the rights actually granted to *political* opposition seem to have been approximately equivalent, but not those granted to other organizations, since unions' and workers' lives were far harder in Chile;[3] and (iii) the franchise widened considerably earlier in Uruguay than in Chile: illiterates and 18- to 21-year-olds have been able to vote since 1918 in Uruguay, and since 1970 in Chile; Chilean women first voted in 1952, whereas the Uruguayans did so in 1934. As a result, extensive suffrage in Chile "is a very recent phenomenon; the enfranchised portion of the population... fluctuated between 7 and 15 percent from the 1880s to the 1940s,"[4] whereas in Uruguay it surpassed 20 percent in 1920. Thus, taking into account Dahl's dimensions of polyarchy—participation and opposition—and an additional criterion within the region—military subordination to civilian rule—we may conclude that by the mid-1960s Uruguay probably was the most democratic polity in South America.[5]

Uruguayan polyarchy was born in 1918, or perhaps even in 1916 (Barrán 1986). Although its life was interrupted twice—"suspended" between 1933 and 1942, and directly replaced by an authoritarian regime from 1973 through 1984—Uruguay is still the Latin American country which has lived longest under democratic regimes. In fact, Uruguay is also the only Latin American nation where the demise of the old oligarchical order brought about a real democratization from the beginning of the twentieth century (Cavarozzi 1981, pp. 9–13). By the mid-1960s the Uruguayan polity had, in principle, all the elements of a mature polyarchy. Exceptional by Latin American standards, that political system was not so surprising in view of the characteristics of Uruguayan society, which fulfilled most, if not all the conditions usually mentioned as prerequisites for democracy.

3. Political Structures and Democratic Stability

The breakdown of Uruguayan polyarchy in 1973 is particularly significant in comparative perspective, for Uruguay is perhaps the most notable instance "in which a relatively long-standing democratic system has been replaced by an internally imposed authoritarian regime" (Dahl 1985, p. 40). If strong, restrictive definitions of polyarchy are considered, then all other cases had experienced "less than twenty years under democratic institutions" (ibid., p. 39). This was so even in Chile because of the relatively limited extent of suffrage until the reforms of 1958 and 1962. The Uruguayan breakdown thus presents a unique opportunity to probe the problems concerning democratic stability. This reinforces the rather obvious point that the discussion of the prospects of democracy in Uruguay after the 1984 restoration must begin with the reasons that led to the 1973 breakdown in the first place.

Some of the political actors involved—particularly those from the left—and some observers as well think that the breakdown was *unavoidable* because of the position of the country in the international system, or its class structure and distribution of resources, or both. This position seems unproductive to me for several reasons. First, it cannot be tested because of well-known difficulties concerning counterfactual statements. Second, it shares a common logic with now discredited ideas on the impossibility of economic development—or even economic growth *tout court*–in dependent countries with market-oriented economies. Because the latter proposition was supposed true, it followed that democracy under conditions of dependent capitalism was ultimately impossible: the choice—in Uruguay as in the third world in general—was between fascism[6] and socialism. Needless to say, the recognized falseness of the premise does not necessarily imply that the conclusion is false as well. Without the premise, however, the conclusion becomes an isolated, atheoretical statement. The history of the argument also suggests that the mechanisms of a self-fulfilling prophecy contributed at least in part to the breakdown. Third, the main fault of the thesis of inevitability is not so much its likely falseness but its sterility. It makes superfluous the really interesting questions concerning *how* the process actually developed, questions whose answers would enable us, I think, to understand *why* things happened as they did. Finally, relaxing the meaning of *unavoidable* does not alter these conclusions. During the process leading to any large accident—that is, any event whose occurrence is not necessary—one or more critical errors occur until a point is reached in which the final crisis becomes indeed inevitable. *Inevitability* might simply mean that this point is reached at an early stage of the process.[7] But even in these terms the no-return stage in Uruguay seems to have happened late enough as to make useless the idea of inevitability. A comparison with Chile is instructive in this regard. The Uruguayan coup of 1973 was not a tragedy in the classical sense that it has been said Chile's was: a situation whose most likely outcome perhaps most of the main actors correctly foresaw and disliked, but felt that they could do nothing to avoid.

Assuming that there were solutions that could have avoided the breakdown, it follows that political elites were not able to find and/or implement them in due time. Uruguay was no exception to Linz's conclusion: "In the last analysis, breakdown is a result of processes initiated by the government's incapacity to solve problems for which disloyal oppositions offer themselves as a solution" (Linz 1978, p. 50). Democratic politicians were absolute majorities within each branch of the legislature. How can we explain that collective failure of most of the civilian political elite? It had several causes. There was plain bad luck and the presence of men particularly unsuited to their first-rank roles in truly critical circumstances—because they were incompetent or lacked democratic commitment or both. In many cases leaders made the wrong choices, and sometimes they attempted to rectify their course when time had already run out. *Democratic authenticity* in Linz's terms was an early victim: it no longer existed five years before the coup of June, 1973. During that period all the factors were present that Linz described as accompanying the process of loss of power of civilian governments, which in turn leads to the death of democracy (Linz 1978, pp. 75 and ff.). That death

> is often recorded . . . as associated with the date of a particular event . . . But in fact, those fateful days or hours preceding the events that marked the end of a regime were only the culmination of a long and complex process. (ibid., p. 80)

The process was indeed long in the Uruguayan case: it took almost two decades. Four general elections, five administrations and their legislatures, and many more cabinets proved unable to solve the constellation of problems which had appeared in the mid-fifties. Not all the parties, fractions, and politicians involved in those cumulative failures were incompetent. This strongly suggests that the problem-solving methods themselves were part of the problem. Confronted with intrinsically difficult problems, Uruguayans also had to deal with ways of doing politics which complicated even more the task of finding solutions to them.

This conclusion underscores the contribution of political processes to the breakdown of democracy. It is a relatively uncommon emphasis, for the analysis of democratic breakdowns

> seems to alternate between an emphasis on the ultimate structural strains (particularly social-economic conflicts, inequality and rapid social economic change, and dependency) and on the period of open strife that immediately precedes the breakdown. This dual emphasis neglects the political process itself, functioning under constraints and often contributing to the conditions that generate rebellion and violent conflict. (Linz 1978, p. 39)

Furthermore, even the studies which do analyze those political processes usually focus on the strategies followed by the political actors and the eventual patterns which emerge from their choices rather than on the *politico-structural* constraints to those strategies and choices. More generally, in the studies on democratic breakdowns "structural problems" normally stand for socio-economic problems. This does not necessarily involve as social or economic reductionist bias. The instoration of polyarchy is by definition a discontinuity which deeply affects the preexisting political system. When a democracy is born at least some of the critical rules of the political process change, and with them all the other components of the system change to some extent as well. The political structures of a very young democracy are thus bound to be in a somewhat fluid condition.[8] This helps to explain their relative absence from the literature on democratic breakdowns for, as Dahl points out, almost all those breakdowns occurred in regimes that had lasted less than one generation. Uruguay's democratic breakdown was perhaps the most notable exception to this rule; because of that it is also reasonable that the Uruguayan case be an exceptional opportunity to study the eventual effect of politico-structural factors on democratic stability.

That is exactly the central concern of this research: the analysis of the effects of politico-structural factors on democratic stability in Uruguay. It will attempt to show that

(i)   some traits of the Uruguayan political system which preceded demo-
       cracy—its presidential tradition, a two-party system, and the fraction-
       alization of the two major parties—remained in place during the initial
       stages of polyarchy and lasted uninterruptedly no less than half a cen-
       tury; they had thus become political *structures*;

(ii) when confronted with severe crises some of those traits— particularly
       presidentialism and the fractionalizatian of the major parties—contrib-
       uted to the loss of efficacy, efficiency, and legitimacy which in turn led
       to the 1933 and especially to the 1973 breakdowns, and

(iii) although by 1973 some of those structural aspects had changed, pre-
       cisely those responsible for the effects pointed out in (ii) remained
       in place. In fact, from a structural point of view the changes—decay
       of two-partyism, increasing fragmentation and polarization of the party
       system—worsened the situation. The 1984 restoration restored that
       worse scenario.

These statements do *not* imply that the politico-structural factors *determined*
the breakdown; they did contribute considerably to it, however. They set a
scenario in which the breakdown became likely if other pressures appeared.
Nevertheless, if (i)–(iii) are true, it follows that at least in some important
regards the prospects for democracy in Uruguay are less than good. The authoritarian regime did not solve any of the difficult socio-economic problems
it inherited, and added some new ones of its own. Socio-economic constraints
have thus worsened, and the politico-structural factors that in the recent past
contributed to the breakdown remain in place; this is more than enough to
conclude that the consolidation of democracy confronts serious obstacles.

Other conclusions also follow from (i)–(iii). The political factors under
consideration are *structural*: in the short run they are relatively independent
of the will of the political actors. In a democratic order the structure of the
party system, for example, simply cannot be modified overnight. Therefore
in the short run democratic stability will depend heavily on the willingness of
the political elite and on the quality of their performance. These are no mean
requirements: the political elite as a whole failed on both counts prior to
1973. What is needed is an extraordinary—in its exact sense—performance
from that elite. Thus, in the short run the critical question is whether the
lesson received, or suffered, by the democratic political leadership during the
authoritarian order will be enough to sustain the overload.

At least during the first democratic government following the restoration (1985–1989), the political elite actually gave, according to several criteria, an extraordinary performance. An extraordinary performance, however,
is by definition limited in time. In the medium run some changes are needed
to attain democratic consolidation. The initial successes of elite cooperation

in sustaining democracy might be extended to tackle some of the most difficult socio-economic problems. Nevertheless, such broad cooperation becomes
less and less likely as a new election approaches, the feeling of the exceptional nature of the historical circumstances fades away, and politics return
to more normal routines. If, however, the elite decided to cooperate, positive
results would not be immediate; reversing a long stagnation and the skeptical
attitude of the population would take time. During that time the reactions
at the mass-public level would become crucial; a strong upsurge of popular
support for disloyal or even semiloyal political actors could easily stop the
cooperative efforts of democratic elites before they could bear fruit.

If the successful cooperation of democratic elites does *not* extend to
social and economic matters, which now seems the most likely course of
events, then it becomes necessary to change the political structures referred
to in (iii) above in order to avoid the restoration of the dangerous pre-1973
scenario. This, in turn, requires a substantial institutional overhaul. Changes,
however, are constrained by the two following factors. First, they need a
solid majoritarian consensus from the political elites. Theoretically it might
seem easier to reach such consensus on *procedural* matters like these than on
the pressing socio-economic problems. Nevertheless, because the short-term
consequences of changes in procedural rules may be different for each of
the actors involved, consensus may not be achieved easily. Some—perhaps
as many as necessary to block any significant change—may resist new rules
which affect negatively, or are perceived as affecting negatively, their position
in the balance of power resulting from the status quo, irrespective of the
long-term, abstract soundness they assign to those rules. The prospects for
any change of that kind depend thus on the elites' views about both the
specific issues involved and their impact on the present positions of the
actors. Second given that any real change of those political structures cannot
be instantaneous even if the elites finally decide to move in that direction,
there is a transitional, relatively extended period during which mass-level
reactions to the events would also be decisive.

Thus, to complete an assessment of the effect of politico-structural
factors on the prospects for Uruguayan democracy two additional questions
must be addressed. They are the final questions this study will discuss:

(iv) Which long-term trends, if any, may be discerned in the political mood
of Uruguayans?

(v) What are the elites' views on the problems identified in (ii) and (iii)
above and on eventual solutions to them? Is there any reason that makes
the kind of agreements the occasion demands difficult or unattainable?

We can now summarize the purpose of this research—and advance its main
findings as well. The central question addressed by this study is that of

democratic stability in Uruguay. Most democratic breakdowns so far have occurred in very young democracies which had experienced a democratic order during less than one generation; the single most important exception is perhaps Uruguay. Uruguayan democracy was born in 1918 and was interrupted twice, in 1933—an authoritarian situation that lasted until 1942—and 1973. The first breakdown belongs to the group of those occurring in young regimes; the second is the exception. Several explanations have been suggested for the two coups, centered essentially on social and economic problems and on the dynamics of short-term political conflicts. Most of them have contributed to a better understanding of those breakdowns. Nevertheless, this study attempts to show that *politico-structural* factors have had a considerable effect on those events as well, for they create a structural predisposition favoring such results. These political structures have been the *fractionalization* of the major parties and the *quasi-presidential* Uruguayan institutions, compounded in 1973 by a moderate increase of the fragmentation and a high increase in the polarization of the party system.

A systematic, comparative analysis of the evolution of the party system during the last thirty years will show that this state of affairs offers no sign of change in the short and medium run, and in so doing it will probe the old problem of the nature of the fractions of the parties from a new perspective. A study of the attitudes of the relevant political elites will explore then the chances of political reform with rather negative but not hopeless conclusions.

From a broader perspective the most important conclusion of the study concerns some structural risks built into the presidential institution. Comparative evidence suggests that fractionalization per se has not had in other places the same effect it had in Uruguay, but that patterns of confrontation similar to those discussed in Uruguay do appear in other instances of democratic breakdown under presidential systems.

4. Methodological Remarks

The goals stated above are rather ambitious; they are truly demanding with regard to the different kinds of evidence they need if a reasonably complete analysis is to be achieved. The nature of the actual evidence has not always matched those needs. The core of this book, written in 1987, is based on the available literature, on several primary and secondary sources, and on two main data sets: a public opinion survey conducted in Montevideo in 1985, and a survey answered by Uruguayan legislators in 1986. A section of the last chapter, written in 1990, discusses briefly the later events, especially the November, 1989, election, and concludes that the main trends identified and described in the book have been so far strongly confirmed by those events.

The first of the main data sets analyzed in this book, the Montevidean public-opinion survey, was conducted in Uruguay's capital city two months after the election of November, 1984, that restored civilian government and democracy.[9] It is not a national sample. Lacking more complete information, however, this survey provides data still highly relevant for the present purpose. On the one hand, Montevideo includes about half the country's population; in particular, in the 1984 election 47.5 percent of the electorate and 46.5 percent of the actual vote was Montevidean. On the other hand, during the present century the country has been governed essentially by urban, Montevideo-base elites. Montevideo has always been the most modern half of the country and usually took the lead or at least accompanied all important political changes; even in the remarkable 1958 election, normally seen as a victory of the rural country, the winning party also won Montevideo. Thus, it might be argued that if the goal is *prospective*, a focus on Montevideo may help to see more clearly the direction of political winds.

The interviews were conducted in February 1985. In retrospect, the timing of the survey was excellent. According to Gallup International, the mood of the Uruguayan population was at its best: the percentage of adult population who thought that, for people like themselves, "the world in ten years' time will be a better place to live in than it is now" was the highest among sixteen nations with comparable data.[10] That mood followed the political events: an overwhelming majority of the population had voted for the opposition to the authoritarian regime; the new legislature was opened on February 15; and the new president was to be inaugurated on March 1. The feeling of overcoming difficult times and the new hopes undoubtedly contributed to an unusual frankness; the level of refused answers to the question on the interviewees' vote was exceptionally low. One thousand interviews were completed—in the interviewees' homes—of a sample of adult residents in Montevideo's urban area. The sample exhibited the relatively small biases usually found in the firm's regular work,[11] and a satisfactory fit was obtained for the question on the vote in the November election and the election's results. Accordingly, the data reported throughout this study is that of the unweighted sample.

The second data set, specifically designed for this research, is a survey answered by the members of the new legislature. Needless to say, legislators cannot be seen as the political elite *tout court*, not even from the view of the most staunch supporters of the positional approach to the study of political elites. For the present purpose, however, a focus on the members of parliament is appropriate for several reasons. First, the legislature, and particularly the Senate, includes at any given time most of the really influential politicians. Parliament thus includes the upper stratum of the party elites. Second, parliament itself has been and still is a relatively powerful institution,

The Vote of Montevideans in the 1984 Election (Percent)

	Sample	Election	Difference
Partido Colorado	33.2	35.5	-2.3
Partido Nacional	25.6	26.6	-1.0
Frente Amplio	35.3	33.2	2.1
Other *	2.1	4.7	-2.6
Refused answer	3.8	–	–
(N **)	(961)	–	–

* Almost exclusively voters of the Unión Cívica, a small, Catholic-based party, both in the sample and at the polls.

** Excludes those who said they did not vote. Montevidean voters were about 900,000.

especially by comparison with most Latin American legislatures. It has been considered—with Chile and Costa Rica—one of the "deviant cases" of the Latin American context. The three legislatures were "relatively influential in a world scale," unlike those of their neighbors, which had "little decisional influence."[12] Third, eventual solutions to the politico-structural problems of (ii)–(iii) require legal and constitutional changes. Parliament would be the central locus of such political engineering. Finally, that political engineering normally does not concern extra-party political elites because of its very nature; those elites are not experts on arcane subjects such as electoral law, and they are not directly affected by them, which explains their relative disinterest. In short: legislators are the main protagonists of the political engineering needed to tackle the problems this study will discuss.[13]

The legislative survey was conducted in the southern hemisphere winter of 1986. No important political events occurred during the field work, which assures the comparability of the answers. The average interview took about one hour, sometimes divided in more than one session. Except for very few cases, the interviewees seemed interested in the contents of the questionnaire. The Uruguayan legislature being relatively small,[14] all legislators were asked for their collaboration. It was possible to complete 107 questionnaires, that is 83 percent of the whole legislature. That figure is remarkably close to those obtained in other comparable studies.[15] Nevertheless, there were noticeable differences between the response rates of the legislators of the different parties. For that reason, data corresponding to the whole legislature or to each chamber considered separately have been always weighted in order to reflect the real political composition of the legislature. The error margin introduced by the weighting is considerably smaller, I think, than the error that would result from considering the set of answers as an accurate picture of the legislature or of each chamber. This point will become clear in later chapters.[16]

Response Rate of Legislators (Percent)

	Senators	Representatives	All
Partido Colorado	69	66	67
Partido Nacional	73	97	91
Frente Amplio	100	100	100
Unión Cívica	–	100	100

Entries are percent of respondents within each cell. The number of legislators of each party in each chamber, in the same order of the table, are Senate: 13, 11, 6, 0; Representatives: 41, 35, 21, 2.

It is difficult to discuss the themes of this study in an orderly fashion. There are disagreements in the literature on some very basic points presented at the beginning of the exposition; I will return to them at different stages of the analysis as new evidence provides fresh arguments. The most notable example of these basic disagreements is the party system itself: some believe that the country has had a two-party system, and others argue that it was a case of extreme pluralism. The discussion will be ordered as follows. The historical arguments concerning the negative effect of certain political structures on Uruguayan democratic stability are presented in Chapters 2 and 3. Chapter 4 establishes the basic continuity of the party system and political elites of the 1984 democratic restoration with those preexisting the 1973 coup. This, added to the continuity of the institutional framework, assures that the democratic restoration will have to confront the same politico-structural problems whose effects were studied in Chapter 3—although this does not imply, of course, that political elites will deal with them in the same ways as in the past. Chapters 5 to 7 provide a considerably more detailed study of the party system as of the 1984 election, pointing out similarities and discontinuities with the past. They allow, on the one hand, an assessment of the effects of those discontinuities on the politico-structural constraints discussed in Chapter 3; on the other hand, they uncover some important long-term trends in the electorate to which any prospective exercise must pay attention. Chapter 8 focuses on the relevant political elite. A collective politico-ideological portrait of the legislators examines the elite's views on the problems discussed in the previous chapters. Chapter 9 summarizes the historical argument and reviews several relevant data on the 1989 election, confirming the trends described in the preceding chapters; finally, it attempts to put together the different threads in a general discussion of the effects of political constraints on the prospects for democracy in Uruguay.

2. Uruguayan Political Structures: Historical Background

1. A Lasting Party System

There is no general, comprehensive history of the Uruguayan political parties. Scholarly literature on parties is scarce; probably the pre-1930 years have been better studied than the later period.[1] Nevertheless, the general traits are well known. The core of the party system, the Blanco (White) and Colorado (Red) parties, is about 150 years old, as old as the country itself. Certainly in the past century they were not political parties in the present sense of the term, but they were strong political organizations with mass following—and even armies—and they survived uninterruptedly to the present. These parties, also called "traditional" parties, were born out of the following of the leading caudillos in the post-independence years. An early civil war, the Guerra Grande, was a decisive moment in their development. As a result of the characteristics of the war and the participation Argentinians and Brazilians had in it, it may be said that Uruguayan parties preceded the truly unified nation-state. At least until the turn of the century, the parties enjoyed more loyalty from a considerable mass of citizens than the institutions that embodied the state. Some of the main traits that were to characterize the traditional parties until after World War II also took form during the Guerra Grande and its aftermath. The Colorados became the Uruguayan version of Latin American liberal parties, being more liberal, cosmopolitan, urban-centered and antichurch than the Blancos, who became the Uruguayan conservative party. But the differences were a matter of degree; both parties were cross-sections of the Uruguayan society. Each party had the support of half the country. Not even foreign nationals—at least the biggest immigrant communities—were indifferent to them: Spaniards tended to be Blancos; Italians and Frenchmen, Colorados.

These traits proved enduring. Religious matters being particularly non-conflictive in Uruguay, the only significant social cleavage associated to some extent with the opposition between the traditional parties is the rural-urban one. The parties have been multiclass-based since the beginning, and their followers have covered a relatively wide ideological spectrum, especially during this century. This blurs even more the possibility of making distinctions

13

between them on objective grounds. Hence the emphasis in most if not all descriptions of the traditional parties is on their personalistic character and on the subtlety of the differences distinguishing a Colorado from a Blanco. Often it is said that such differences can be really perceived only by direct participants in Uruguayan political culture.

Blancos and Colorados between them won about 90 percent of the vote until the mid-sixties. Several parties shared the remaining 10 percent. After World War II the Blancos held office from 1959 through 1966, while the Colorados governed during the remaining years until the 1973 coup. In principle, a two-party system was defined, for two large parties controlling 90 percent of the electorate rotated in office and the several minor parties sharing the remaining 10 percent never entered—nor were they asked to enter—into coalitions with the governing major party. Nevertheless, this broad historical picture of the Uruguayan party system has been subjected to two major criticisms.

The first criticism is that the two major parties occupied very different positions in the system during most of their existence. According to Sartori, Uruguay was a case of a predominant-party system within a two-party format, not a two-party system (Sartori 1976, Section 6.5, passim, especially p. 197), for in his view the Colorados were a predominant party from 1868 to 1959, and again from 1967 on. It is important to keep in mind the nature of Sartori's distinctions: the *format* is simply the *number* of relevant parties. Irrespective of the format, if there is a party capable of winning at least three consecutive majorities in the lower chamber in actually free and open elections, then we have a predominant-party system (ibid., pp. 195 and 199). The distinctive characteristic of a predominant-party system is that one party governs alone without caring much about the other political actors' views—the only limit being, of course, that of maintaining democracy. A two-party system is a two-party format working with the logic (or "mechanics") resulting from reasonably frequent alternation in government and/or lack of legislative majorities; it is clear that either way the situation naturally imposes on the government party the need to take into account the opposition, hence the idea of *system*, and it is equally clear that these traits are not determined merely by a two-party format, hence the distinction between the two concepts—*format* and *system*. The difference is often blurred by the common practice of using the term *system* in a purely descriptive manner, as a simple synonym for "the existing configuration of parties," irrespective of the actual "mechanics" according to which they interact.

Using Sartori's own definition of predominance, however, Uruguay was *not* a case of predominant-party system because: (i) Real electoral guarantees did not come until 1918, which leaves the period 1868–1918 out of the discussion. Furthermore, I think that no Uruguayan historian would subscribe to the thesis that had elections been actually competitive during that period, the Colorados would have been a predominant party in Sartori's sense. (ii) From 1918 to the 1933 coup the Colorados never obtained "three consecutive majorities" in the lower chamber; they won an absolute majority in 1919 and 1922, lost it in 1925, and were unable to recover it later. The same happened in the powerful Senate: in 1925 the Colorados had only 42 percent of the Senate seats, and from then through 1933 they always won less than 37 percent of the seats. (iii) The authoritarian situation initiated in 1933 may be considered completely superseded by 1942; the four following elections—1942, 1946, 1950, and 1954—were all won by the Colorados, but in 1946 they failed to win an absolute majority in the lower chamber. (iv) The Blancos won in 1958 and 1962. (v) The Colorados won again the three following general elections, 1966, 1971, and 1984, but in the two latest they got little more than 40 percent of the seats in the lower chamber, and they lost the 1989 election to the Blancos. Thus, according to Sartori's definition the Colorados never became, strictly speaking, a predominant party. Nevertheless, this conclusion seems equally misleading when confronted with the data. Although the 1946 election broke the chain of three consecutive majorities required by the definition, it seems reasonable to consider the Colorados a predominant party from 1942 through 1958.[2] If this is so, under *democratic* governments Uruguay has indeed had a two-party system most of the time so far, but the Colorados managed to become a predominant party during about a third of the country's democratic life.[3] Political life continues under nondemocratic governments, however, and it is a politically relevant fact that from 1868 to 1917 and from 1934 to 1942 the Colorados always controlled the (nondemocratic) government.[4] The last third of the nineteenth century, in particular, should be considered as a failed Colorado attempt to become an hegemonic party in Sartori's sense. In short: Sartori's view contributes to a better understanding of a certainly complex process; according to his own definition and to the data, however, the traditional picture of a two-party *system* still remains true during a full half of the democratic life of the country.

The second criticism of this traditional view concerns the internal structure of both parties. Throughout the present century the traditional parties have been, and still are, highly fractionalized.[5] In fact, most of the time both parties have been rather loose coalitions of fractions. Frequently the ideological distance between certain fractions of different parties—measured against the left-right continuum—turned out to be smaller than the one existing between fractions within each party. Stressing the ideological undifferentiation of the traditional parties, a keen observer wrote in 1930 that within them,

> they can accommodate individuals who support all kinds of ideas, even the most disparate among them . . . , thus, the case of the coexistence

of two opposing groups [i.e., fractions belonging to rival parties] both professing, however, exactly the same ideals. (Martínez Lamas 1946, pp. 116–117)

As a result, it has been said that this apparent bipartyism badly disguised an actual multiparty system. One of the most forceful arguments is Lindahl's. He wrote that the Colorado fractions during the 1920s were *parties* because "they all had independent party organizations and because there was no common, permanent organization for all the Colorado parties," and, even though Colorados claimed to have a common program, "this was more a way of speaking." From the vantage point of the early 1960s he concluded, with regard to both traditional parties, that "a multiparty system has been in existence in Uruguay for four decades" (Lindahl 1962, pp. 40 and 273 respectively). Sartori agrees with Lindahl. In a footnote to a passage on the parties' possibility of being as organizationless as their own fractions, he wrote: "the extreme case appears to be Uruguay, whose (dubious) two party system is . . . only an electoral façade with respect to the real actors, i.e., the *sub-lemas* of the Blanco and Colorado parties" (Sartori 1976, p. 107, n. 11). Ten years later he reaffirmed this view: considering a seven-country list that included, in his judgment, all contemporary two-party systems, he pointed out that he deliberately excluded Uruguay because that system, and "even more Colombia," are "façade two-party arrangements that fail to meet even the relaxed defining characteristics [of two-party systems]" (Sartori 1986, p. 67, n. 20).[6] This view on the structure of the party system is widely held among intellectuals, particularly those of the left.

Nevertheless, I think the case for a "disguised multipartyism" is wrong. The first reason against it is the sheer endurance of the traditional parties in the face of numerous challengers. In the nineteenth century the Unión Liberal (1855), the Partido Radical (1873), and the Partido Constitucional (1880) were short-lived. The attempts in this century have been far more long-lived, but during two-thirds of the century third parties remained in an electoral ghetto. The Partido Socialista (PS) was born at the turn of the century. It split in 1921: the left wing became the Partido Comunista (PC). The Unión Cívica was born in 1910; half a century later it split as well, its left wing majority becoming the Democracia Cristiana (DC). This is the set of parties which by the mid-1960s had been able to win parliamentary representation. Apparent or real, then, the two traditional parties proved capable of successfully surviving numerous attacks against their preeminence during a very long time—measured against the life span of contemporary party systems.

The second reason concerns the ideological argument. Fractions within the same party may be ideologically very different, whereas the parties themselves may exhibit, on the whole, little difference; hence, it is said, we actually have two *coalitions* of parties. This is not necessarily so, however. In fact, this may be expected when two large catch-all parties—in Kirchheimer's (1966) sense—compete against each other. But the idea, if not the name, of both traditional parties as catch-all parties has been long established. Early observers like Melián Lafinur and Ariosto González described them as unprincipled, with few ideological differences, or directly as nonideological vote maximizers; both writers lamented, as Kirchheimer did, this de-ideologization of politics (Ariosto González 1922; Melián Lafinur 1918). Martínez Lama's comments quoted above make the same point.[7]

Third, the organizational argument favoring the multiparty thesis does not seem convincing. Even if Lindahl is right in his point on the organization of the traditional parties, there existed an important link between the fractions: the process that determined which fractions would run together under each party label. This process was normally directed by the fraction or coalition of fractions which presumably controlled a majority of each party's votes. It was not an arbitrary process, because tradition set limits on the possible outcomes and the minorities, as will be seen below, usually had real leverage. The limits set by tradition were very real; at least since the birth of polyarchy in 1918 fractions might appear or disappear, might even abandon—temporarily or not—their party; but a fraction of one of the traditional parties never became a fraction of the other. The outcome of this process was important in two senses: whether an agreement was reached or not proved sometimes decisive in winning or losing elections; besides, the agreement itself was obviously a crucial step in the nomination of the candidates of each party. This nomination is precisely what has emerged "as the most important function of the present day catch-all party" (Kirchheimer 1966, p. 198), and not only of catch-all parties; this may even be used to define political parties (LaPalombara 1974, pp. 509–510). After the election party lines were relevant for the nominees actually elected. Under normal conditions there were no interparty alliances between fractions for conducting regular government business; ministers belonged to the party in government, usually to different fractions within the party. Fractions and parties defined, then, frontiers of a different kind. It is true that there was little parliamentary discipline; nevertheless,

> unlike Colombia, where dissident factions from both major parties often formed a legislative alliance to oppose the factions supporting the regime, there were no such permanent divisions in the Uruguayan Congress. Individual members could cross party lines in voting, as they do in many countries, but it was an ad-hoc process. (McDonald 1978, p. 236)

Under exceptional circumstances (as the 1933 coup and again before the 1973 coup) alliances that crossed party lines did appear; they are, in my view, the exceptions that confirm the rule, because they indicate how heavy a pressure was needed to break party lines in a systematic manner. Summing up: it must be conceded that this does not amount to a formal organization. Nevertheless, it seems utterly impossible to consider the historical continuity of these links merely as a series of coalitions among minor parties. They suggest that the traditional parties have been indeed parties, although very loosely structured parties.[8]

Fourth, the view Uruguayans themselves had on their parties also supports the latter suggestion. Lindahl was aware of this fact: "for a Uruguayan," he wrote, "it is natural to regard the various traditional parties . . . as factions of the Partido Colorado and the Partido Nacional [Blanco]." But he dismisses the point: "this is due to the power of language over thought," without further comments (Lindahl 1962 , p. 269). The fact that voters indeed perceived them as parties throughout several generations, however, goes a long way towards concluding that they have actually been parties.

Finally, most foreign students of Uruguayan politics have shared this view, as Lindahl himself recognized:

> Nearly all foreign writers on Uruguay seem to have regarded the Colorado Party and the Nationalist Blanco Party as united parties with several factions. Particularly since 1919, this view is obviously erroneous. . . This is understandable in North American observers, accustomed to the rudimentary organization of the American parties, and the poor unanimity in political questions on the Congress level. (Lindahl 1962, p. 340, n. 32)

I think the last commentary is revealing. The case denying the traditional parties the condition of parties has been obscured by definitional problems. In Lindahl's view, certain types of catch-all parties simply are not parties at all. Real de Azúa had already pointed out the same definitional character of several criticisms of the traditional parties:

> it appears obvious, in short, that those who denounce the nonexistence of parties in Uruguay are appealing to a model whose lack of relevance can be seen, not only in all of the Latin American nations, with the possible exception of Chile and Venezuela, but in societies with party systems as old as the United States. (Real de Azúa 1971, p. 230 and passim)

Within the richer nations, Italy and Japan, besides the United States, exhibit an "unusual and somewhat extreme standing in fractional and factional performance" (Sartori 1976, p. 92). Both the Italian Christian Democrats and the Japanese Liberal Party have been described as federations or coalitions of subparties. Sartori's view on the Italian Christian Democrats (for example, Sartori 1966, especially p. 151) is particularly striking to any student of the

Uruguayan parties because of the obvious parallel involved.[9] From a comparative perspective, if we consider those parties—as well as the U.S. Democrats and Republicans—as real parties, the rationale for denying that condition to Blancos and Colorados is unclear. In the end, as Sartori wrote precisely on the Uruguayan case, "the question is . . . whether [Uruguay's] parties . . . are significant units" (Sartori 1976, p. 215, n. 127). I have attempted to show that this has been indeed the case.

The conclusions of the whole discussion may thus be summarized as follows: Uruguay has had two major *parties*, Blancos and Colorados, since the nineteenth century; these parties competed within a two-party *format* until the mid-sixties, and under democratic governments they defined a two-party *system* most of the time.

2. The Institutional Framework

Uruguay's institutional setting has experienced tumultuous changes since the birth of polyarchy, as may be seen from the history of its constitutional law. The 1918 Constitution, which established democracy, was the second in the country's life; the first, founding Constitution was enacted in 1830. Since 1918, however, the Constitution was reformed in 1934, 1942, 1952, and 1966.[10] The sheer frequency of the reforms was compounded by some rather dramatic changes of the highest executive authority: from the presidentialism of the 1830 Constitution to the mixed form established by the 1918 Constitution, which included a president and a bipartisan National Council of Administration in charge of some of the duties formerly attributed to the president; from that mixed form back to a single president in 1934 and again in 1942; from there to a pluripersonal executive again, this time in its purest form,[11] and from this *colegiado* once more to a single president in 1966.

Below this agitated surface, however, two keystones of the Uruguayan institutional setting have remained constant since the birth of democracy. The first I will call, lacking a better term, the *quasi-presidentialism* of Uruguayan Constitutional tradition. The second constant consists of a few, far-reaching core principles of Uruguayan *electoral law*. I will argue later that these constants have deeply shaped Uruguayan ways of doing politics. These foundation stones, their relationships, and their consequences across the years became *political* structures particularly relevant for the present discussion.

We may begin with a brief definition: the essential characteristic of a presidentialist system is that the president is a directly elected chief of state who also governs.[12] It may be added that the president cannot be removed by the legislature except in truly extraordinary circumstances, as through impeachment in the U.S.; it is a criminal procedure which cannot be the result of disagreement on policies. Other characteristics are also more or less typical of presidentialist regimes; some of them have indeed important consequences regarding the mechanics of system, but none has the central, defining role of those mentioned above. In particular, ministers are not supposed to be removable by the legislature; theoretically they are truly "secretaries" of the president.

How does the Uruguayan system appear in the light of this definition? Uruguay's *legal* framework has exhibited since the beginning, in varying degrees of intensity, several of the secondary traits usually attributed to *parliamentary* systems. Under democratic regimes the legislature usually has had the right to interpellate and even to remove ministers. For that reason it has been said that the Uruguayan system has a strong parliamentary basis or that it is, or was, a quasi-parliamentary system. Gros Espiell (1956, pp. 90 and 105 and ff.) called semi-parliamentary or "rationalized parliamentarism" the system defined by the 1934 and 1942 Constitutions. Sanguinetti and Pacheco Seré (1971, pp. 108–109) agreed with that judgment and used the term "neo-parliamentarism" regarding both Constitutions. They argued that the 1952 Constitution—the *colegiado* Constitution—was a return to the quasi-presidentialism of the 1830 and 1918 Constitutions and, finally, that the 1966 Constitution restored a neo-parliamentary system (ibid., pp. 115 and 121, n. 8). According to them, thus, the present Uruguayan system is neo-parliamentary.[13]

In spite of its importance, a legal approach alone is not enough to assess these matters. In its classical sense a Constitution is far more than written or unwritten law: it also includes the set of expectations, mores, and institutions—in sociological terms—describing the mode in which a state is organized. The real Constitution may be very distant from the state of affairs assumed, described, or prescribed by any written text. This is exactly what happens regarding the presidency and the 1830 Constitution. According to the text it was not a truly presidential system, partly because of the position of the ministers and partly because the president was elected by the legislature. In practice, however, most of the time all of this was a juridical fiction. The president was a de facto *first elector* and enjoyed more real power than the president of any democracy. Irrespective of the differences—which were important—in the approaches, values, and behavior of the nineteenth-century presidents, the presidency itself became a very powerful institution. For precisely this reason José Batlle y Ordóñez sought to destroy it, dividing its power among the members of a pluripersonal body. The 1918 Constitution was, as it is well known, a transactional solution that preserved a president deprived of some of his previous power but still in charge of Interior (including the appointment of the chiefs of police in the *Departamentos*), Defense,

Foreign Affairs, and, to some extent, Finance as well.[14] It has been said that as an additional caution Batlle y Ordóñez always used his great political weight to avoid "really popular candidates" becoming presidents, as a further means "to reduce the prestige attributed to the presidency" and, presumably, to reduce the risks that would result from too many power resources clustering in the presidency. All told, he

> failed completely. Immediately after his death it became clear that the majority of his party had forgotten his views on the nature of the presidency. (Lindahl 1962, pp. 203–204)

Four years after Batlle's death in 1929 a democratically elected Colorado president headed a coup and later reformed the 1918 Constitution.

The 1934 and 1942 Constitutions are still viewed as neo-parliamentary systems for, although they established a single chief of state and of government popularly elected and suppressed the National Council of Administration, they also gave the legislature the power of censuring ministers, and the president the symmetrical power of dissolving the legislature and calling general parliamentary elections—provided that less than two-thirds of the General Assembly had voted the censure. If the General Assembly resulting from that election maintained the censure, then the president and the ministers would fall. The president thus appeared as a prime minister in a parliamentary regime. Nevertheless, these theoretical possibilities remained as such. Under the 1934 and 1942 Constitutions that dissolution never occurred, and the whole mechanism was not tested. In practice this would have been extremely difficult; after 1942, in particular, it should be remembered that the Colorados were a predominant party: a large Colorado support would have been needed to oust a Colorado president.[15] The real point is not what could have happened if either Constitution had had time enough to deploy its full potential. In the medium or long run any of them could have weakened the presidency. This did not happen, however, and the presidency was, if anything, more powerful than it was during the so-called quasi-presidential system of the 1918 Constitution.

Once more, this fact is one of the explanations of the 1952 reform. The 1952 Constitution was possible because the politicians who promoted, and finally obtained, the reform sought three different but not contradictory goals: some of them were true believers in the virtues of the pure *colegiado* finally established by the new Constitution; others sought to expand the opportunities of the runner-up party to participate in and control the administration; and still others saw in the reform the only legally available way of blocking another Batlle, Luis Batlle Berres, from acceding to a powerful presidency, for he was expected to be a presidential candidate and the likely winner of the following election (Gros Espiell 1956, pp. 114 and 116; Sanguinetti and

Pacheco Seré 1971, pp. 7–8). The 1952 Constitution satisfied all three groups. Regarding the present concern in particular, it could not avoid the electoral victory of Batllismo, but it left Luis Batlle with considerably less power. In a nutshell, the new Constitution instituted a ceremonial chief of state renewed every year and a four-year collective chief of government, the *colegiado*; the chief of state was simply the presiding member of the nine-person *colegiado*. Batlle became in fact the first among nine equals. In more general terms, the 1952 Constitution produced the weakest chiefs of state since 1918. It would have been far more difficult for a member of the *colegiado* to head a coup like that of President Terra in 1933; according to Batlle y Ordóñez this was, in fact, one of the most interesting virtues of the *colegiado*. From the point of view of the voters, however, they were still voting for president—only that this time there were four, one for each year—and the candidates were the most important leaders of the competing parties and fractions.

During the early sixties many political leaders began to think that the virtues of such diminishing risks of authoritarian temptations no longer outweighed the shortcomings of government by assembly.[16] These feelings led to the inter-party agreement which finally produced the 1966 Constitution. According to its text the presidency became a more powerful institution than it was in any of the Constitutions since 1918. The president, as in the initial definition, is a directly elected chief of state who also governs. His mandate was expanded to five years, and he no longer might be removed by the legislature for political reasons, as the 1934 and 1942 texts at least theoretically allowed. Arguing that the resulting system is neo-parliamentary because the legislature may censure ministers seems to me an erroneous assessment of the global situation. It is true that the legislature may remove ministers for political reasons, unlike what happens in the U.S., but the president of the U.S. cannot dissolve the legislature, whereas the Uruguayan president can. On the other hand, it is clear that the institutional position of the Uruguayan president is stronger than that of a prime minister: the president remains in charge during the whole of his mandate, no matter how difficult a time his ministers might have with the legislature. The actual working of the system reinforces this view. The procedure eventually leading to dissolution was initiated on just one occasion, in 1969. The General Assembly censured a minister, and the president observed that decision. An absolute majority of the Assembly was against the minister, but the majority was not enough to supersede the presidential veto. When that veto came to a vote, however, the Colorado majority voted against its own government "for political reasons which did not imply withdrawing its support to the government," thus surpassing the three-fifths threshold necessary to override the veto and precluding dissolution and the resulting new legislative election. The commentarists I am quoting concluded that "the special characteristics of the vote and the absence of a general election did not oblige a change of policy...which was reasserted by the President" (Sanguinetti and Pacheco Seré 1971, pp. 118–119). The president had thus to change his minister, but not his policy, and a little tactical voting in the legislature was enough to produce that result. A president without a legislative majority could impose his policy; the opposition in fact accepted its defeat at least partly because it was already unsure—the exact word is perhaps *frightened*—about how far the president was willing to go to assert his views. It seems to me that a system that works in this manner simply cannot be called *neo-parliamentary* in any meaningful sense.

The conclusion that follows from this discussion is, I think, clear: under democratic governments Uruguay has been essentially a quasi-presidential system; *quasi* points to the *colegiado* system and to the secondary traits typical of parliamentary systems it has exhibited—some of which still remain. Nevertheless, irrespective of the judgment the *colegiado* may deserve, it is important to notice that both the 1933 and 1973 coups occurred under a more definitely presidential system.

The second foundation stone of the Uruguayan institutional setting is to be found in electoral law. Leaving aside some relatively minor changes—at least by comparison with the huge variations just described—Uruguayan electoral law has had four major characteristics during a long time:

(i)   proportional representation in the election of both chambers;

(ii) closed and rigid lists;

(iii) double simultaneous vote; and

(iv) simple plurality to decide which party wins the presidency.

Since 1934 a further trait was added,

(v)   all elections occur together, once every four years before 1966, and once every five years since then—except during the authoritarian regime.

Proportional representation (PR) has been in force in the lower chamber since 1918, except for the fact that each *Departamento* must elect at least two representatives. It has been in force in the upper chamber as well since 1942. The two chambers differ because the Senate election considers the whole country as a single constituency, whereas representatives are elected separately for each of the nineteen *Departamentos*—although votes are in fact pooled after a first stage of allocation of seats in order to assure global proportionality. The mechanics of allocation of seats in both chambers is based in the D'Hondt system. This PR system has been always a closed and rigid list system. Any alteration of the lists provided by the parties makes the ballot void.[17] Nevertheless, the double simultaneous vote (DSV) system, in force since 1910, does allow intraparty choice. Voters cannot alter party lists, but they can choose among several party lists which compete for the same posts. DSV means that voters vote at the same time for a party and for a specific set of candidates within the party, although they have to select lists—which cannot be modified—among those presented by the rival fractions within each party. Once they choose the party, they have as many options as the lists presented by the party. An obvious consequence of voting for a party is that split tickets are not allowed. Regarding the presidential competition the system may be described—in U.S. terms—as running primaries and the actual election at the same time. A remarkable feature of the system is that the winner of the presidential race is not necessarily the most voted candidate, for the winner is the most voted candidate of the winning party. The party that obtained a plurality of votes is the winner; the winner of a plurality within that party becomes president. Since 1934, finally, all elections occur at the same time.[18] This simultaneity obviously reinforced the effects of the ban on split tickets resulting from the DSV rule.

From the point of view of the voter a party has to be chosen and then, within the party, there are further options exhibiting an arborescent structure. At the top there are a few presidential candidates—between 1952 and 1966 a short list of candidates to the *colegiado*—who usually head the party's main fractions. Below this level there are several options to choose from for each presidential candidate. More than one list to the Senate is usually linked to each presidential candidacy, and more than one list to the lower chamber is usually linked, in turn, to each of the lists to the Senate. A similar picture occurs at the subnational level—i.e., within the *Departamentos*.[19]

All told, this set of rules defines a rather sui generis electoral system. It must be underscored that it is indeed an old structure. Even though its main characteristics did not appear at the same time—and below this structural level there have been other minor changes as well—all its main components have remained stable for a long time, as measured against the life span of contemporary party systems. Except for the composition of the Senate—and its accompanying electoral rules—this structure has been in place since 1934, and two of its central pieces are even older: PR at the lower chamber level since 1918, and the DSV principle since 1910.[20] This means that the whole structure has had a long time to deploy its eventual effects on the Uruguayan polity.

3. Two-Partyism and Fractionalization

We may now return to the main characteristics of the party system. Uruguay had a two-party format until the mid-sixties. Both parties, Blancos and Colorados, were loosely structured catch-all parties. A first question is, how can we explain the high degree of fractionalization of the traditional parties? A second, more general question follows from the fact that the party system was very stable in comparative perspective, particularly taking into account that there were no important, clearly marked social cleavages capable of explaining its formation. How can we explain this stability?

Rival explanations on these matters may be sorted in three main groups: there are two common, diametrically opposed views which may be called the "optimistic" and "pessimistic" views, and a third group which mixes elements of both types. The optimistic view is majoritarian in the center of the political spectrum, and at least in the last twenty years it has been expressed mainly through the press, in the context of political debates; it has had little, if any, supporting scholarly work. According to this view the emergence of the traditional parties, but not their permanence, resulted from historical accident. They enjoyed real popularity because they expressed the feelings and needs of the population at large. Throughout a difficult learning process, the parties became convinced of the virtues of peaceful life under democratic institutions. From then on, the stability of the party system is essentially a consequence of the traditional parties' capability of expressing people's aspirations, eventually evolving and modifying themselves in the process. The two traditions became two distinct, although not antagonistic, historical identities.[21] They were catch-all parties because they truly reflected Uruguayan society: as there were no contradictory ideologies, no deeply rooted divisions, both the Blanco and Colorado followings were recruited independently of existing social cleavages. Even fractionalism has its logic:

> the justification for the traditional parties . . . makes a virtue of necessity and maintains that, being "parties of free men," all "legitimate differences" fit "within "them (as opposed to "among" them . . .).[22]

In short, the essential traits of this view are the adaptability, dynamism, and responsiveness of Blancos and Colorados. These characteristics explain the permanence of the party system and, at the same time, the birth and consolidation of Uruguayan democracy. The fractionalization of the dominant parties simply results from a highly developed internal democracy.

The pessimistic view is dominant at the extremes of the political spectrum and it has received more attention from the intellectual community as well. It has two main components, the first being its characterization of the Uruguayan political system as a "non-policy oriented system," that is, a system in which "the stakes tend to be personal and private satisfactions of motivations (e.g., jobs, favors)" (Biles 1972, p. 441). Somewhat caricaturizing the position, Uruguayan politics appears as a giant patronage system. Political entrepreneurs exchange private favors for votes and political loyalties. On ideological issues, politicians' stands do not matter very much, as long as favors continue to be delivered. The main political parties are then co-operatives of political entrepreneurs seeking to maximize their vote-collecting capabilities. These themes have appeared repeatedly in the literature on the Uruguayan traditional parties. Solari wrote about the "extremely important non-political functions" fulfilled by those parties and, in particular, on the characteristics of the patronage system built upon the creation of jobs in the public sector, which helped to create and maintain electoral clienteles and to mitigate social tensions (Solari 1964, p. 147; 1967, p. 147 and passim). According to Weinstein, these traits were as old as polyarchy itself. Writing about the elections held during the 1920s, he observed that

> the close victory margins and the frequency of elections made for a frantic search for votes. It was soon apparent to all that political patronage would now make the difference between victory and defeat. The growing state bureaucracy . . . was both a source of votes and a payoff for the loyalty of party fractions.[23]

Besides the clientelistic issue, the pessimistic view has a second component: the role assigned to electoral legislation as a central device for maintaining the dominant role of the traditional parties. A recent writer put it concisely:

> The predominance of the traditional parties was assured through complicated electoral legislation which stimulated factionalism, even as a means for expanding the "hunting ground" of each party, and blocked the emergency of a multi-party system . . . Thus, a biparty system—product of the formal restrictions on party competition—was the axis around which the political system was articulated.[24]

The "clientelistic" and "electoral legislation" components of the pessimistic view complement each other. Historical accident produced two main parties which, once they reached a certain critical point without competition, established a duopolistic control over the resources that sustained patronage, precluding access to them for new parties. The electoral legislation, enacted by its direct beneficiaries, contributed to stabilizing the duopoly by further elevating the barriers to entry. We are very far from the conclusions of the optimistic view: we now have corrupt political machines which perpetuate themselves by tampering with electoral legislation and monopolizing the sources of patronage. In this view the stability of the party system is explained in terms of both clientelistic practices and electoral law, whereas the fractionalization of the traditional parties results essentially from electoral law.

Both the optimistic and pessimistic models have more than some grains of truth—in other words, I believe that the best model belongs to the third, "mixed" family. The optimistic view has truth if only, as Solari put it, because:

> The idea that religion is a fraud invented and maintained by the priests for their own benefit, has long been abandoned as an explanation for the phenomenon of religion, even by the most recalcitrant atheists. Nevertheless, a large part of the Uruguayan left refuses to abandon an analogous principle to explain the survival of the traditional parties . . . believing that they exist and are maintained primarily by means of an immense fraud effected for the good of politicians themselves. (Solari 1964, p. 147)

I think that two central facts cannot be seriously doubted: both democracy and the early Uruguayan welfare state were a result of the action of the traditional parties. Democracy was essentially a result of the equilibrium depicted in the optimistic view. The Colorado attempt to become a hegemonic party failed, and by the turn of the century a significant part of the Colorado elite was ready for a new approach; Blanco tenacity had borne fruit even after military defeat. Democracy slowly evolved, as in Rustow's discussion, as a means of solving intense internal conflict (Rustow 1970). The early welfare state instead was to a large extent a result of the efforts of the Colorado *Batllista* elite (Barrán 1986). In short, the strength of the traditional parties during the first quarter of the century needs no explanation other than their own impulse.

The optimistic view can thus explain the consolidation of the dominant role of the traditional parties during the first years of the century. It may also be accepted that the fractionalization of the parties preceded the birth of democracy: it was a natural result of extremely turbulent times and little or no organizational resources to govern a political party in time of peace. In spite of their very real mass following, at the turn of the century the parties were structured as parties of notables. Thus, the fractionalization of the parties during the initial stages of democracy was simply the survival of the old status quo.

Nevertheless, the optimistic view does not really explain the continued dominant position of the traditional parties nor the permanence—in some respects, the increase—of their extremely high degree of fractionalization. Seventy years have elapsed since the birth of polyarchy, including nine years of "authoritarian situation," in Linz's terms, and eleven of authoritarian military rule. The performance of the traditional parties did not live up to the expectations generated at the beginning of the century, but only during the last twenty years have credible challenges to their position finally, and slowly, begun to evolve. The situation is even more intriguing with regard to the fractionalization of the traditional parties. Parties as fractionalized as the Blancos and Colorados—like the Italian DC and the Japanese Liberals—have existed during far shorter periods, and there is no direct term of comparison. At any rate, whatever their age they are uncommon. When they do exist, however, all the major parties of the system tend to be fractionalized. Hence party fractionalization seems to be a systemic attribute rather than a characteristic of isolated parties. There is something in their milieu that fosters and maintains fractionalization.[25]

We may then turn to the pessimistic view for an explanation of the continuity of these political structures, continuity which is not accounted for within the optimistic tradition. The pessimistic view offers two explanations for those continuities: the clientelistic and electoral-law arguments. The latter addresses both the stability of the party system and the fractionalization of its main parties, and the first, the clientelistic argument, has been offered essentially as an explanation of the stability of the party system. The clientelistic thesis does not look very promising as an explanation of the stability of the party system or even as a factor capable of normally deciding electoral outcomes. Solari pointed out that as a system for generating electoral support, clientelism is self-defeating: the more institutionalized the system becomes, the more the citizens will tend to perceive it as a right that does not actually generate political loyalties (Solari 1967, pp. 162 and ff.). This seems all the more true when voting has the appropriate procedural guarantees, as in Uruguay. Gillespie has argued that no simple model of patronage can explain landslide shifts of votes such as the 1958 Blanco victory, nor the poor performance of old clientelistic fractions in later elections, nor the survival of the traditional parties' appeal after eleven years of authoritarian order during which they did not have access to the resources needed to allow patronage (Gillespie 1983, pp. 13–14, 30). In fact, the groups that did have some access to these resources were the big losers in the 1982 intraparty *elecciones internas* and in the 1984 general election. Moreover, the arguments are not restricted to the relatively recent past. If patronage had had decisive importance the Blanco electoral strength during the 1920s, after more than forty years in the opposition, would be utterly incomprehensible. It has been said that clientelistic practices peaked during the 1930s. But then they should not be a permanent trait of the system; what is more, if it were argued that clientelism during the 1930s and 1940s helps to explain why the Colorados became a predominant party after 1942, then it would be difficult to understand their 1958 debacle. In short: the point is not to deny the existence of such practices; they did exist, sometimes blatantly. They even had political relevance. What seems untenable in face of the available evidence is to assign them a decisive role in stabilizing the party system or regularly winning elections.[26]

The electoral legislation issue offers a priori more interesting possibilities. It is widely accepted now that "the electoral system may determine the number of parties and to some extent their coherence and structure" (Butler 1981, p. 11), which is precisely the contention of the pessimistic view.

Nevertheless, the arguments that have upheld this line of thought have been plagued by three major faults. First, usually they are not explicit about the exact nature of the mechanisms producing the alleged effects; sometimes it seems as if the authors had applied Butler's general dictum above without probing the specifics of the Uruguayan case—in fact, some authors simply state the conclusion, without really attempting an explanation. Second, this lack of precision is particularly inexcusable given the fact that Uruguay has a PR system. Arguing that a PR system produced a two-party system— against well-known, strong empirical regularity and against an increasingly consensual view on the literature as well—would require, so it seems to me, a particularly careful discussion.[27] Third, more often than not the debate has been charged with moral overtones: we do not really have a systematic argument—i.e., one that explains why electoral law consolidated or even pro- duced a two-party system, irrespective of the identity of those two parties at any particular time[28]—but a criticism of the particularism of rules addressed to maintain the dominant positions of the oldest players, which happened to be just two, Blancos and Colorados, hence the resulting two-partyism. Le- gal manipulations favoring the position of the traditional parties have indeed existed, but they have been comparatively minor obstacles—as, for exam- ple, the distinction between "permanent" and "non-permanent" *lemas*, which the birth of the Frente Amplio proved unimportant—and they are relatively common in other democratic polities as well. Their net effect is simply to increase somewhat the entrance costs, but they are incapable of arresting real changes in the political mood of the electorate.

Very recently a new approach has emerged which cannot be assigned to any of the three groups—optimistic, pessimistic, and mixed—although its policy implications tend to agree with those of the optimists. The main thesis of this new approach is simply that electoral law has little effect on its own on the party system. Quoting Nohlen, Solari argues that "both electoral and party systems are variables which depend on social and political structures in any given society," and concludes that comparative analyses show "very clearly that the characteristics of the party systems depend on very different factors among which there is the electoral system, whose importance is variable."[29] According to the first statement, any relationship between electoral law and party systems may be suspected to be spurious; according to the second, there is no general rule governing those eventual relationships. This general skep- ticism is accompanied by another, more particular skepticism that associates the view that electoral law has important effects on the party system with a more general fascination of Uruguayan elites "towards the magical powers of legal solutions, in spite of repeated frustrations" (Solari 1986, p. 150).

I think Solari is wrong in saying that his view is "representative of the most current thinking on the problem" (ibid., p. 120); this opinion seems to be common among those who share his approach. At least since Rae (1971) published his reexamination of Duverger's "laws," Butler's remark quoted above reflects the dominant view on the subject. Almost everybody agrees that there are clear empirical regularities supporting the kernel of Duverger's argument—strong regularities, according to the probabilistic criteria of the discipline—and a few counterexamples. The law-like nature of the relationship has indeed been discussed, as well as the meaning of the counterexamples, but those discussions have been more methodological than substantive. Rae's findings on the whole supported Duverger's point; more generally, they reinforce the view that electoral law does contribute to shape party systems. Since then this has been a widely shared idea. In Dahl's view the party system "is dependent to some degree on electoral arrangements. And these can be deliberately manipulated in order to maximize or minimize fragmentation" (Dahl 1971, pp. 223–224). Linz agrees: electoral laws can contribute "to shaping the party system" (Linz 1978, p. 89). It seems to me that Sartori's conclusion in his reexamination of the matter might well reflect a consensus within the profession:

> Can we be as parsimonious as Duverger? The reply is yes, provided that we replace the neatness and logical force of necessary and sufficient conditions with the laxity of *facilitating* versus *obstructive* conditions . . . we can indeed settle almost everything with just two very simple laws, namely:
> *Tendency law 1*: Plurality formulas facilitate (are facilitating conditions of) a two-party format and, conversely, obstruct (are an obstructive condition of) multipartysm.
> *Tendency law 2*: PR formulas facilitate multipartysm and are, conversely, hardly conducive to two-partysm.
> The above . . . is just about all that Duverger said. (Sartori 1986, p. 64; his emphasis)

My case for the enduring two-party format of the Uruguayan party system may now be easily presented. I have argued—as the optimistic view does—that a purely historical argument is enough to explain the dominant role of the traditional parties during the first quarter of the century. Since then, electoral competition has been conducted within an institutional framework which has exhibited certain stable traits. The quasi-presidentialism of the Uruguayan polity is perceived by most voters, needless to say, as presidentialism *tout court*. Whatever the importance attributed to other elective posts, it is clear that the most important among all of them is the presidency; attention is thus naturally focused on the presidential race, which is decided by a plurality—or relative majority—of votes, hence Sartori-Duverger's Tendency law 1 applies.[30] Since all elections occur simultaneously, the central effect of PR on the party system is blocked, for the ban on split tickets imposed by DSV assures that the plurality rule of the top race—the presidency—dominates electoral logic. In fact, the mere conjunction of presidential and legislative elections—without an explicit ban as that provided by DSV—seems enough to produce the same result: most presidential systems with concurrent presidential-legislative elections are two-party systems as well (Shugart 1989). This is a well-known fact at the voters' level: in Uruguay, the idea and the term *voto útil* (useful—as opposed to wasted—vote) is a commonplace, and it encapsulates the core of this reasoning.[31] When the Uruguayan historical context and the theoretical principle are considered simultaneously, the result is far stronger than the Tendency law alone. "Tendency" laws are such because the formal argument per se does not work in every circumstance. In particular, a nonstructured party system may cancel any effect resulting from electoral laws. If the party system *is* structured, however, and it *already has* a two-party format, as was the case in Uruguay, then the following rule applies:

> A plurality system cannot produce by itself a nationwide two-party format . . . but under all circumstances it will help *maintain* an already existing one. Hence, whenever a two-party format is established, a plurality system exerts a brakelike influence and obtains a freezing effect. (Sartori 1986, pp. 58–59; his emphasis)

The stability of Uruguayan two-partyism is thus the result of the combined action of the institutional setting and of electoral law. This conclusion agrees with the more general view according to which the constitutional system is one of the "manipulative factors" of the party system (Sartori 1982, pp. 311–312). It also agrees with an old thesis that sees the U.S. party system as a result of the American constitutional *and* electoral system. The theoretical principle backing this thesis is the same of Sartori-Duverger's tendency laws; Morris Hillquit, Socialist Party leader, wrote in 1910 that in the U.S.

> the ticket handed to the voter . . . contains the names not only of candidates for the state legislature or congress, but also for all local and state officers and even for President of the United States. And since a new party rarely seems to have the chance or prospect of electing its candidate for governor of a state or president of the country, the voter is inclined in advance to consider its entire ticket as hopeless. The fear of "throwing away" the vote is thus a peculiar product of American politics, and it requires a voter of exceptional strength of conviction to overcome it.[32]

That fear was not "a peculiar product of American politics," but simply the particular American expression of a general principle: any mass-scale election involving a single, indivisible major prize will tend to produce, after a learning process of the elites and the voters, the same result. Whenever the constitutional arrangements—be they parliamentary or presidential—and electoral law establish a particular instance of that general principle, the same conclusion will obtain.[33] Finally, it should be noted that not all three major traits of electoral law involved in maintaining two-partyism play the same role. One of them acts "positively": the plurality rule in the presidential race is the active element pushing towards a two-party format, whereas the other two—DSV and the simultaneity of all elections—act "negatively," i.e., cancelling the eventual effects of PR on the party system.

The initial discussion of the structure of the party system had concluded that the traditional parties were already fractionalized when democracy was born, and that the persistence and even increase of such fractionalization during three quarters of a century could not be accounted for as pure systemic inertia. It should be noted in the first place that circumstantial causes promoting fractionalization are always present in any conceivable democratic polity. Sheer competition for political power among elites is enough to produce a constant, latent risk of fractionalization within all more or less democratically organized parties, and even within parties definitely non-democratically organized. In polyarchies, parties loosely organized—as the Uruguayan traditional parties—are molded by the structure of the competition they are engaged in, that is, essentially by extra-party rules and forces. Polities differ widely in this regard. Some in fact penalize fractionalization, while others allow some or even much of it. In the limit, certain systems seem to foster—not merely to allow—fractionalization. Such systems may be said to cause fractionalization. I will attempt to show that Uruguay has been a system of this kind since the birth of polyarchy and, in particular, that electoral law actively fostered fractionalization.

As it has been noted above, the DSV makes Uruguay a member of the family of electoral systems which allow intraparty preference voting, although the DSV itself has been extremely uncommon outside the country.

For all such systems,

> Whether or not cohesion is the "natural" state of a political party, effective intraparty preference voting creates a powerful incentive to disunity. (Katz 1986, p. 101)

Candidates cannot rely solely on their party; they must distinguish themselves from competitors within their own party. They must develop at least a minimal organizational base of their own. As a result, if successful they will control power resources independent of the party as such—and they will have compromises and debts of their own as well. Such heterogeneities obviously affect internal cohesion. Besides these theoretical considerations, "there is substantial evidence that preference voting is associated with intraparty disunity" (ibid., p. 102).[34]

Nevertheless, given the atypical nature of the DSV such general considerations are not enough to settle the issue. I think that the mechanics at work in the Uruguayan case may be described as follows. The DSV allows different candidates to compete for the same posts without wasting votes, since all of them belong to the party. But this competition differs from that of other systems of the intraparty preference voting family for two reasons: first, at the national level it may be conducted at three levels of political importance—candidates for president, for senator, and for representative—with increasing opportunities at the lower levels; and second, since whole lists compete against whole lists the rivalries are not individual, but involve teams whose structure quite naturally reflects that of the hierarchy of positions at stake. The most important places are occupied by the most important politicians. In other words, the nature of the intraparty competition in the Uruguayan case goes far beyond the creation of a series of *individual* rivalries on the basis of which the involved politicians may or may not constitute fractions; it directly creates the fractions, for only teams may play the game. The stimulus provided by the DSV is reinforced by PR, which assures that it is not necessary to get the first prize to stay in the race; a modest electoral success is enough to provide some important posts for the top leadership of the fraction or subfraction, which in turn may "trickle down" to their lesser associates.[35] As a result, this system continuously creates new challengers to the established leaders who, if moderately successful, will become in turn the leaders of new fractions or subfractions. In organizational terms the crucial point is that the system allows the would-be leader to skip one step in the party hierarchy, opening a parallel, competitive candidacy or set of candidacies. Within certain limits, the most important party leaders cannot oppose this state of affairs. They gain little attempting to "discipline," and risk losing votes instead. If they deny the new splinter group the use of the party's name and symbols, they risk an exit and a loss of votes which, added to the already existing competition, could be decisive even if small.[36] In the long run, then, the expected trend is towards a greater number of candidacies.

Such a logic looks simple a posteriori. To fully develop its potential it reasonably requires a series of trial-and-error tests capable of demonstrating the dynamics of the system. The political events of the 1920s provide fine opportunities for that learning process. In 1925 the Colorados lost the National Council of Administration election because the Vierista fraction voted outside the party. The numbers were eloquent: the Colorados obtained 116,000 votes, the Blancos 119,000, and the Colorados Vieristas 7,000. In 1926 Herrera and the Blancos he led lost the presidency to the Colorados because the Blancos Radicales voted outside the party. This time the figures were even closer: 141,500 votes for the Colorados, 140,000 votes for the Blancos, and 4,000 votes for the Blanco dissidents. Almost the same figures appeared again in 1928, when the Blancos lost the National council of Administration because of the Blanco Radical dissidence. In the end, the Colorados learned their lesson somewhat more quickly than the Blancos. The Blancos paid for Herrera's intransigence with Blanco minorities by remaining for a long time out of the highest office; the Colorados won it through democratic bargaining with their own minorities—the bargaining being expensive to the majority but beneficial to democracy within the party. This practical experience and the logic of the system produced an enormous expansion of candidacies after the democratic reequilibration following the 1933–1942 authoritarian situation. The number of *listas* (lists) for the lower chamber—nationwide—was 153 in 1946 and 554 in 1971. A Montevidean citizen, in particular, had to choose one list for the lower chamber among 39 in 1946, and one among 110 in 1971, and this taking into account the two traditional parties alone.[37] Each of these 110 lists could, in principle, elect 43 representatives.[38]

Fractionalization thus appears as a result of the DSV and PR. These do not play the same role, however; the DSV is the active principle fostering fractionalization, and PR is the facilitating condition, because by making more prizes available it diminishes the expected costs of actual competition. This completes the examination of the reasons explaining the structure the party system exhibited until the mid-sixties.

3. Political Structures and Democratic Breakdowns

1. The 1933 Coup

In 1933 a democratically elected Colorado Batllista president, Gabriel Terra, dissolved parliament and began a de facto regime under the banner of a supposedly needed constitutional reform. The coup was supported by part of the Colorado party and by the Blanco majority, the Herreristas—those who followed Luis Alberto de Herrera. The coup has been widely regarded as a reaction from the conservative upper classes, and particularly the landed elites, against a steady decline of their economic fortunes since the end of World War I, further aggravated by the consequences of the Great Depression (e.g., Finch 1880, pp. 21–26). Although many aspects of those events are still polemical, there are some relatively consensual points particularly relevant for the present purpose.[1]

Terra's coup may be seen to a good extent as a result of the pressures generated by the Great Depression on a still consolidating young democracy. Between 1930 and 1936 just one South American independent country managed to maintain its political stability—Colombia, which was not a democracy. Nevertheless, the coup and Terra's later policies were unnecessary to solve the problems generated by the Depression; it has been argued that at least in several important respects the country had already begun its recovery when the coup took place. It also seems that a strictly national political dynamics greatly contributed to the coup, although there is probably no agreement about what aspects of that dynamics are to blame.

The role of at least some of those aspects, however, seems reasonably clear. In the first place, there was a president whose democratic faith proved weak. That president has no legislative majority: the Colorados were a minority both in the lower and upper chambers, and even within his party the president's support was dwindling before the coup. Since the beginning of his presidency Terra had campaigned against the Constitution; he argued that "no one knew who governed Uruguay—the government was divided among so many instances" (Lindahl 1962, p. 178). His real problem was not only in those divisions, of course, but also in his lack of political majorities to control any of those instances. For example: the Agrupación de Gobierno

Batllista was, according to the regulations and customs of the fraction, entitled to formulate recommendations to all Batllistas in government posts, though formally they were not binding; but soon after Terra was inaugurated as president, he dismissed a recommendation of the Agrupación on the basis that. "the group was not competent to give him instructions, regardless of how many persons supported its recommendation, for he recognized his responsibility only to the party and the country" (ibid., p. 173).[2] In practice this meant, of course, that he was going to do as he pleased. This was his fraction and its regular coordinating and governing body; whatever the problems Terra had with them, it was certainly not a matter of division of authority.

It is debatable whether Terra's policies to overcome the crisis were better than those that would have been followed without the coup. What is certain is that he actually had—and so he felt—little power to enact them. This was partly an explicit purpose of the 1918 Constitution, and partly a result of the lack of majorities supporting him. Whatever his reasons, the fact is that Terra no longer wanted to abide by the rules which had made him president. To impose his views he began to circumvent the law and established practices. Therefore, his conflicts with his intra- and extra-party political rivals became institutional conflicts as well, and mounting tension followed. A rather incredible scenario of Communist menace was staged by the president and his followers; this scenario was added to disquieting signals from the traditional parties themselves. Those signals were also very dubious, but at least they were more along the lines of national traditions, which made them more credible.[3] Several problems, including the arrest of one of the two Communist representatives, led to increasing tensions between president and legislature; ministers were criticized in parliament, but it was clear that the real target of the criticisms was the president. A few weeks before the coup, a Montevideo newspaper that was Terra's mouthpiece, *El Pueblo*, published that

> superstitious faith in constitutions was a mistake, for if such blind faith had always existed, monarchies would still dominate. It was the healing violence that had given people democratic-republican governments. In questions of popular government it was hopeless stupidity to hesitate when faced by the words of a constitution. (Lindahl 1962, p. 182)

The coup finally came by means of an agreement whose details are still controversial, but its central piece assured the acquiescence of the Blanco majority to the coup in exchange for certain guarantees and greater influence in the government. Those aspects of the pact were later institutionalized in the 1934 Constitution. The coup was an entirely civilian matter: Terra had neutralized the army, which remained in its barracks, and used the police force instead. In spite of the frightening rhetoric quoted above, the actual behavior of the de facto regime was comparatively mild. There were several excesses,[4] but

> the regime cannot really be regarded as a reign of violence. It has been characterized as *dictablanda*, from *dictadura*, dictatorship, where *dura*, "hard," has been replaced by *blanda*, "soft." (Lindahl 1962, p. 186)

In other words, it was closer to an "authoritarian situation," in Linz's terms, than to a truly authoritarian regime. In fact, leaving aside some very specific aspects—as the composition of the Senate, for example—the structure of the Constitution the regime produced remained unchanged in the later reforms (Gros Espiell 1956, pp. 83 and 84–85) enacted by Terra's political enemies.

The Constitution addressed directly Terra's two central problems. Its solution to the institutional problem consisted of returning to a single chief of government—the president, who also was the chief of state—and suppressing the National Council of Administration. This solution survived the 1942 reform, was replaced in 1952 by the *colegiado*, and was finally reinstated in 1966. The second problem, that of obtaining legislative majorities supporting the president, was mainly a result of the fractionalization of the dominant parties. The new Constitution addressed this point with a simple solution: it greatly strengthened the position of the main fractions within each of the traditional parties, thus discouraging fractionalization.[5] This aspect of Terra's reform is often overlooked because in the circumstances surrounding the reform such strengthening implied a direct reinforcement of the position of the two allies who led the regime, that is, the Blanco majority and the Colorados who followed Terra. The more general contents of the reform was somewhat lost behind its more spectacular, immediate implications for the status quo. Those implications, of course, led to the abandonment of Terra's solution in 1942; it was never reinstated.

The exit of the de facto regime required another coup, the "good coup" of the liberal tradition. The 1942 coup, however, was a clear example of disjunction between legality and legitimacy leading to democratic reequilibration:

> The new regime might be established illegally, but it must be legitimated by the democratic process afterward, and above all, it must operate thereafter according to democratic rules. (Linz 1978, p. 87)

Both conditions were satisfied, and in this sense the value judgment of Uruguayan liberal tradition is right. The 1942 election proved that most of the population was against the politicians linked to the de facto regime; besides, voting abstention as a political instrument completely disappeared. The quarter of a century that followed the 1942 reequilibration was perhaps the cleanest period of Uruguayan democracy thus far, though not its most creative one.

2. The 1973 Democratic Breakdown

Forty years after the dynamic 1920s things were very different. The two decades that preceded the 1973 coup were characterized by economic stagnation and slowly but steadily growing social unrest. The depth and persistence of Uruguayan economic debacle has no parallel among democratic politics during that period; in fact, it probably has very few terms of comparison during the whole of the present century, Great Depression included. The average gross domestic product (GDP) per capita decreased regularly from 1951–1955 through 1966–1968; assigning a base of 100 to the first period, its best historical level until then, it fell to 89.7 in the second; it had returned to the post-war level twenty years back–an average of 88.3 in the period 1946–1950.[6] Among the 135 nations whose per capita gross domestic product and growth rates between 1961 and 1965 are included in the *World Handbook of Political and Social Indicators*, only two (Malawi, -1.5; and Dominican Republic, -2.0) experienced more serious negative growth than Uruguay (−0.9); only one other country actually had negative growth in the same period (North Vietnam, -0.8). Gross domestic fixed capital formation

> during 1955–66 represented 12.9 percent of GDP, and in 1967 it was 11.4 percent. The significance of these figures is best understood in relation to the comparative ratios for Europe's market economies. In 1960, they invested an average 20 percent of their domestic products, while centrally-planned economies invested as much as 25 percent. (Gillespie and González 1989)

In comparative terms this amounted to a relative de-industrialization of the country. Among market-oriented economies in 1968, 19 countries could be considered as semi-industrial nations according to the per capita value added of industrial production. Uruguay was the third most industrialized country within that group in 1953, and twenty years later, in 1973, its relative position had fallen to the twelfth place.[7] The Uruguayan average annual growth rate of industrial production 1953–1978 was 1.5 percent, the lowest rate among those 19 countries, and less than half of the second-lowest rate—that of Argentina, 3.3 percent (Obradovic 1984, p. 39). The real wages of urban workers fell accordingly, though they began to fall slightly later. The real salary in the manufacturing industry peaked during 1955–1959, and by 1970–1972 it had returned to pre-1950 levels. Rural wages and particularly retirement pensions were in even worse circumstances.

These developments led increasing social agitation and political polarization. Relatively strong urban unions became more active and the number of workers affiliated or at least sympathetic to them increased; by the 1960s they finally became united in a single federation, the Convención Nacional de Trabajadores. During the 1960s, however, this process was not visible in electoral terms. The middle classes reacted in heterogeneous ways. In some sectors "certain signs of right-wing authoritarianism" appeared (Filgueira 1973, p. 110), in some ways following the pattern of the interwar years in Europe. In others a radicalization developed in the opposite direction. Some typically white-collar unions—as the bankworkers, for example—shifted to highly combative positions that situated them in the left of the trade union movement.

The electoral behavior of Uruguayans reflected their increasing impatience with the crisis. In 1958 they voted the Blancos into government, terminating the predominant role of the Colorados since 1942. In 1962 they gave another chance to the Blancos, this time to a rival fraction, not the 1958 winners. In 1966 they supported the return to presidentialism and elected a Colorado president; the Blancos had wasted their chance. In 1971, for the first time since 1954, the same party and the same fraction within the party won the election. Nevertheless, this was *not* a sign of continuity, appearances notwithstanding; as it will be seen later, this election showed deep transformations of the Uruguayan party system. The formal continuity of the winning fraction in 1966 and 1971 obscures some of the main changes. Perhaps the most notorious of those changes was the birth of the Frente Amplio (Broad Front). Before 1971 the left made two attempts at coalition-building, both with scarce electoral success: the Unión Popular, formed by the Partido Socialista and small groups from the traditional parties, and the FIDEL (Frente Izquierda de Liberación), a coalition led by the Partido Comunista—more properly described as the Comunistas plus a few very minor allies. The Frente Amplio unified the whole legal left: the socialistas and the Comunistas, the Partido Demócrata Cristiano, a fraction from the Colorados led by Zelmar Michelini and Hugo Batalla (the Lista 99), and a rather heterogeneous group—which in 1971 used the *sub-lema* Patria Grande (Great Fatherland)—including Blanco dissidents led by former Minister Enrique Erro and enjoying some support from the radical left. Both in its composition and in its advocated policies the FA was more center-leaning than the Chilean Unidad Popular. In the 1971 elections the FA won 18 percent of the national vote, and 30 percent in Montevideo. This was the first serious inroad into the old status quo.

The mass-level answers to the crisis were not the only relevant answers. Since the early 1960s a small, radicalized group of left-wing militants began to build an urban guerrilla movement, the Tupamaros.[8] They became convinced of the futility of peaceful efforts towards social progress, and concluded that armed struggle was unavoidable—the only way towards that goal. Their views were obviously influenced by the Cuban Revolution and by Guevarismo; in theoretical terms they were close to Régis Debray's *foquista* thinking—that of *Revolution in the Revolution*. The group remained small until their final defeat, but their impact on the Uruguayan political system was very strong for at least two reasons. First, although in retrospect it seems clear that they never had any chance of success, they conveyed the image—as a minimum—that the police alone were no match for them. On the one hand this contributed to the feeling that the "security of the state" and that of the existing order was to some extent endangered; on the other hand, this state of affairs quite naturally led to the military's involvement in the antiguerrilla effort. Second, the Tupamaros were the immediate, true revolutionary option; as such they were the left opposition to the legal left, which was thus caught between opposite forces upon which in the short run it had no influence at all. By the time of the 1971 election the sympathies of the left towards the Tupamaros appeared clear. The Comunistas in particular had repeatedly asserted that the only basic disagreement they had with the guerrillas was a procedural one. Some smaller groups were so radical in their language that it was not clear what disagreements, if any, they had with the Tupamaros. As later events showed, one of these smaller groups was in fact organically related to the guerrillas. As a minimum, then, these groups linked symbolically the legal left with the guerrillas, and the bulk of the left did not want, or did not dare to sever those links. That inaction had several causes—including the worries of some of the groups of the legal left about the Tupamaros' relatively successful recruitment among youths. Needless to say, the effects of such positioning on the polarization of the system were very large. From the perspective of those in charge of the fight against the guerrillas, the 1971 election showed that nearly a fifth of the national population, and a third of Montevideo's, were disloyal to the established order. This was a situation potentially much more dangerous than anything a relatively small guerrilla band alone could create. On the other hand, the remaining four fifths of the population who in 1971 had voted for the traditional parties were definitely opposed to the guerrillas. In short, the military confronted a situation of high potential risk, but they also had a massive mandate to defeat subversion. That mandate did not define the *methods* of their work, but the *goal* was clear.

Such a situation was the final result of a long series of decisions and non-decisions taken by all the important actors and of several constraints affecting those decisions. From the perspective of the FA founders, the forces to their right appeared as maintaining a status quo the left was denouncing as deeply unjust; those forces were represented by parties whose organization and ways of doing politics were the polar opposites to those of the left—the large, fractionalized, pragmatic catch-all parties that had always governed the country versus the small, highly ideological and militant parties which at their best had been the country's goad parties. Tupamaros instead were simply a branch of the left: a new group whose founding members came from the left, as well as most of their new recruits, and whose views on the status quo and on the just, desirable society—though this in a rather loose manner—were similar to those of at least part of the legal left. *Before* 1968 the ultimate decision the left confronted was particularly thorny, for its opposition from the right defended an unequivocally democratic order, and this was not an empty symbol among at least a large part of the left. *After* 1968 things changed quickly, however, as a result of the actions of the traditional political elite; the already semiloyal left was openly pushed to plain disloyalty by the government and most of the leadership of the major parties—with the significant exception of the Blanco majority. Besides, by 1971 the very idea of loyalty was unclear: the government itself did not abide by the existing rules.

There are two different problems concerning the behavior of the traditional elite. The first is this: Why were they unable to solve the pressing social and economic problems the country faced during the two decades preceding the 1973 coup? This was essentially a responsibility of the traditional parties, because they alone were successively in charge of government. They proved incapable of establishing any coherent and stable set of policies. This may be seen even in the most remarkable attempt at developing a new approach, that of the Blanco government elected in 1958. The Reforma Cambiaria y Monetaria Act of Novembar 1959 was a clear departure from the Batllismo of the late forties and early fifties; its central idea was that overcoming stagnation required reinforcing the export-oriented rural sector. The whole project, however, was not given enough time to determine whether the new approach was better than the status quo: the fractionalized Blancos could not abandon their urban constituency even if only for a while. The project was defeated by the internal problems of the governing party well in advance of the next election.[9]

The second problem concerning the behavior of the traditional political elite is this: Why were they unable to stop the rather obvious downward spiraling which ultimately led to the 1973 coup? There were several remarkable similarities with the events surrounding the coup that had taken place forty years before. Instead of a president whose democratic faith proved weak, as in 1933, before 1973 there were two consecutive presidents whose democratic faith proved very weak. The first, Jorge Pacheco Areco, was President Gestido's, vice president; he became president when Gestido died shortly after his inauguration. Pacheco's presidency was thus an accident in more than one sense: according to several independent reports Gestido had offered the vice-presidential candidacy to at least two other politicians, and both declined his offer. Pacheco was neither a first-rank leader nor a particularly respected politician; his power within the party had to be built after he became president—but in this endeavor he was helped by the most presidentialist of the Constitutions the country has had since 1918. Nevertheless, he was not able to coopt many important leaders from the other fractions into his own. In fact, he never really became an influential leader of the Colorado elite; he did become powerful, but these are different things that should not be confused. His political strategy was simple: he turned to the right and became the champion of the established order against subversion, and in so doing he—as Terra before him—no longer respected the rules of the game that had elected him president. He did not have parliamentary majority and did not really lead his own party, but he had his own ideas on the fight against the guerrillas and on several other matters as well. He used the guerrillas as the justification to impose Medidas Prontas de Seguridad, a kind of siege which he used to circumvent parliament and to impose his policies on the most disparate subjects. In this manner he at least partially solved one of Terra's problems—his difficulties in obtaining parliamentary majorities. But in so doing he, like Terra, repeatedly violated the spirit and the letter of the law, including an attempt—forbidden by the Constitution—to run for reelection. Terra's second problem—the relative weakness of his institutional position— had already been solved by the 1966 Constitution. Finally, Pacheco did not need to invent a scenario of Communist menace: he had at hand very real Tupamaros.

Pacheco's reelection attempt failed, but his political strategy, which had exacerbated polarization, succeeded in returning his fraction as the Colorado majority in the 1971 elections. The candidate he had chosen, Juan María Bordaberry, became the new president. If Pacheco's position within the Colorado elite had never been very strong, Bordaberry's was much weaker. He was not a truly Colorado politician: before the 1971 election he had been elected to the Senate on Blanco lists.[10] Pacheco handpicked Bordaberry for his own purposes; Bordaberry had little control over the electoral campaign, that was designed for Pacheco's benefit, and little or no influence of his own on the party that had elected him president. He was not even able to become powerful in the sense Pacheco was, partly because, assuming he had the necessary personal talents, he did not have time enough to try his hand, and partly because the politicians of his own fraction were already loyal to Pacheco, not to him. The turmoil of the fifteen months he served as civilian president obscured the fact that he could only govern thanks to the other Colorados' decision that the lesser evil in the circumstances was to help him in the hope of avoiding even greater disasters. At least in this sense, when he became caretaker president of the military his role was not so different from the one he had already been playing.

The year of Bordaberry's inauguration, 1972, was also the year of the final confrontation between the military and the guerrillas. The Tupamaros decided that the time for an offensive against the army had come, and the army took about six months to completely destroy the guerrillas' organization and military power. They acted essentially on their own: their theoretical chief, the president, could not control even his fraction in his party, much less the army. By the beginning of 1973 it was clear that the guerrilla menace had been terminated and that the military were acting autonomously. An initial attempt to recover some degree of civilian control over the army—in February 1973—ended in a defeat that prefigured the events of the next four months. After concluding the military operations against the guerrillas, the army leadership became more interested in its politico-ideological roots—or in what they saw as such—in order to avoid any chance of reappearance of left-wing insurgence. Their behavior and demands were unacceptable for a civilian independent legislature, and the first important rejection of the army's demands produced the coup. The president had chosen the army's side.

3. Learning from the Crises

A first lesson from the history of the two coups is that the single most important substantive problem conditioning Uruguayan political stability lies perhaps in the country's relationship with the rest of the world. This is quite obvious with regard to the 1933 coup, but it was no less true forty years later. The economic and social crisis described above is strikingly similar, though some of its traits appear even more marked, to that experienced by Argentina beginning about the same time.[11] What went into crisis was the import-substituting industrialization process, which had accelerated as a response to the Great Depression first and then to World War II. In Uruguay the left and the right—at least since the 1950s—agreed on the central problem, though their explanations were different: where the left saw imperialism and dependency the right saw the consequences of large-scale intervention of the state in the economy.

The economic policy implemented during the late 1940s and early 1950s was closer to the left's views; it combined strong state intervention and high tariff barriers in an effort to foster import-substituting industrialization. In fact, if not in theory, the strategy assumed that a focus on the internal market was the best way to industrialization and development. This approach, as shown in the previous section, proved wrong, but from the mid-fifties on the political elites were unable to develop any alternative strategy, though at least some failed attempts were made. It may thus be said that the crises which led to the two interruptions of democracy had an important external dimension, but it is erroneous to consider those crises as exogenously determined. In particular, the dismal Uruguayan performance by comparison with all other semi-industrialized countries during the two decades preceding the 1973 coup shows that external constraints were not the only causes of the crisis.

As a result, two problems should be distinguished regarding the specific reasons for democratic breakdowns: on the one hand the inability of political elites to cope with the problems of development; and on the other hand their inability to resist and eventually overcome within a democratic framework the accumulation of problems resulting from the first failure. Let us call them, for the sake of brevity, the *developmental* and *democratic* questions. The first question refers only to the 1973 breakdown; it cannot be properly asked with regard to the 1933 coup. Not only is the term inappropriate, but the whole situation could not be perceived from that perspective by contemporary actors and observers. Uruguay was doing fairly well before the Great Depression; the country could even be proud of its relative position in the world, not merely in Latin America, both on economic and political grounds. The obviously exogenous origin of the crisis posited the question not as a failure of national policies but instead as a transitory effort of adjustment to purely external events. Forty years later the picture was entirely different: the developmental question was in the center of public debate, and the feelings of frustration widespread.

Let us begin with the developmental question. As we have seen, the first election after the onset of the crisis—that of 1958—ended the predominant role of the Colorados; since then no party has obtained a stable parliamentary majority.[12] The winning *sub-lema* within the winning *lema* won executive power. In the four elections from 1958 through 1971 those winning *sub-lemas* obtained between 43 and 58 percent of the votes their *lemas* received, which amounted to 21 and 27 percent respectively of all voters—the latter figures being also the lowest and highest percentages of the period. What is more, those *sub-lemas* were further subdivided, i.e., added different lists to the Senate and even more to the lower chamber. An example will illustrate the situation. In 1971 Pacheco's *sub-lema* won the presidency (Bordaberry), obtaining 56 percent of the Colorado votes, which amounted to 23 percent of all voters. Nevertheless, the *sub-lema* included three lists for the Senate, two of which obtained seats, and thirteen lists for the House in Montevideo alone, two of which obtained seats. Even that 23 percent of the total vote, then, was not a single block, but an alliance of subfractions each of which could consider quite legitimately that its share of power should be no smaller than its share of the electorate.

These facts suggest two simple and cumulative reasons explaining the elite's inability to build and sustain coherent policies to overcome stagnation. First, a party without a legislative majority cannot maintain controversial policies, and the kind of policies capable of successfully confronting a long, hard crisis cannot but be controversial; otherwise the crisis would be neither hard nor extended. Inasmuch as since the beginning of the crisis the winners at the polls did not obtain parliamentary majorities and, as mentioned in

Chapter 2, interparty government-sharing agreements have been exceptional in Uruguay, it follows that the format and logic of the parliamentary party system tended to block the kind of policy-making necessary to fight the crisis.[13] Second, the two parties that governed during the crisis have always been fractionalized parties. As the core constituencies of their main fractions have usually been different, covering a wide spectrum of interests (Aguiar 1977, passim), either party was bound to find internal oppositions capable of blocking almost any conceivable policy bold enough to confront the crisis. Those who felt condemned to pay a disproportionate share of the initial cost of the new policies could, and did, react quickly to stop the unjust role their own party was assigning to them. The interplay of subfractions within the fractions opened even more room to internal blockages. Thus, the inner structure of the two major parties also tended to block the kind of policy-making necessary to fight the crisis.

It seems clear that any of these factors considered in isolation could produce political stalemates. Hence the result of their simultaneous, cumulative action was a powerful force towards political immobilization. Nevertheless, such a situation did not necessarily lead to a total blockage; at least theoretically a series of short, unstable governments could have tried different approaches, some of which could have resulted in significant improvements. A further factor cancelled even this theoretical possibility: the Uruguayan quasi-presidentialism froze the stalemates generated by the structure of the parties and of the party system. That freezing effect of quasi-presidentialism—or of plain presidentialism since 1966—on political stalemates has at least two dimensions.

The first and most obvious is that election dates are fixed; in Uruguay neither presidential nor legislative elections have ever taken place, under democratic governments, outside their legally preestablished dates. The stalemate produced by all elections since 1958 was thus frozen during the four years—five since 1966—in between elections. The second dimension of the freezing effect of quasi-presidentialism concerns its lack of flexibility for coalition-making. Parties entering a governing coalition they do not lead necessarily take some risks beyond the ordinary attrition of governing. If things go well they do not receive the most important political credit, but if things go wrong as a result of actions they do not control they may have to take part of the blame. The mechanics of a parliamentary system, however, provides a crucial resource to coalition partners: they are not powerless vis-à-vis the prime minister because they are literally owners, so to speak, of a share of the prime minister's position equal to their own share of the votes of the coalition in the legislature. The prime minister is always politically responsible, and a no-confidence vote may terminate his or her tenure. The power of the members of the coalition is thus directly expressed in a highly visible indicator, their share of the seats of the governing coalition. The vulnerability of the prime minister acts as a guarantee for the other members of the coalition, reinforcing or eventually replacing mutual trust among top politicians who are, by definition, adversaries. This guarantee is always zero in a presidential, or quasi-presidential, system. A president is not the *primus inter pares* a prime minister is, and cannot be replaced because of disagreements on policies, whatever their intensity. To achieve such a result a truly politico-criminal procedure such as impeachment must be followed.[14] Such a procedure is never part of normal, if agitated, political life; as Nixon's case illustrates, it is, in and by itself, an instance of deep crisis. Not every system may be strong enough to absorb that crisis. The institutional position of a president thus necessarily implies that the minority partners in a governing coalition have to participate in a subordinate position which is politically damaging for them and that they lend political capital without any guarantee. If the coalition breaks down the president simply returns to the starting point, deprived of the additional parliamentary support the coalition gave him, but the other members may have well been used in the president's benefit.

It may be argued that those characteristics of presidential systems affect even intraparty relationships as well, particularly when the president's party is fractionalized. The Members of Parliament (MPs) of a governing party have more influence on a prime minister than they could have on a president. Backbenchers' rebellions are not frequent, but they may and sometimes do happen; in this sense a prime minister is always re-creating his or her leadership. The institutional position of a president spares him those needs; his position cannot be affected by such rebellions, at least not in any immediate sense as that of a prime minister. It might be expected that because the institutional position of a president is stronger than that of a prime minister he should be more successful, other things being equal, in establishing his leadership within the party, if only because of the sheer opportunism of lesser politicians. Nevertheless, exactly the opposite is true for the other first-rank leaders of the president's party: they have to mark differences with respect to the president precisely because he already is in a qualitatively higher position—otherwise they risk losing too much precious visibility of their own, hence reinforcing the president's predominance and weakening their own political future. Needless to say, leaders of important fractions are always, by definition, first-rank politicians and competitors of the president; this has obvious implications concerning the fractions' behavior, implications which at least in Uruguay have always been clearly visible.

Finally, it should be underscored that the theoretical considerations involved in this discussion of the effects of Uruguayan political structures on the developmental question assume a structured party system *and* party government. (*Party government* means that the top decision-makers belong to the same party, though usually to different fractions. This upper echelon normally includes the ministers and the chiefs of the main fractions of the party.) This is an important remark because in Uruguayan tradition the term *coparticipación* (coparticipation) has several different meanings and it is sometimes understood as the opposite of party government. For the present purposes it will suffice to point out that Uruguayan democratic governments have always been party governments, whatever the level of coparticipación that may have existed according to some of those different meanings.[15] The same remark holds true concerning the effects of Uruguayan political structures on the democratic question—that is, the inability of political elites to confront the developmental question within a democratic order. To this problem we turn now.

It may be observed in the first place that democratic breakdowns occurred when men of weak democratic faith had become presidents. Although these men had the direct, personal support of about a quarter of the electorate or less, they felt that the system blocked their presidential rights and duties and began to ignore the rules, opening the road to authoritarianism. Nevertheless, the importance of personal attributes—underscored by the obvious fact that most Uruguayan presidents since 1918 did not stage coups—should not obscure the fact that Terra, Pacheco, and Bordaberry were indeed presidents. In at least partially consolidated polyarchies the institutional position of the president conveys a mix of resource and pressures which is by definition unique. He has material means, institutional resources, personal legitimacy and, when lacking parliamentary support, some arguments which provide him at a minimum with a ready-to-use rationalization for his eventual antisystem behavior. A prime minister lacks the relative independence of presidents from the legislature, lacks the legitimacy resulting from being directly elected by the whole electorate and, if leading a minority government, is subject to clearly defined rules governing the situation; in particular, a minority government can endure only as long as the majority allows. A politician who is at the same time chief of government and chief of state is more powerful *ceteris paribus* than another who is chief of government alone. Nevertheless, the difference between presidents and prime ministers does not boil down to power differentials. The presidential position seems to involve a greater expectation of leadership, irrespective of the political context. This seems to be related to the rules governing minority governments: there are well-defined rules concerning them in parliamentary systems, but not in presidential ones. As a result, the prime minister of a minority government has an explicitly caretaker role; this is not true for presidents in a comparable situation. The president has thus more power and more pressure to deliver.

In fact, in a polity sophisticated enough to become a relatively consolidated polyarchy it is difficult to stage a coup against the president—except in the case of a particularly inept one. The 1973 coup was led only nominally by the president, but it was not an exception to this rule. Leaving aside whether Bordaberry was inept or not, civilian institutions and the rule of law were seriously weakened by Pacheco, who had much more control of the situation than Bordaberry later did. By the time of the Tupamaros' defeat the political crisis had reached such dimensions that only a widely supported president who also was a skillfull politician and sincere democrat could have avoided the breakdown, but Bordaberry was not a sincere democrat and was probably one of the most isolated presidents—at the political elite's level—since the birth of democracy. He continued the encroachment that Pacheco had initiated of the executive branch on the whole government and allowed even more autonomy and power to the military. As a result, when he attempted to stop the military—in February, 1973—nobody trusted him and, accordingly, nobody was willing to help him. Unable to stop the military he negotiated with them: he managed to remain as president of the de facto regime by lending to their coup the prestige of his post.

The importance of the purely institutional factor beyond the effect of personal attributes is underscored by the role parliament played in both coups. In both 1933 and 1973 the breakdown followed clashes between the legislature and the president, and in both cases parliamentary majorities denied what the presidents were asking from them; the legislatures were an obstacle to presidential will, and their last sessions before their illegal dissolutions, which marked the final step of the respective crises, recorded their antiauthoritarian stance. Although inefficiently and too late the legislatures stood for democracy against the presidents who did not.

The two coups thus exhibited a Munich-like path during which parliamentary majorities—those that were to stand for democracy in the final confrontation—proved unable to stop presidents whose antidemocratic behaviors were increasingly clear. On the one hand this points out once more a crucial difference between presidential and parliamentary regimes: a no-confidence vote and the replacement of the chief of government by a more trusted leader could have taken place at an earlier stage than that of the final conflict between the president and the legislature, lowering the risk of breakdown. On the other hand, it shows crudely the compounding effects of the fractionalization of the major parties. The 1933 coup was unavoidable once Terra and Herrera reached an agreement, because Herrera was the leader of the major Blanco fraction. But even before that agreement things were difficult for the democratic Colorados. Without a common organization they had to reach an agreement with the Blanco minority, which was no better organized, to begin the almost impossible task—on practical grounds—of toppling a president of their own party. In 1973 the Blanco majority was definitely prodemocratic, but this time the democratic Colorados were a minority within their parliamentary party. This meant that an eventual early agreement against Pacheco or later Bordaberry was very difficult for the democratic Colorados because it would have involved a high risk of strengthening too much the Blancos' position—who, besides, also had their own nondemocratic right wing minority. When things became so obvious as to make such possibilities perhaps thinkable, then the possibility itself was pointless—time had run out and any such agreement would have led to the coup anyway.[16]

For the present purpose the most important conclusion of this analysis is the presence of the same themes in the answers to both the developmental and democratic questions. When the country confronted acute social and economic crises the increasing fragmentation and fractionalization of the party system led to persistent political stalemates which in turn inhibited the enactment of policies capable of dealing with those problems.[17] Uruguayan quasi-presidentialism worsened and froze those stalemates. The same factors reappear in the democratic question, although in the opposite order of importance and in a context in which short-term issues and almost aleatory events acquired more prominence than they had regarding the developmental question. The high-risk factor involved in the two breakdowns was Uruguayan quasi-presidentialism; the fractionalization of the major parties compounded its effects. Two of these common themes—quasi-presidentialism and the fractionalization of the major parties—are stable, structural traits of the Uruguayan polity. The third—the increasing fragmentation of the party system—is not; it is a relatively recent phenomenon to which I will return in the following chapters. It is important to note, however, that the historical parity of the votes received by the major parties, added to PR, often made the combined vote for the very small *parties of ideas* enough to deny a parliamentary majority to the governing party. At any rate, if the essentials of the preceding discussion are right, it follows that fractionalization alone was a severe obstacle to solving successfully the developmental question, and that it made credible checks on the behavior of unreliable, undemocratic presidents very difficult.

The lessons from the breakdowns may now be easily summarized. Two political structures proved adverse to democratic stability. The *fractionalization* of parties blocked the enactment of policies capable of confronting serious crises. *Quasi-presidentialism* first and then plain presidentialism provided the means untrustworthy men needed to impose their will against the rules and in so doing terminating democracy. Both breakdowns occurred when undemocratic politicians became presidents amidst severe crises; the Great Depression in the early 1930s, and the protracted crisis of the import-substituting industrialization process and its political sequels—including relatively successful urban guerrillas—forty years later. Either of the two factors separately considered increased the risk of breakdown during a crisis, but taken together the net effect was multiplicative, not additive, for each of them accentuated the negative effects of the other on democratic stability. It cannot be said, however, that these factors and their interactions *caused* the breakdowns. This is so for at least two reasons. First, both breakdowns were preceded by economic and social crises which had an important external dimension domestic policies could not alter.[18] Second, the surrounding circumstances and personality of the main actors—first and foremost those of the presidents—also played an important role.[19] But they did define a political framework particularly unsuited to withstand deep crises: Uruguayan democracy broke down under the pressure of the two great challenges it experienced since its birth.

The case on the consequences of these political structures is thus completed. In order to avoid misunderstandings, however, let us add a few remarks on the historical bounds of the argument. Concerning presidentialism, in particular, it is very obvious that it was the only republican alternative available in 1830, and that the creation of new monarchies was against the thrust of the revolutionary wars which emancipated the former Spanish colonies. It is certainly no accident that Brazil, which was spared an independence war, was the only South American country that actually tried nonrepublican institutions. As a result, the Uruguayan quasi-presidentialism initiated in 1918 was itself an important departure with respect to national tradition. This departure probably went as far as circumstances permitted; therefore the negative effect of quasi-presidentialism on the 1933 breakdown would have been unavoidable. That inevitability, however, was less and less so from 1942 onwards—as attested by the very discussions on the parliamentary aspects of the Uruguayan system summarized in Chapter 2. The 1966 constitutional reinforcement of presidentialism was simply the solution that the political elites thought best fitted Uruguayan political predicaments. Assuming—as I do—that democratic political stability was a central goal for them, according to the present argument they were wrong.

Fractionalization, on the other hand, greatly helped democratic instoration—particularly in its initial stages. It forced continued bargaining within the parties, bargaining which strengthened considerably intra-party democratic practices. There was no central party machine overpowering the minorities; the access to leadership was, at least in relative terms, extremely competitive, and the decisive admittance ticket was paid in votes. Furthermore, by making the minorities vitally interested in clean electoral practices—because their power was in their votes—and, more generally, in the strengthening of fair democratic procedures, it provided a considerable stimulus to democracy. Its contribution to the relatively early elimination of electoral fraud under a widely extended franchise seems to me particularly evident.[20] Fractionalization made all but the majority within the winning party—which always was a minority—directly interested in honest elections (*la pureza del sufragio*). It is difficult to overestimate the importance of such self-sustaining mechanisms in the early phases of consolidation of democracy.[21] In broad terms this view was shared by many first-rank politicians. If this picture was essentially right during the first third of the century, then, once more, there were no reasons to fight party fractionalization before the 1933 coup. By the end of the 1960s, however, party fractionalization had reached grotesque levels, and many political leaders worried about the eventual consequences of such a state of affairs.[22] Nevertheless, no change of the DSV was ever seriously considered. Electoral law is not a sacred matter, of course; changes were not considered because many did not see links between DSV and fractionalization, and others believed that the beneficial consequences of the DSV far outweighed its eventual shortcomings.[23] Critical views on the role of the DSV were widely known, however; its permanence was then a collective choice of the political elite.[24] Assuming, again, that democratic political stability was a central goal for this elite, according to the present argument they made the wrong choice.

In short: two of the central pillars which allowed the *building* of Uruguayan democracy proved unsuited to *maintain* it. How does this conclusion look in comparative perspective? Regarding the role of fractionalization little can be said. The performance of the highly fractionalized Italian and Japanese systems during the post-war years was truly outstanding; this means that fractionalization alone does not necessarily lead to stagnation. It is difficult to specify the factors that made the difference because there are many possibilities and too few cases. Regarding presidentialism, however, this analysis clearly supports some recent, though tentative, critical discussions of the presidential institution. In Linz's view "the consequences of the 'presidential' versus the 'parliamentary' game in democracies deserves further and more systematic analysis" (Linz 1978, p. 74), for the very institution of the presidency is at least part of the explanation of the recurrent crises of most presidential regimes. Almost all his considerations do apply, I think, to the Uruguayan case (ibid., pp. 71–74). According to Sartori presidential systems involve additional risks for the stability of highly polarized polities (Sartori 1982, p. 311). The critical point concerns the position of the president in the governing *blocco*: if the president is to the right of a right-wing bloc, or to the left of a left-wing bloc, then it is likely that further polarization will develop and that the system will approach breakdown (ibid., p. 313). As will be shown in Chapter 6, before the 1973 coup Uruguay had become a relatively highly polarized system, and Sartori's remarks on the relative positions of presidents that reinforce polarization and create breakdown risks fit perfectly Pacheco's and Bordaberry's positions in the political scene. Regarding the relationship between the two political structures, at least from a certain perspective the multiplicative effects of presidentialism and fractionalization are scarcely surprising. In a presidential Constitution the link between president and legislature is uncertain. The U.S. Constitution

> could never have been made to work if some of its vital deficiencies, not least the link between the executive and the legislature, had not been remedied by the political party. (Hofstadter 1969, p. viii)

The fractionalization of the governing party makes that linkage more difficult. This allows, or even fosters, conflicts between the executive and legislative powers—as was exactly the case in Uruguay before the 1933 and 1973 coups.

4. The 1984 Election: Restoration

1. Authoritarianism and Transition: 1973–1984

The initial years of the authoritarian regime (1973–1975) may be described as a *commissarial dictatorship* in its classical sense. Both government and opposition perceived the regime as an emergency solution which was not aimed at changing the institutional framework of the polity significantly. According to Zelmar Michelini, leader of the former Colorado group Lista 99 and cofounder of the Frente Amplio, at the beginning everybody within the military thought their government should not last beyond 1977. It was not until 1975—two years after the coup—that this idea began to be contested.[1]

The military decision of going ahead by themselves was the first step of a wider strategy that dominated the second phase of the military regime, from 1976 through 1980. The central goal became the building of a new political order, something like a *democradura* in Schmitter's terms; political repression increased again, probably in order to clear the way for the future regime. According to a report from a commission of the Chamber of Deputies issued in 1985, after democratic restoration, the majority of the political kidnappings that involved the military and whose victims remained "desaparecidos" occurred between 1975 and 1978.[2]

In spite of those somber facts, the projected regime was a real hybrid: in a nutshell, the military would have a last-instance control over a government which otherwise would be very much like that of the preceding democratic regime, including an explicit role for political parties. The attitude of the military towards democracy, or towards some of its aspects, was truly ambivalent. For they looked for the consent of the population to found their democradura: the project was to be completed and legitimated via a plebiscite. In an important respect this was not merely paying lip service to the idea of control by the citizens, as may be seen by comparing the approximately contemporary plebiscites in Chile and Uruguay. In both countries there was "structural fraud," in the sense that the campaign preceding the actual vote was extremely biased; the voice and actions of the opposition were curtailed in a similar manner in the Chilean plebiscites of 1978 and 1980 and in that of Uruguay in 1980. But in Chile the military were prepared for, and actually

53

committed, direct fraud: votes were not counted honestly.[3] The Uruguayan military simply acknowledged their defeat instead.

That defeat was the first step of the Uruguayan transition to democratic restoration (1980–1985), third and last stage of the military regime. The Uruguayan political parties played an important role in the military's defeat and its aftermath. In the first place, all significant leaders took sides in the matter. A majority of the political leadership had opposed the regime since its very beginning; that opposition increased and turned more explicit when it became clear that the regime no longer considered itself a transitional, emergency solution.

The line dividing those for and those against the regime ran across the parties except for the left, which opposed the military unanimously. Though internally divided, Blancos and Colorados did not act in the same ways towards the regime. The coup was headed at least nominally by a president elected from the Colorado majority, and its most important civilian support came from the former Colorado president, Jorge Pacheco Areco, and from his followers. Some first-rank Colorados worked for the military government in more or less technical roles. According to the relative positions obtained in the 1971 elections, the rightmost fractions of both major parties, the Colorado majority (the "pachequistas") and the Blanco minority supported the coup more or less explicitly and later also supported the constitutional project of the military. The Blanco majority (the "wilsonistas," from Wilson Ferreira, its leader) and the Colorado minority formed the core of the opposition to the regime. Thus the Blancos were the main political force within the opposition.

In fact, the Blancos also became the most radical opposition to the military. Ferreira carried on a tireless international campaign against the regime with the help—outside the country—of the left, a particularly unacceptable step from the point of view of the military. Hence, thanks partly to their own actions and partly to the forced local inaction of the left,[4] the Blanco majority increasingly appeared as the "hard" nucleus of the opposition. The regime itself—probably its "informal" supporters, not its formal leadership—reacted accordingly. Though nobody in the opposition had a peaceful living, the only leading politicians from the traditional parties that actually lost their lives to political violence were Blancos.

The pro-regime votes in the 1980 plebiscite amounted to 43 percent of the valid votes; this was just 6 points above the 37 percent the pro-regime political forces had obtained in the 1971 national election. Taking into account what I have called "structural" fraud this result did not look particularly impressive, and it did not bode well for the pro-regime political forces either. What is more, it should be underscored that at the time the defeat of the government looked far more impressive than now. The Chilean experiences had been successful from the point of view of the military, and in wider terms there were no comparable precedents of governmental defeat under harsh authoritarian conditions.[5] Ten years later, however, the electoral dimension of the Eastern European revolutions and other circumstances in Latin America as well have made us more familiar with that kind of event. But at the same time most observers, both Uruguayans and foreigners, thought until the very end that the military were going to win, eventually using direct fraud if needed.

After the defeat it took almost one year and a lot of suspense for the military to put in place an alternate plan. The new timetable assumed a reorganization of the political parties—except those of the left—through direct popular vote in 1982, and national elections in 1984. In spite of the dramatic political events of the following three years the plan worked until the end, leading to democratic restoration in 1985.

The 1982 internal elections within the legal parties (Blancos, Colorados, and the small Unión Cívica were an even greater political defeat for the military. A relatively high turnout of 60 percent of the registered electorate—the vote was not mandatory, as in ordinary national elections—produced a complete defeat of the pro-regime fractions within both major parties: opposition leaders won 78 percent of the Blanco votes and 70 percent of the Colorado votes. The Frente Amplio had called for a blank vote with poor results. All in all, the pro-regime fractions obtained a mere 23 percent of the votes. Hence the main result of the "internal" elections was that, according to the regime's own legality, the civilian opposition to the military became its only valid interlocutor.

Long, difficult negotiations between the military and the strengthened civilian opposition led to the so-called Naval Club Agreement which opened the way to the November, 1984, national elections. That agreement defined a case of *reforma pactada*, in Linz's terms, mixed with what Stepan called extrication led by the military as institution (Linz 1990a; Stepan 1986). In other words, the agreement was indeed a transaction; it was not imposed, in any meaningful sense of the term, on any of its participants. Everybody obtained something and conceded something. The military conceded almost everything except for two things: the Blanco leader Wilson Ferreira could not run for president, and at least in the short run the civilian leadership would not be able to change the top military leadership at its discretion.

The Naval Club Agreement was remarkable with regard to the role of the parties as well. The negotiating position of the Blancos was intransigent particularly with regard to the issue of *proscripciones* (banned political leaders). The military, who had taken a crash course in politics in 1980 and 1982, and the Colorados recognized that they alone could not strike a deal (for the Colorados were not a national majority), but the only other available partner was the left. The military were able to extract the necessary conclusions and to act accordingly. They changed their old line towards the left, allowing it to enter into the conversations, and the final result was the Naval Club Agreement. The Blancos did not take part in that agreement; confronted with the fait accompli, though, they reluctantly took part in the resulting election. Leaving aside the details, a particularly important point is that for the first time a political pact of great national significance was decided without the participation of one of the traditional parties. This reflected, of course, the new realities emerging from the 1971 elections, but it is ironical that the military were necessary for that first recognition of the new political world.[6]

At least at the party level the 1984 election reproduced the situation that first appeared with the results of the 1971 election. The Colorados won the election, as in 1971, but this time its liberal wing won comfortably within the party; the Batllista candidate, Julio María Sanguinetti, became the first president of the democratic restoration. The party system exhibited again the "two-and-a-half" pattern acquired in 1971: the two major parties winning each about 40 percent of the electorate, and the united left—the Frente Amplio, the "half party" of the system according to its share of the vote—winning the remaining 20 percent.[7] The results within the parties showed that the defeat of the military and their political friends was even greater than in 1980 and 1982. Within the Colorados they obtained less than a quarter of the votes of the party. Within the Blancos they disappeared: in spite of PR, they were not able to elect a single representative. On the whole, the pro-military 43 percent of the vote in 1980, which had decreased to 23 percent by 1982, by 1984 had boiled down to 11 percent of the vote.

As noted above, the 1984 election was not open to all candidates. Among other *proscriptos*, the most prominent member of the civilian opposition, the Blanco Wilson Ferreira, was banned from running for president. He was not even allowed to campaign for his party, since he was jailed until after election day, whereas another famous *proscripto*, the recently freed Frente Amplio leader Líber Seregni, worked hard for his coalition. Nevertheless, everybody accepted the results of the election, though probably for different reasons. Irrespective of the nature of those reasons, everybody was also convinced that in spite of the limitations of its origin the spirit of the new government was truly democratic and that the *proscripciones* had ended. The three following chapters and the remainder of this one will examine in a more detailed manner the political landscape of the democratic restoration as it emerged from the 1984 election.

2. A Restored Party System

All Uruguayans would probably agree that the thirteen years preceding the 1984 election—beginning with the last general election before the coup, in 1971—have been by far the harshest, most traumatic years the nation experienced since the end of the last civil war in 1904. Therefore the resemblance between the 1971 and the 1984 electoral results looks particularly striking. Many Uruguayan commentators, however, have taken this continuity for granted, as a more or less natural result of national idiosyncrasy; others have even assumed that in the aftermath of an authoritarian regime the preceding political alignments tend to reappear. This last argument confuses the problem. On the one hand, it is true that nobody expected any fundamental change in the structure of the party system. This expectation was based both on national experience and on some comparative evidence available. Considering the age of the party system and the historically observed strength of party identifications, the most reasonable forecast was obviously the stability of the party system. The events during the transition also pointed against big surprises.[8]

Nevertheless, all of the above applies to the broad picture, not to the concrete vote alignment. Knowing that the party system was going to be essentially the same as before did not tell much about the election returns or the identity of the winner. What is more, under comparable circumstances the close similarity of electoral results pre- and postauthoritarianism is the exception, not the rule. It did not happen either in Spain or in Brazil or, for a closer term of comparison, in Argentina in 1983. Thirteen years is a relatively long period: it is longer that the whole life of the Third Reich, for example. The Second World War was even shorter; nevertheless, in studying electoral volatility in postwar Europe, Pedersen took 1948 as his starting point precisely because of

> the highly irregular character of the elections immediately after the Second World War . . . In many countries also the outcome of the first election was highly atypical for the country . . . Thus 1948, which is the year when the second round of elections after the war really began, seems to be the natural starting point for a mapping of patterns of change and persistence. (Pedersen 1983, p. 34)

According to those experiences, then, a close resemblance between the 1984 and previous election returns was a rather unlikely event. The remaining argument favoring such a resemblance, the "idiosyncratic" theme which reduces the question to national tradition simply evades the problem. To put some order into this discussion it is necessary to answer at least two questions: First, which is the "local idiosyncrasy" on this matter? Second, what exactly is meant by saying that the 1971 and 1984 election results are very similar?

Table 4.1 presents Pedersen's index of aggregate (or net) volatility for the eight general elections from 1946 through 1984. The index "is simply the cumulated gains for all parties in the party system" (Pedersen 1983, p. 33) expressed as percentage differences. Computing either the losses of the parties or one half of the sum of the absolute values of the difference of vote shares for each party gives of course the same result.[9] The table shows that "national idiosyncrasy" on this matter is indeed relatively low volatility, at least by comparison with European data. Pedersen reports a total average volatility of 8.1 for thirteen European countries during the years 1948–77. The Uruguayan average (7.1) is thus lower. Five out of Pedersen's thirteen countries show lower means than Uruguay (Austria, 3.7; Switzerland, 4.0; Sweden, 5.2; United Kingdom, 5.9; and Finland, 6.8); the remaining eight countries have higher means than Uruguay (ranging from Belgium and Ireland, 7.9, to France, 16.8). It should be underscored that the Uruguayan data include two somewhat extraordinary elections: 1942, the first really "normal" election after the 1933 coup, and 1984 itself. Without them the average is slightly lower (6.8).

TABLE 4.1
Net Electoral Volatility, 1946–1984

1942–46: 10.6	1958–62: 5.3
1946–50: 5.9	1962–66: 7.2
1950–54: 2.1	1966–71: 8.6
1954–58: 11.5	1971–84: 5.2

Average volatility: 7.1
Standard deviation: 2.9

Values of Pedersen's index (cumulated gains of all the parties which improved their share of the vote from the first election to the second, expressed as percentage differences) computed on election results as reported in Rial (1984a, 1985) and Balbis (1984). Splinter fractions from traditional parties which later returned to their original trunks were not counted separately. The year 1966 is considered in different ways to compute 1962–66 and 1966–71 volatilities. The votes for the small parties which formed the Frente Amplio in 1971 are counted together in 1966 to compute the 1966–71 volatility; this is necessary to avoid an artificially high volatility. They are counted separately, however, to compute the 1962–66 volatility, as well as during the whole period 1942–62. Not doing so does violence to the substance of political events.

Second, the 1971–84 net electoral volatility is indeed low by comparison with Uruguay's own previous experience. Only one of the elections of Table 4.1 shows a lower value (1954: the 1950–54 volatility was 2.1). Furthermore, there is only one election substantively comparable—at least to some extent—to 1984: the 1942 election, which also followed a coup. The last election where all relevant parties competed before 1942 was in 1931; the gap 1931–42, eleven years, is also comparable to the gap existing between the 1971 and 1984 elections. Pedersen's index for 1931–42, however, is 10.2:

it almost doubles the 1971–84 value, and it is the third highest value of the computed indexes, nine in all.

In short: Uruguayan electoral volatility has been relatively low since World War II, and the 1984 election exhibited a particularly low volatility with regard to Uruguay's own electoral history during the past half century. This last result is somewhat unexpected, at least when considering some relevant experiences in other countries and Uruguay's only comparable election in the past. This does not mean that the election returns surprised Uruguayans.[10] It means that the reasons which explain the resilience of the parties' share of the vote are indeed powerful, and that most probably they should shed some light on Uruguay's political prospects. The conclusion I think this analysis has already substantiated is simple: the 1984 election was a remarkable restoration of the party system.

3. A Restored Political Class

The authoritarian regime did not like the behavior of the political parties during the precoup years. This was particularly true of the civilians who occupied government posts. Beginning with the ideas of the first president of the regime, Juan María Bordaberry, the elected civilian president who also nominally headed the coup, there were several different proposals to suppress or significantly reduce the role of political parties.[11] Nevertheless, even though some of those civilians had real influence on the regime, this influence resulted merely from their personal skills. The final decisions were always taken by the military, and on this matter their decisions were clear and consistent: the parties themselves were not responsible for the misdeeds of the politicians who circumstantially had led them. The parties had to be reformed, not suppressed.[12] As early as 1974 the military declared their aim of moralizing and democratizing the political parties. In 1976, after a much publicized polemic with Bordaberry that ended with the ouster of the president, they declared that they did not want to share "the historical responsibility of suppressing the traditional parties" (Zubillaga 1985, p. 92). Even though not all the civilians who supported and served the regime shared Bordaberry's views, there is more than a small irony in this spectacle of the military defending, in their own manner, the political parties against the attack of some noted politicians, including a democratically elected president.

Most of the politicians themselves, however, did not enjoy this military benevolence. In 1976 the Institutional Act #4 suspended for fifteen years the political rights—except the right to vote—of all successful candidates for legislative office in the 1971 and 1966 elections. The same measure was taken against all candidates for executive office, even the unsuccessful, as well as all candidates for legislative office, successful or not, of the parties "associated" in those elections with organizations outlawed later on. The candidates of the outlawed groups could not even vote. It has been estimated that this decision proscribed politically about 15,000 persons. Had Brazil applied the same rigor, in relative terms, as the Uruguayan military, half a million Brazilians would have been deprived of their political rights instead of the five hundred actually proscribed.

Most of those proscriptions were revoked before the 1984 election.[13] They show eloquently, however, the dominant mood within the military towards the political elite. Politicians tended to be perceived as members of a closed group that retained its dominant position thanks to manipulative, nondemocratic practices, that perpetuated itself through cooptation and was thoroughly pervaded by corruption. Did the military succeed in their attempt to renovate the political leadership?

Table 4.2 shows that half the members of the new legislature had no previous experience in elective office, and that only one-third of the members had been legislators before the coup. In other words, the turnover for the legislature as a whole was two-thirds.[14] The table also shows that there are large differences between the political careers of representatives and senators, differences to which I will return later. To ascertain the meaning of these figures it is necessary, first, to establish some criteria for comparison, and second, to take into account the thirteen years elapsed since the preceding election.

TABLE 4.2

Previous Elective Office of Legislators (Percent)

Elective office prior to the coup	Representatives	Senators	All
None	56	40	53
Sub-national level only	18	—	13
Representative once	17	5	14
Legislator twice	7	23	11
Legislator three or more periods	2	32	9
(N)	(84)	(23)	(107)

Entries are column percentages. Answers weighted according to main fractions.

According to the only published work on the subject, the Uruguayan average legislative turnover for the six elections from 1950 through 1971 was fifty percent.[15] This is a very high figure by comparison with old and established legislatures. Both West German and British lower houses had about fifty percent turnover immediately after World War II, but in both cases it dropped steadily to level off at about 25 to 30 percent in West Germany and 15 to 25 percent in Britain. Analogously, the turnover of the first regular legislative election in Italy after the War, in 1948, was 56 percent (with respect to the 1946 *Costituente*), but in the following election (1953) it had already dropped to 36 percent (Somogy 1963, p. 17). The average turnover in the U.S. House of Representatives during the years 1950–68 was just 16 percent (Loewenberg and Patterson 1979, pp. 106 and ff.). By the end of the sixties almost all lower houses in democracies had turnover rates of less than 30 percent (Blondel 1973, Appendix C). In fact, turnover rates as high as the Uruguayan average tend to be associated—at least in democracies— with major disruptions of national life. Post-World War II Britain and West Germany, as quoted above, provide good examples. More generally:

> Major constitutional changes or radical alterations in the pattern of so-cial and economic power in a country are likely to produce a high proportion of new members in a legislature. The turnover indicates a disruption of the legislature's way of doing business. In 1930, 40 percent of the members of the German Reichstag were new, although during the 1920s the turnover rate had averaged 25 percent. (Loewen-berg and Patterson 1979, p. 108)

It should be emphasized that these comparisons understate the Uruguayan figures. First, most of the non-Uruguayan data are based on the more re-stricted definition of turnover, which does not consider simply previous parliamentary experience, but presence in the *immediately precedent* leg-islature. Most probably this definition should produce higher turnover rates if applied to Uruguay; in any case it cannot produce lower rates. Second, the non-Uruguayan data refer to lower houses. The corresponding Uruguayan figure is 59 percent, not 50 percent. In short: Uruguay's turnover rates since the 1950s double most of the highest rates of other democracies. All of this, I think, is more than enough to substantiate the statement above: at least by comparison with other democracies Uruguayan turnover has been exception-ally high since 1950.

It is also necessary to consider the thirteen years elapsed since the last parliamentary election, in 1971. This would have included more than three legislative terms according to the 1952 Constitution, or more than two and a half according to the present Constitution.[16] It is difficult to handle this problem in a systematic way. It might be argued that the freezing of polit-ical activity under authoritarian conditions does not favor the replacement of former political leadership. Quite naturally, the freezing conserves old leaders because it does not provide opportunities for new potential leaders to compete for leadership positions. This reasoning, however, does not fit actual Uruguayan conditions. Open political activity began in 1980 because of the plebiscite, and by 1982 it had become very intense because of the *elecciones internas* to choose party leadership within the traditional parties and the small Unión Cívica. As a result, some of the most important leaders of both traditional parties had no political experience before 1980—e.g., the vice president elected in 1984, Enrique Tarigo, began his political career fighting against the regime's projected constitution.[17] Thus, it seems that a rather negative point might be made: the impact on Uruguayan politicians of the extended period with no parliamentary elections may have produced more withdrawals from political careers than more normal times. This is so simply because at least some of the politicians who in normal times would have developed successful political careers became so involved in other endeavors that they did not wish, or simply could not attempt to return to full-time political life. It should be remembered that political activity from 1980 onwards was "amateur" in the sense that politicians could not earn a living at it.

Thus, in order to discuss the 1984 "turnover" two steps should be taken. First, data from a more normal thirteen-year period should be collected. This may be done as follows: choose a starting point (the first year of a legislature, for example) and establish how many of its members had already been legislators thirteen years before, yielding a "thirteen-years turnover" minimum estimate. Second, to obtain a more realistic estimate it would be necessary to expand that minimum estimate according to some "corrective factor" in order to take into account the extra-withdrawal effect mentioned above. This procedure would produce an empirically based estimate of the effects on the political class of thirteen years with neither parliament nor professional politics. Once this were done, the resulting estimate might be directly compared to the 1984 observed "turnover." If the observed turnover were greater than the estimate then the difference would measure the success of the military in renovating the political leadership. If the difference were nil, or negative, then the military's efforts would have been a failure, or would even have had the opposite effect than intended.

Unfortunately, this cannot be done. The second step, the transformation of the minimum into a more realistic estimate, is probably impossible in Uruguay as everywhere because there is no simple way to decide which should be the required "corrective factor." The minimum itself, however, would provide a useful baseline. But the data necessary to compute this minimum are not available in the Uruguayan literature. Thus, all that can be done is to look elsewhere for an admittedly rather crude comparison. There are at least two different approaches for such a comparison. One is to estimate the just-mentioned baseline in a contemporary, well-established democracy. British data show that 40 percent of the MPs elected in 1983 had first entered Parliament in the 1970 general election or before. The "turnover" that could serve as a baseline for comparison with the 1984 Uruguayan election was then 60 percent. This figure amounts to 2.6 times the "regular" British turnover, which was 23 percent.[18] Thus, according to the preceding discussion the theoretical "thirteen years-no Parliament" turnover corresponding to the British data should be higher than 60 percent. The other approach is a comparison with the "turnover" resulting from a more similar context—i.e., before and after a relatively comparable regime with no elected legislature. From this perspective, Primo de Rivera's dictatorship in Spain provides in principle a reasonable term of comparison. Eight years elapsed from the last legislative election of the constitutional monarchy (1923) till the first of the republic (1931); 14 percent of the *diputados* elected in 1931 had served in the legislature of the monarchy (Linz 1972, p. 385). The "turnover" following Primo de Rivera's dictatorship was thus 86 percent. As Linz has shown, however, there was a large discontinuity between the pre- and postdictatorship Spanish political elites. The Weimar republic would seem to be a more appropriate reference. The last legislature of the empire, before the 1918 revolution and the military defeat, was elected in 1912; ten years later, in 1922, the first ordinary legislature of the republic was elected: 27 percent of its members had already been in the Reichstag before 1918. The "turnover" was 73 percent.[19]

The two approaches lead to consistent results: upper and lower bounds of 86 percent (the Spanish second republic) and 60 percent (British contemporary data) respectively, and a "reasonable" turnover estimate of 73 percent (the Weimar republic). We can turn now to the 1984 Uruguayan election. According to Table 4.2, the 1984 "turnover" was 66 percent.[20] This does not seem very far from the average level 1950–71 (50 percent). A first striking point regarding this "turnover" is how close it is to the estimate computed on British data ("higher than 60 percent"). This is particularly remarkable when considering that the average British turnover for the 1950–71 period— 24 percent—was less than half the Uruguayan corresponding figure. In fact, the 1984 Uruguayan turnover figure (66) is precisely midway between the lower bound (60) and the "reasonable" estimate (73). The obvious conclusion, then, is this: the military's attempt to renovate the political class failed in the sense that influential politicians at the time of the coup returned to Parliament in greater proportion than what could reasonably be expected for such an extended period.

A closer look at Table 4.2 shows the real extent of that failure. The Senate, as in most bicameral presidential regimes, has always been the most important and prestigious chamber. Normally it includes the upper stratum of the political elite. An example will suffice to illustrate the point: the presidential candidates of the most important fractions of the traditional parties more often than not also run at the top of their fractions' lists to the Senate. Because of that it is not surprising that the Senate's turnover has been consistently far lower than the lower chamber's. Guidobono's data show that the Senate's average turnover from 1950–71 was 21 percent, while the House's was 59 percent (Guidobono 1986, p. 159). The 1984 election was no exception to the rule: most of the top political leaders won seats in the Senate, whose "turnover" was just 40 percent.[21] This is far lower than the British 60 percent "baseline." It might be argued that a direct comparison is not appropriate because of the low average turnover, in normal times, of the Uruguayan Senate. This objection is easily circumvented. The British "thirteen-years" turnover was 60 percent, that is, 2.5 times the average of the period 1950–71. The same rate (2.5) applied to the average Senate turnover for the same years—that is, 21 percent—yields 52 percent, lower than the 60 percent "baseline" but still far higher than the observed turnover. With regard to national precedents, finally, Guidobono pointed out that the 1984 Senate turnover was in fact close to the turnover of the 1954 and 1962 elections, two entirely normal elections, and that this was a surprising finding given the circumstances of the 1984 election (Guidobono 1986, pp. 159–160). In short, the military's efforts to renovate the political leadership did not merely fail—they backfired.

Backfire is indeed an appropriate term, for on the one hand the turnover was lower than could have been expected given the length of the period without parliamentary elections, and on the other the actual turnover was in part due to the political decline of the friends of the military. The proauthoritarian fractions disappeared within the Partido Nacional, and shrunk from being the majority to being a quarter of the vote within the Partido Colorado.[22] These changes opened spaces to be filled by the antiauthoritarian fractions, thus improving the chances of comparatively inexperienced politicians to gain office. Perhaps the most striking example of the antimilitary backlash is this: only one of the members of the new legislature had been in the legislature directly appointed by the authoritarian regime,[23] and none had occupied high-ranking positions in its administration.

In fact, most legislators had personal grievances against the authoritarian regime. When asked whether they had been harassed for political reasons, almost three quarters of them answered affirmatively. The answers to the question asked regarding what troubles they had experienced were revealing in several ways. Most of them took for granted the conflictive, adversarial nature of their relationship with the military; only a handful of the interviewees, for example, bothered to mention that they had had their political rights suspended.

Even though the legislature certainly did not act vindictively, the data reported in Table 4.3 may help to understand why its first action was to free all political prisoners, including former guerilla members, but only two years later did it pass a law granting amnesty to the members of the security forces for human rights violations during the authoritarian regime. Politicians experienced directly the repressive harshness of the regime in greater proportion than the population at large. The more prominent the politician's position, the more likely he was to experience the regime's political persecution; this explains the differences between representatives' and senators' answers.

TABLE 4.3

Political Harassment Experienced by Legislators (Percent)

Harassment	Representatives	Senators	All
None	35	4	28
Threats, arrests for cross-examination; other forms of intimidation*	33	34	33
Fired from public and/or private jobs	21	19	21
Prosecution, prison, exile; harassment directed against family	10	42	18
(N)	(84)	(23)	(107)

Entries are column percentages. Answers weighted according to main fractions.

* The other forms of intimidation mentioned in the table included wired phones, shadowing, different types of economic sanctions, etc. Comparatively few interviewees—just 6 in 107—had lived in exile, all of them Blancos or Frentistas. Four had been living for some time in Argentina, though only one stayed there uninterruptedly until 1984.

Table 4.4 shows that party affiliation indicated significant differences in the nature of the politicians' relationships with the military regime. Even though differences in the attitudes towards the authoritarian regime and particularly towards the transition period may influence the answers, it seems impossible for differences as large as those reported to be reducible to differences in perception. The Colorados were the *blandos*, the softliners capable of leading the transition at least in part because they had experienced less harassment. Their differences vis-à-vis their fellow politicians were not merely ideological. Nevertheless, it is still true that within the new legislature the senators as a group—that is, the leading politicians—were harder hit by the military regime than the members of any particular party.

Finally, this restored political elite had few personal ties with those who had governed the country during the authoritarian regime. Three-quarters of the new legislators had neither friends nor relatives among them. Two out of ten had personal ties—mostly family ties—with military officers, and only one out of ten had ties with the civilian elite of the former regime. Social ties *within* the political elite not linked to the authoritarian government were

TABLE 4.4
Political Harassment and Party Affiliation of Legislators (Percent)

Harassment	Colorados	Blancos	Frentistas
None	46	25	–
Threats, arrests for cross-examination; other forms of intimidation	34	35	30
Fired from public and/or private jobs	13	10	56
Prosecution, prison, exile; harassment directed against family	7	30	18
(N)	(36)	(42)	(27)

Entries are column percentages. Answers weighted according to main fractions.

far stronger: six out of ten interviewees said they had political leaders among their closest friends or relatives.

The differences in the frequencies of personal ties reported in Table 4.5 cannot be due merely to the different numbers of members of each of the three elites—i.e., the military, civilians who worked for the authoritarian government, and the political elite. By any reasonable account there are more military officers—about 3,500 in 1985—than political leaders. A generous estimate could put the number of political leaders at about 500; this is an

TABLE 4.5
Legislators and the Military Regime: Personal Ties (Percent)

Personal ties	Representatives	Senators	All
None	77	69	75
Military officers only	14	14	14
Civilians in important government positions only	4	9	5
Both	6	8	6
(N)	(84)	(23)	(107)

"Could you tell me whether there is . . . among your closest friends or relatives?" (any military officer; somebody who occupied important positions in the military regime). Entries are column percentages. Answers weighted according to main fractions.

upper bound for almost every sensible definition. As for the civilians who occupied high-ranking posts during the authoritarian regime, that is, ministers, under-secretaries, directors of public enterprises, and members of the *Consejo de Estado*, they were less than one tenth of the number of military officers— probably about 250. Considering size,[24] then, the less connected group were the military. Their civilian collaborators were less isolated from the political elite. It should be added that in this regard party affiliation made no difference: the percentages within each of the major *lemas* do not differ more than one point, on average, from the totals reported in Table 4.5. The military and their collaborators were isolated from the political class as a whole, independent of party affiliations.

4. Summing Up: Military and Politicians

The authoritarian regime did have an impact on politicians. On the one hand, although its efforts backfired, thirteen years elapsed between 1971, the last previous general election, and 1984. The mere passage of time increased legislative turnover to higher levels than in the recent post-World War II past. On the other hand, this hiatus disrupted the normal career patterns of politicians. Table 4.2 included the answer "Representative once," not "legislator once," because there were legislators who had been representatives once, but not just "senators once." All of those who had been senators before 1984 had previously been representatives. In fact, the answers show very clearly that the general pattern of a successful political career was from local elective office to the House to the Senate, including eventual passages through nonelective office. This was not true in 1984, as Table 4.2 shows: 40 percent of senators—or at least one-third, according to Guidobono and Rial—had no previous experience as legislators.

The first, most general conclusion on the 1984 election is its remarkable restorative character. At the party level the election exhibited an unexpectedly low volatility, and the parliamentary "turnover" was also lower than it would have probably been without the authoritarian irruption. The military regime slowed the pace of renovation of the political leadership, even though this was not the most reasonable course of events. Behind this "unreasonable" development lies the collective will of the opposition leadership to resist the military, even though before 1980 they did little more than the time-honored practice of retreat and wait. That will did not work in a vacuum; it was reinforced by other factors. On the one hand, the officer corps was a relatively isolated group, at least with regard to the politicians. The military harassed most politicians and relied on mostly nonprestigious civilian collaborators. This strengthened a feeling of solidarity within the opposition; the military were the common enemy, the usurpers. Not able to coopt opposition politicians, the military probably did not realize the need to do so until it was too late—that is, until after the plebiscite of 1980.

The picture I have attempted to describe shows an antimilitary restoration, and I think it responds to the facts. It leaves us, however, with a paradox: the leader of that restoration was precisely the Colorado Party, the party which elected the President who at least nominally headed the coup. The Colorados also were the party of the strongest ally of the military, the former President Pacheco, who still leads a strong fraction and who ran for president as the favorite candidate of the military. This paradox is related to another, less blatant but no less important: at least since 1950 Uruguay has combined a comparatively low electoral volatility and a comparatively high parliamentary turnover, particularly in the lower chamber. The next chapter will begin to discuss these paradoxes while addressing the nonrestorative aspects of the 1984 election.

5. The 1984 Election: Changes

1. Changes within the Parties

At the party level the 1984 election had two particularly obvious and important characteristics. The first was the confirmation of the trends that appeared during the transition. The 1982 *elecciones internas* that chose the leadership of the legal parties penalized the proauthoritarian fractions; their defeat in the 1984 election was even more pronounced. The leaders of the Colorado majority in the 1971 election were the main civilian supporters of the authoritarian regime. While they had obtained 56 percent of the Colorado vote in 1971, they fell to 31 percent in the 1982 *elecciones internas* and to a mere 24 percent in 1984; they experienced a thirty-two-point decline during the period. Because of the complexities of the Uruguayan electoral system and the shifting alliances of minor leaders, these figures are reasonable approximations of the electoral strength of the proauthoritarian fractions, not exact data. The 1971 figure is Bordaberry's share of the Colorado vote. Bordaberry won the 1971 election and remained president after the coup, until he was ousted by the military. The 1982 figure is Pacheco's share of the Colorado vote. Pacheco was president from 1967 through 1971. He was Bordaberry's political mentor; he decided on Bordaberry's candidacy, supported the coup, and in 1980 supported the proregime vote. In fact, from the very moment of the coup Pacheco himself, not Bordaberry, was considered the military's most important civilian ally.[1] The 1984 figure is, quite naturally, Pacheco's share of the Colorado vote.[2] Both before and after the election he was widely perceived as the military's preferred choice. Blancos and Frentistas pointed to Pacheco as the military's candidate, and the Pachequistas neither bothered to answer this claim nor looked particularly upset by it. After the election the press reported enlightening details: overwhelming Colorado-Pachequista majorities were obtained at some polling booths that because of their placement were almost exclusively used by military personnel.

The same trend may be seen within the Blancos. The fractions which supported the authoritarian regime obtained 34 percent of the Blanco vote in 1971, 26 percent in the 1982 *elecciones internas*, and just 3 percent in 1984. They experienced, then, a thirty-one-point fall during the period. Estimates are also approximate in this case. The 1971 figure is Aguerrondo's share of the Blanco vote. Aguerrondo was a retired general, presidential candidate of the conservative fractions; he was widely seen as a nationalistic, conservative hard-liner. From one of the *sub-lemas* which supported his candidacy came some of the most prestigious members of the authoritarian regime's *Consejo de Estado*. The 1982 figure includes the votes of Gallinal, an influential Blanco who supported the regime in 1980, and all the smaller fractions not linked either to Gallinal or to the oppositionist Blancos.[3] The 1984 figure, finally, is Paysée's share of the Blanco vote. He was the only proauthoritarian Blanco candidate. The military had appointed him *Intendente* of Montevideo, that is, a weaker equivalent of a provincial governor.

The voters of both traditional parties thus followed parallel trends: the proauthoritarian fractions lost roughly one-third of their parties' vote from 1971 to 1984. Were these changes abnormal in the context of Uruguayan political history? Not with regard to the last thirty years. Since 1954 the governing fractions have always lost the elections, either to the rival party or to a rival fraction of the same party, with a particularly notable exception in 1971. What was indeed new was the similarity of the trends within both traditional parties, and the authoritarian regime deserves most, if not all, the credit for such a result.

The discussion so far has been restricted to the traditional parties because of the obvious fact that the Frente Amplio did not have proauthoritarian regime fractions. Nevertheless, the 1984 election had a second characteristic, related but not reducible to the first, that affected the three main *lemas* in the same ways. As many commentators pointed out in the days that followed the election, the winners within the three parties were their political centers.[4] Within the traditional parties the losers were their right wings; within the Frente Amplio the loser was its left wing. This process was related to the decay of the proauthoritarian fractions because all such fractions belonged to the right wings of their parties; the two processes were not identical, however, for two reasons. On the one hand, not all the leaders of the right wing fractions were proauthoritarian; on the other hand, the leftmost fractions weakened by the second process certainly did not support the authoritarian government—they were in fact its main victims.

The displacement towards the center within the Frente Amplio may be assessed in two somewhat different ways. First, let us consider the electoral strength of the most radical Frentistas, the proguerrilla vote. This is not an easy task. It has been argued that most such voters voted the Patria Grande *sub-lema* of the Frente in 1971, but not all of this *sub-lema*'s voters were proguerrilla. The Frente's *sub-lema* that in 1984 inherited at least this reputation was the Izquierda Democrática Independiente (IDI). Patria Grande obtained 23 percent of the FA vote in 1971, whereas IDI obtained just 7 percent in 1984. A second, far more diluted but also more dependable comparison may be made between the 1971 and 1984 votes of the Frente's left wing as a whole—that is, the above mentioned fractions plus the communists and their allies (the Fidel in 1971, and Democracia Avanzada in 1984) and the Socialist Party (which was avowedly "Marxist-Leninist" in both elections). In these terms the left wing vote fell from 68 percent of the Frente total in 1971 to 50 percent in 1984. Both measurements, then, lead to the same conclusion: about a fifth of the Frente's voters shifted towards the center of the political spectrum.

This process of displacement towards the center within the three main *lemas* is more general than the first process—the decline of proauthoritarian fractions—because it involves at the same time all the relevant parties of the system. It also leads to more optimistic short-term forecasts for democracy because it weakened all the antisystem forces of the political spectrum. At least a significant part of the leftmost fractions weakened in the process cared very little about what they called contemptuously "bourgeois" democracy. Furthermore, the importance of those fractions was greater than their actual electoral strength, because at least in symbolic terms they were highly successful in pulling the whole Frente towards the left. The radical left which sought social revolution eventually at the expense of "bourgeois" democracy and the theoretically peaceful Frente Amplio became allies in the eyes of friends and foes.[5] In short: the process of displacement towards the center reduced the polarization of the system because it simultaneously reduced the electoral strength of the proauthoritarian fractions of the right and the prerevolutionary fractions of the left of the political spectrum. I will return to this point in the following chapter.

From a methodological point of view, however, previous discussions concerning the positions of parties and fractions in the left-right dimension have been too subjective.[6] Even though most of the published analyses tend to agree, writers seldom mention the reasons they have for their ordering of parties and fractions along the left-right continuum. The resulting lack of precision has blurred the distinction between the two processes, that is, the electoral decline of proauthoritarian fractions and the displacement towards the political center of the voters within each of the main *lemas*. Often one or both processes are referred to generally as the voters' choice for "moderation." Thus, a more solid basis for these analyses is needed. I will attempt to provide such a basis for analyzing elite and mass public opinions in the following sections and the next chapter.

Finally, these changes on the left-right continuum are certainly related to the history of the authoritarian regime, if only because they are related to the decline of the proauthoritarian fractions. In some relevant senses, however, they may be seen as the crystallization of processes that began before the authoritarian order—in fact, processes of which the authoritarian order itself was one of the results. Within this broader perspective the changes occur not merely within the parties; what is in process of transformation is the party system.

2. Changes within the Party System

Chapter 2 provided a brief history of the traditional parties. The more liberal profile of the Colorados since last century and the enduring impact of José Batlle y Ordóñez on Uruguayan political life put the Colorados to the left of the Blancos until 1971. Twenty years after the death of Don José in 1929 his nephew, Luis Batlle Berres, who also became president, reinforced this historical place of the Colorados. Luis Batlle was a dominant political figure of his times, and his policies and style are often referred to as populist, even though within an entirely democratic polity—an exceptional combination in Latin America. In short, seeing Batllismo, and with it the Colorados, to the left of the Blancos is not a black-and-white matter, but on the whole the picture is reasonably clear and most students of Uruguayan politics agree with this judgment.

Towards the end of the fifties and throughout the sixties a relatively slow displacement towards the right of the political spectrum became increasingly visible within both traditional parties. This rightward drift affected the Colorados more severely. One symptom of the displacement, and of its greater impact on the Colorados, was the exit from both traditional parties of several politicians who built alliances outside the traditional parties with the left, the "parties of ideas." The first relevant losses were experienced by the Blancos (the former Blanco Minister Erro, who made an electoral alliance with the Socialist Party—the Unión Popular—in 1962), but the most important was experienced by the Colorados (Zelmar Michelini and Hugo Batalla, cofounders of the Frente Amplio). The loss of left wing leaders and the displacement towards the right stopped first in the Partido Nacional. The 1971 election returns showed that Wilson Ferreira had conquered the Blanco majority; he was the undisputed leader of his party. But Ferreirismo was by then the dominant political force of the center-left section of the political spectrum; the Blancos were thus to the left of the Colorados. The Colorados dominated the right and the center-right, although the two parties had at least some relevant politicians in all three sections, from the center-left through the right. The authoritarian regime finally stopped the Colorados' rightward drift. The 1971 election was the rightmost mark; 1984 signaled that the pendulum was swinging to the opposite direction.

Those displacements towards the right within the traditional parties were accompanied by several attempts at popular front building. Two preliminary and unsuccessful experiences—the Unión Popular and the Fidel in the 1962 and 1966 elections—led to the birth of the Frente Amplio a few months before the 1971 election. The Frente was a wider coalition than the Chilean Unidad Popular (UP) because it included the Christian Democrats and its program was in principle more reformist and less revolutionary than the UP's. Nevertheless, the Tupamaros played a role similar to the Chilean MIR's. In practice, both the UP and the Frente appeared as legal movements which were at least tacitly allied to the revolutionary, armed left, and at worst they appeared as having, more or less in disguise, their own armies waiting for a good opportunity. Needless to say, the political right and the military saw the situation in the latter terms. To many activists in the left the difference with such a view was merely semantic: the armed left was there "just in case," and it was certainly better having it than not having it.

Whatever the case, the Frente Amplio obtained nearly a fifth of the popular vote in 1971, after just a few months of political activity. In the context of Uruguayan political history this was a significant success. In retrospect, perhaps the most important question about that success is whether it was obtained thanks to, or in spite of, the ambiguous relationship between Frente Amplio and the guerrillas. But it was undoubtedly a success, even though many expected an even stronger showing of the left on the basis of its remarkable capability of mobilizing its electoral support in street demonstrations. The left had, and still has, a higher ratio of militants to voters than the traditional parties. This success may be epitomized through three facts unheard of in Uruguayan political history prior to 1971:

(i) never had a third force gained a fifth of the national electorate;

(ii) never had a third force relegated one of the traditional parties to third place in the most important electoral district of the country, the capital city, Montevideo; and

(iii) never had a third force acquired the effective arbiter capability in the legislature that the Frente obtained in 1971.

Whenever the traditional political elites split in two groups of comparable strength, following or breaking party lines, the Frente could tilt the scale. In this sense it may be said that for the first time in its history the Uruguayan party system had become a "two-and-a-half" system.

In this manner the 1971 election bore witness to two major changes in the party system: on the one hand, it had become a "two-and-a-half" system; on the other hand, its two major parties, the traditional parties, had changed positions in the left-right dimension. This second change is a very rare occurrence in comparative terms; theoretically, at least in a truly Downsian model, this is *not* supposed to happen (Downs 1957). These changes, however, could have been anomalous, transient occurrences due to a more or less exceptional

combination of circumstances. What the 1984 election proved, in the light of
the conclusions of the preceding chapter, was that those changes were neither
anomalous nor transient. Their notable permanence after thirteen years of social and political upheavals points definitely to a party system in transition.
If the causes which led to the 1971 changes were enduring enough to survive
those upheavals, then the party system itself was changing. The share of the
electorate obtained by the Frente in 1984 confirmed the new *format* of the
party system appearing in 1971. Its new *logic*—that is, the Frente could tilt
the scale in the event of a division of the traditional politicians—had already
been confirmed by the participation of the Frente in the Club Naval Pact. The
displacement towards the center within all the *lemas* maintained the change
of positions of the traditional parties in the left-right continuum, for, as it
was simultaneous and of similar extent in both parties, it could not alter the
configuration of 1971. It is time then to check whether the data support these
contentions. Of course, they cannot say whether the historical processes just
described have been correctly assessed; at a minimum, however, they can
say whether the final stage corresponds to the expectations.

3. Left and Right in Parliament

Exactly 100 of the 107 legislators (93 percent) answered the question of
self-placement in the left-right dimension. Three interviewees who answered
this question did not answer some or all of the questions asking for placement
of parties and fractions on the scale.[7] Eighty-six percent of the Colorados,
95 percent of the Blancos, and 89 percent of the Frentistas answered the
whole set of questions concerning the left-right scale. Several interviewees
who answered the question were skeptical, however, about the usefulness of
the exercise. Some commented that the task was very difficult; others, while
placing some of the groups of the Frente well to the left, added "if left is
progress, then this is false."

The data allows three different ways of analyzing the position of the
parties in the left-right scale. First, it is possible to consider all the legislators as a balanced, qualified set of judges, and to average their answers for
each party and fraction. Second, it is possible to consider that a particularly
appropriate set of judges consists of the members of each party or fraction,
thus computing the average of the answers of the members only. Third, it
is possible to consider that a more objective measure results not from the
opinions of any set of judges, but simply averaging the self-placement of
the members in the scale. Needless to say, the comparison of the results of
the three methods is particularly interesting. For this purpose, however, it
is unreasonable to consider the thirteen fractions of the three main *lemas*,

because some of them returned very few legislators. The position of some fractions would depend thus on the opinion of just one or two legislators. A practical solution is taking into account only the right and left wings of each of the three *lemas*. These wings, however, are different units: within the Frente the wings themselves are composed by parties, even though comparatively small parties; within the traditional parties they are in principle just wings—fractions of a major party. The wings were defined with a simple rule: for each *lema*, the fractions that according to the self-placement of its voters—to be discussed in the next chapter—were to the right (or to the left) of the total average of the *lema* were considered part of its right (or left) wing. This rule produced a classification that many observers of Uruguayan politics would consider sensible. Within the Colorados, the left wing is made up of Sanguinetti's voters, and the right wing Pacheco's. Within the Blancos, the right wing includes the voters of the two Herrerista (from the late Blanco leader) fractions—Lacalle's and Ortiz's—and the left wing is the rest of the party (not including Paysée, who did not obtain parliamentary representation). Within the Frentistas, finally, the left wing contains the two avowedly Marxist-Leninist parties plus the IDI, the group within the Frente Amplio closest to the former guerrillas, and the right wing includes the Christian Democrats and the Partido por el Gobierno del Pueblo, Batalla's and Michelini's ex-Colorado fraction.

The data presented in Table 5.1 allows several conclusions. To begin with, the *lemas* do appear in the expected order according to all three methods. It is unnecessary to discuss which method is most appropriate in this case, because all of them lead to the same result: the Colorados are to the right, the Frentistas at the left, and the Blancos in between. The table allows other conclusions which are true for all three methods as well. The first, directly linked to the positions of the *lemas*, is that the distance between Colorados and Blancos is consistently smaller than the distance between Blancos and Frentistas: depending on the method, the second is 2.5, 4.4, or as much as 5.0 times larger than the first. No matter which method is used in the comparison, the traditional parties are far closer to each other than to the Frente. This may be seen in other characteristics of the table as well. The traditional parties overlap, for according to the three methods the Blanco right wing appears to the right of the Colorado average, but there is no such kind of overlapping between Blancos and Frentistas. The Blanco left wing is approximately two points to the right of the Frente right wing according to all of the three methods.[8]

A second conclusion, also invariant with regard to the three positioning methods, is this: even though the Frente is explicitly a *coalition* and the Colorado and Nacional Parties are *parties*, the distance between the Frente wings covers a shorter space on the left-right axis than its equivalent in

TABLE 5.1
Left and Right in the Party System according to Legislators

Average position of the three *lemas* and their wings in the ten-point left-right scale

| | Position according to | | Ideological self-placement | |
	All members of Parliament	Members of evaluated fractions	of members of evaluated fractions	(N)
Rightmost possible position: 10				
PC right wing	8.7	5.8	6.2	(4)
Partido Colorado	7.1	5.4	4.8	(31)
PC left wing	7.1	5.3	4.5	(27)
PN right wing	7.9	6.5	5.7	(6)
Partido Nacional	5.9	5.0	4.3	(40)
PN left wing	5.4	4.6	4.1	(34)
FA right wing	3.3	2.6	2.4	(16)
Frente Amplio	2.9	3.0	2.1	(24)
FA left wing	2.1	2.4	1.7	(8)
Leftmost possible position: 1				
Maximum difference:	6.6	4.1	4.5	

Answers weighted according to main fractions. The totals are the minimum number of answers included in each row's averages; a few interviewees reported their self-placement but did not answer some or all of the questions on the position of the groups. The total N includes the answers of the two Unión Cívica Representatives. The first column is based on the total N, including ninety-seven or more answers for each entry. The composition of the lemas' wings is discussed in the text.

any of the traditional parties. The average distance, considering the three methods, between the Colorado left and right wings approximately doubles the corresponding distance in the Frente; the Blanco figure is about three times the Frente's. These differences cannot be explained merely by the fact that the Frente share of the vote—and of parliamentary seats—is about half the traditional parties'.[9] The Blancos appear, on the whole, as the most extended *lema* along the left-right scale, even though according to the third method, self-placement, they are slightly less extended than the Colorados—but just by one percentile of the scale: 1.6 vs. 1.7.

From a comparative perspective the relevant point is not that Blancos and Colorados are overextended, but that the Frente is rather tightly tied. At the level of legislators there is not much comparable published evidence, but the existing data suggest that the dispersion of Colorado and Blanco legislators is not uncommon.[10] At the mass public level, as it will be seen in the next chapter, there is enough data available to support a simple conclusion:

the dispersion of the voters of the traditional parties is similar to those found in most parties of all other democracies.

A third, important conclusion is linked to the differences between the distributions produced by each of the three methods. Comparing the first and third columns of Table 5.1—that is, the distributions resulting from averaging (i) the judgments of all the legislators on each group, and (ii) the self-placement of the members of each group—it is easily seen that, first, the range of the positions shrinks considerably, and second, that the whole range experiences a leftward drift. From the first to the third column the range of the positions is compressed from 6.6 to 4.5 units; it loses almost a third of its initial length. While being compressed this range drifts leftwards in such a way that the initial distribution, approximately symmetrical with respect to the center of the scale, is transformed into a distribution entirely biased towards the left: it simply has no right. All the wings and parties experience this displacement towards the left. It is relatively small in the Frente, and it increases towards the opposite end of the spectrum. For the Frente it amounts to .8; for the Blancos it doubles this figure, and for the Colorados it is three times the Frente's figure. The most affected group is the Colorado left wing, that is, the Batllistas (2.6).

Neither the drift nor the leftist bias seems to be peculiarly Uruguayan. Discussing the self-placement of French representatives on a seven-point left-right scale, Cayrol et al. remark: "the wish not to appear conservative seems evident. This is revealed in the rejection of the term 'right.' "[11] According to their data just three percent of the representatives self-identified with the *droite*, and none at all with the *extrême droite*. An even better comparison is provided by Converse and Pierce's study on representation in France because, like this research and unlike Cayrol et al.'s, they asked about the position of each party and self-placement in the left-right scale.[12] They found that the candidates of a given party

> located it on the average farther to the left than did outside opponents. The effect is slight among the left, in part because there is little room for such displacement. . . As we move to parties and candidates of the right, however, the leftward displacement of estimates for the respondent's own party became quite striking. . . Thus a very generalized preference prevailed among those elites to envision their own parties as being farther to the left than outsiders would have assumed. (Converse and Pierce 1986, pp. 130–131)

This is what may be seen comparing the first and second columns in Table 5.1. What happens in France when we turn to the comparison between the second and third columns? On average, politicians tended to consider themselves as personally falling still more to the left of the position they ascribed to their party, a position already left-biased. (ibid., p. 131)

This was not true for the "far left," but the effect became already visible within the moderate left, and in the "parties of the center and the right, this personal flight to the left again [became] marked" (ibid., p. 131). On the whole, a few details notwithstanding, this is a fine description of the Uruguayan results presented in Table 5.1. Discussing explanations for their findings, Converse and Pierce seem to choose a rather idiosyncratic, specifically French historical argument. The French Revolution "pitted a heroic left against a decadent right;" this legacy, "reinforced by traumas like World War II," explains the facts just described. It is essentially a problem about symbols: "although somebody must defend the status quo in the eternal political conflict, it may be more comforting in France to do so under the most leftist symbology possible" (ibid., p. 132). This seems, at least in part, a sensible explanation. Nevertheless, the same pattern appeared in Uruguay—a small Spanish-speaking Latin American country—seventeen years later. This suggests, I think, that the pattern itself is not a peculiarity of French political culture. In this vein, for example, during the seventies Sartori wrote in general terms about "the current victory of 'left'—its ever-growing evaluative positiveness," which he sees as a sequel of "the defeat of the Fascist 'rightist' regimes [and] the decline of religion." This victory is important for "it renders left the most crucial word in the *war of words* with which political battles are fought" (Sartori 1976, p. 335).

The striking similarity between both data sets suggests that there is a problem deserving a more general discussion than Converse and Pierce's. Surely singular historical events played a role in the development of that pattern, and diffusion effects followed. Sartori and Converse and Pierce mention the impact of fascism and World War II on this pattern; the waves generated by such events undoubtedly reached Uruguayan shores. National, first-hand experience—the impact and consequences of the authoritarian regime—reinforced the effect of those waves. But I think this is not enough to account for what the data say. It seems to me that Sartori is right at least with respect to the *scope* of the problem.

With regard to the differing details mentioned above, perhaps the most visible difference between the French and Uruguayan data is that in Uruguay the left also positions itself more to the left than the average parliamentary view sees it. This is related to another peculiarity of the Uruguayan data. The data exhibits two clear patterns: first, shrinkage on the range of the positions; and second, leftward drift of the whole range. Thus, the lines going from the positions of wings and parties according to all members of parliament to the positions determined by the self-placement of members tend to converge towards the left. This trend, however, has two symmetrical exceptions precisely in both ends of the spectrum. The members of the Frente's left see their wing more to the center—instead of more to the left—of the position the average parliamentary opinion assigns to it. But they self-place themselves neatly at the left not only of the position they assign to their own group, but at the left of the position resulting from the average parliamentary judgment as well. Exactly the opposite occurs at the other end of the spectrum. The members of the Colorado right wing view their fraction at the left of the position resulting from the total average, thus following the general trend, but they self-place themselves to the right of the position they assigned to their fraction, thus breaking the trend. This may happen either because left-wing Frentistas and right-wing Colorados simply perceive their wings to the center of their own position, or because they think that for tactical reasons their groups have to temper their "true" positions. To put it in somewhat different terms, realizing that on average they perceive their fractions to the center of their own positions may be surprising even for themselves, or may be the result of a deliberate *aggiornamento* effort—whether successful or not is another question. In either case the net result reveals pressures towards stretching the ideological space. At both ends of the spectrum, then, there are symmetrical deviations from the general trend which signal the presence of centrifugal forces.[13]

Finally, in order to check both the dependability of comparative references I have just begun to make and the usefulness of the results of the present research for comparative purposes, it is necessary to establish whether the left-right dimension actually taps what it is supposed to among the Uruguayan political elite. There is wide consensus within the literature on which are the core components of the left-right dimension. To quote just one example,

> *Left* and *Right* originated . . . to distinguish, respectively, those who supported egalitarian changes and those who resisted them. Now, as then, attitudes towards egalitarian change are the essence of this ideological dimension . . . . by the end of the nineteenth century, government intervention had come to be seen as an essential tool of redistributive politics and opposition to state intervention became a conservative stance. Thus, during the twentieth century, support for state intervention and support for social reform have been strongly correlated.[14]

In short: state participation in the economy and egalitarianism are very important components of the left-right dimension. According to the data presented in Table 5.2, it is clear that the self-placement of legislators in the left-right scale actually taps what it is supposed to tap with regard to state participation in the economy. The more state participation is deemed desirable, the more to the left the legislators place themselves. The two variables are strongly correlated.[15] Besides, the data is interesting for at least two reasons. On the one hand, it is obvious that the results are not biased towards one end of the scale as is the case with self-placement. Each half of the scale gets approximately half of the answers. On the other hand, the Batllista historical answer to this question is undoubtedly the fourth alternative.[16] This is still the mode of the distribution, but 48 percent of the legislators are to the right of such a view.

TABLE 5.2
Role of the State in the Economy and Left-Right Dimension

	Respondents (percentages)	Average self-placement in left-right scale	(N)
1. Support free enterprise; reduce state intervention to a minimum	10.3	5.9	(9)
2. Provide economic guidelines for the private sector	11.6	5.1	(10)
3. Provide incentives for private firms in selected areas, maintaining a small public sector	26.0	4.5	(24)
4. Support important public sector, including nationalizations to develop selected areas	30.1	4.0	(30)
5. Control of main areas of the economy, including investment	20.5	2.4	(24)
6. Full, direct control of the economy	1.6	1.0	(2)
(N)	(106)	4.1	(100)

Answers weighted according to main fractions. The question was: "Which should the role of the state in the Uruguayan economy ideally be in your opinion? Please indicate which of the following options is closer to your view." A card was presented containing the options listed above.

The issue of egalitarianism must be studied indirectly, because the questionnaire did not include a specific question on it. Nevertheless, one of the questions asked the respondents to pick the three most important goals for the Uruguayan government from a listing of eight options covering a broad range of themes. One of the options was "to improve living conditions quickly, especially for the most deprived"; another was "to secure a fair [*equitativa*] distribution of existing goods." The latter is a very strong egalitarian statement; there is a qualitative difference between this and the former, which may even be interpreted in terms of compassion. The second option rejects any qualification (e.g., "first it is necessary to enlarge the pie, and then . . .") or delay; it is a purely distributive statement. The interviewees were asked to select and rank the three most important items of the listing. This leads to a simple way of constructing a seven-point scale of egalitarianism: from most to least egalitarian, the first three positions are assigned to those who mentioned the strong egalitarian statement in first, second, or third place respectively; positions four, five, and six are analogously assigned to those who only mentioned the weak statement (in first, second, or third place respectively), and the last position, the seventh, is assigned to those who mentioned none.

Table 5.3 shows that the scale of egalitarianism performs as expected, even though its fit is not as satisfactory as in the case of the role of the state in the economy. The distribution of the answers suggests that the scale itself is rather crude; in particular, the last category looks too large for a residual class. In spite of some imperfections,[17] the trend is clear and in the expected direction, and the correlation between the two variables is still strong.[18]

TABLE 5.3
Egalitarianism and the Left-Right Dimension

	Respondents (percentages)	Average self-placement of respondents in left-right scale	(N)
1. Most egalitarian	2.3	3.2	(2)
2.	9.1	3.0	(11)
3.	22.2	3.4	(23)
4. Middle	20.9	4.0	(24)
5.	14.6	4.3	(15)
6.	8.3	5.0	(7)
7. Least egalitarian	22.5	4.9	(18)
(N)	(107)	4.1	(100)

Answers weighted according to main fractions. The scale of egalitarianism is discussed in the text.

The general conclusion is thus reassuring: the left-right dimension means to Uruguayan legislators what it is supposed to mean. The self-placement in the left-right scale is strongly correlated with two basic components of the dimension as discussed in the literature. As a final check, a standard regression shows that a full half of the variation of self-placement is accounted for by the beliefs on the role of the state in the economy and on egalitarianism. In Uruguay these variables are, then, empirically central in order to define positions in the left-right spectrum.[19]

4. Parties in Transition: A Preliminary Assessment

The data have confirmed that at the elite level the Colorados are to the right and the Blancos at the center of the party system. All three indicators based on elites' views about their own positions and the positions of parties and fractions in the left-right scale lead to the same conclusion. The data cannot show whether the present positions involved leapfrogging or not; this must remain a historical judgment. Some cues suggest that such leapfrogging actually occurred. The Colorados see themselves at the left of the Blancos, even though at a small distance from them. The average Colorado opinion assigns the Blancos 6.1 points in the left-right scale; all the Colorado fractions and the party itself are seen by their members to the left of that position. Fortunately, what was really in discussion—as these Colorado opinions prove—was the present position of the parties in the left-right dimension. Nobody argues seriously against the historical role of Batllismo as the center-left of the system—or even as its left *tout court*, given the meager importance of the "ideological" left.

Another interesting question that these data cannot answer is what kind of leapfrogging this was. Leapfrogging may in principle occur in several different ways. In one possible scenario one of the parties remains in a fixed position and the other changes enough so as to pass over the first. The other possibilities assume that both parties change their respective positions, leapfrogging in the process. A relevant distinction would be whether both parties experienced similar changes or not. According to the historical account both traditional parties changed in opposite directions, but that account is too imprecise to estimate by how much. On this the data provides some mixed, scarcely dependable signals.[20]

The main fractions within each of the traditional parties appear clearly differentiated in ideological terms. This means that political winds may change, sometimes considerably, without changing the governing party. This has been indeed the case. At the beginning of this chapter it was noted that the observed changes in electoral support for the fractions of the traditional parties from 1971 to 1984 were not uncommon in Uruguayan recent political history. In fact, at least since the 1950s the leading fractions of the governing parties had not been able to remain in power during two consecutive terms except in 1971. Either the governing party lost the election or it remained in power but with another majority or plurality fraction—and with this, also changing the holders of executive power. This goes a long way in explaining one of the paradoxes mentioned in the preceding chapter: that since 1950 Uruguay has combined low electoral volatility and very high parliamentary turnover. The first is measured at the party level, whereas the second depends most upon the electoral success of the fractions.[21] This result is consistent with the available comparative evidence. It has been observed that in countries allowing intraparty preference voting

> party processes (list ordering and preference voting) are slightly more important as sources of turnover than is interparty competition; more incumbents lost to members of their own parties than lost to members of other parties. (Katz 1986, p. 99)

Since the Uruguayan DSV is an atypical, extreme form of intraparty preference voting, it seems reasonable that its impact on parliamentary turnover be extreme as well. Those ups and downs of fractions and the relevance of their ideological differences also help to understand the second paradox noted in the previous chapter, i.e., that the party which led an anti-military democratic restoration was the party of the favorite candidate of the military.

There is another central point with regard to which this peculiar logic of fractions appears as decisive. It has been pointed out that leapfrogging is empirically a very rare event and theoretically an almost impossible event, at least from the point of view of a strictly spatial model. When the now Blanco majority began its leftward drift it was nothing particularly different from politics-as-usual within the traditional parties. When it conquered a very neat majority within its party it was not so usual, but still it was not abnormal. When the whole Colorado party drifted to the right following its then majority it also was politics-as-usual. The unusual facts were, first, the simultaneity of both processes, and then their crystallization thanks to the political conflicts developed around the birth, development of, and exit from the authoritarian regime.[22] Now, at this stage of the process, it is clear that nobody built purposefully the whole chain of events, and it is very reasonable that the Uruguayan political landscape would seem so strange to many: everybody senses that important things have changed, but it is very difficult to point at a particular event and say "eureka, this is what happened."

Finally, the newest member of the system, the "half" of the two-and-a-half present party system, appears isolated at the left end of the spectrum. All indicators show the same picture. This seems particularly notable when considering that the Frente's most voted member was a splinter fraction of the Partido Colorado. The Frente also appears more cohesive ideologically than the traditional parties. With regard to the past it has been said that the Uruguayan left historically languished in a small electoral ghetto. Its impact on political life was indirect, through its limited capability of affecting the traditional parties; it was the goad part of Uruguayan society. Now it is not small and it no longer languishes, but in terms of elites' ideologies it still remains relatively isolated.

6. A Polarized and More Fragmented Party System

The preceding chapters discussed the most visible continuities and changes that resulted from the 1984 national elections. This and the two following chapters, though still based on 1985 (mass-public) and 1986 (elites) data, complete the picture of a new party system. As will be seen below, the system described by these data already was clearly in place by the 1971 election, remains so twenty years later, after the 1989 national election, and most probably will still be in place by the next national election (November 1994).

The discussion begins with an analysis of the parties' ideologies as seen through their voters' self-identification in the left-right continuum. The implications of that analysis are probed through several international comparisons; those comparisons are based in a formally defined concept of "families" of political parties. Those comparisons lead naturally to the idea of a polarized party system, which is then documented by means of the concepts and measurements developed by Sani and Sartori (1983). The final step applies the ideologically based concept of political families to an analysis of the fractionalized structure of the major parties and of the Frente Amplio coalition as well. The whole discussion provides a fresh approach and new insights on that old and difficult problem.

1. Left, Right, and the Voters

The question on self-placement on the left-right scale posed to parliament members was also posed to the sample of Montevideo adult residents described in Chapter 1. The format of the question—the standard ten-point scale used throughout all of Western Europe since at least the early seventies—was the same for both elite and mass-public interviews. A card containing a long, flat rectangle (with the words "Left" and "Right" on its corresponding extremes) subdivided into ten consecutive cells was presented to the interviewees. Both legislators and ordinary citizens were asked to place themselves in that rectangle according to their "political ideas"; those who did answer the question thus obtained values ranging from one (the leftmost position) to ten (the rightmost). Legislators, as discussed in the previous chapter, were also asked to position all Uruguayan significant parties and fractions in the same scale. Voters were asked only for their own position ("self-placements") instead. As will be seen below, though, voters' self-placements play a central role in this analysis: on the one hand, they define the left- or right-wing character of the fractions of each party and, more generally, the position of all parties and fractions in the left-right dimension; on the other hand, they allow a precise definition and measurement of the polarization of the party system.

A full 86 percent of Montevidean voters answered the question on left-right self-placement.[1] This is not far from the corresponding figure among the elite—93 percent—and it is also very close to the 88 percent of Madrid residents who answered the same question in the fall of 1977, near the first election of the Spanish return to democracy (Linz 1980, p. 128). It is similar to the average found in several Western European democracies during the 1970s, and higher than the values reported for the U.S. in 1973 and 1976 (Klingemann 1979, p. 229). Thus, Montevideans—and, more generally, Uruguayans[2]—recognize the terms "left" and "right" and are willing to place themselves in a left-right scale in ways similar to those of European publics. They are more familiar with the left-right dimension than U.S. citizens, and probably even more so than most Latin American publics.[3]

Do voters and political elites see the same political map, at least in terms of the ideological, left-right dimension? The data reported in Table 6.1 provides an answer to this question. On the one hand, the table presents the average self-placements in the left-right scale of the voters of each of the major fractions (or members of the Frente Amplio coalition) and those of all of each party's voters. A fraction is to the right (or the left) of its party simply if the average position of its voters is to the right (or the left) of the average of its whole party. The right and left wings of each party, the discussion of which began in the previous chapter, are the sum of all the respective fractions. On the other hand, for comparative purposes the table also presents the average position attributed to fractions and parties by all the legislators. Note that the criterion is not the same, i.e., in the case of politicians the data are not average self-placements of the involved legislators (members of each fraction or party), but the average judgments of all the legislature instead. This is so because of practical reasons: among legislators, for some of the minor fractions there are only one or two "self-placement" available answers, too few for a meaningful, unbiased average.

The fractions mentioned in the table may be succinctly described as follows. Sanguinetti, the winner in the 1984 election, began as a proxy for Jorge Batlle, leader of the Batllista fraction Lista 15 (founded by former president

TABLE 6.1

Lemas and Fractions in the Left-Right Scale: a Detailed Map

Parliamentarian judgments on the position of parties and fractions in the left-right scale and self-placement of the voters of each of them in the same scale

	Parliamentarians' judgments (averages)	Voters' self-placement (averages)	(N of voters)
Rightmost possible position: 10			
Pacheco	8.7	7.9	(39)
P. COLORADO	7.1	6.4	(267)
Tarigo	6.9	6.3	(93)
Sanguinetti	7.2	6.1	(91)
Flores Silva	5.9	5.6	(36)
Ortiz	8.4	7.8	(6)
Lacalle	7.7	5.6	(36)
P. NACIONAL	6.0	5.3	(214)
Pereyra	5.6	5.2	(68)
Ferreira	5.3	5.1	(93)
Dem. Cristiana	3.6	3.6	(22)
Batalla	3.2	3.6	(135)
F. AMPLIO	2.9	3.1	(310)
P. Socialista	2.7	3.0	(54)
Izq. D. Indep.	1.6	2.5	(22)
Dem. Avanzada	1.9	2.3	(71)
Leftmost possible position: 1			
All	—	4.8	(855)

Parliamentarians' answers weighted according to main fractions. Each entry in the first column includes 97 or more answers. The total N in the last column includes all interviewees who answered the question on self-placement. 84, 87, and 91 percent respectively of Colorado, Blanco, and Frentista voters answered the question of self-placement in the scale.

Luis Batlle Berres, his father). Tarigo was elected vice president; he had founded his new, successful fraction in the aftermath of the 1980 plebiscite. Both fractions ran a single presidential candidate, Sanguinetti, under the *sub-lema* Batllismo Unido. Flores Silva also supported Sanguinetti's presidential candidacy, but he ran a separate *lista* for the Senate headed by himself—and he was actually elected senator. Within the Blancos, Ortiz and Lacalle led her-rerista fractions; Pereyra is the leader of the Movimiento Nacional de Rocha and was Ferreira's running mate in 1971. Within the Frente, finally, Batalla headed the former Michelini's Colorado fraction Lista 99 (now Partido por el Gobierno del Pueblo, PGP). Democracia Avanzada is the name the Communists and their closest allies adopted because their former coalition—the Fidel—was banned. The old name was selected because of obvious reasons, and because of no less obvious reasons its eventual return seems now highly unlikely. The Izquierda Democrática Independiente (IDI) was the coalition of small leftist groups mentioned in the preceding chapter.

The table establishes several important facts. First and foremost, the political landscape objectively embodied in the voters' self-perceptions is essentially the same landscape the politicians see. What matters most is the order, and in this regard in only four of the sixteen positions displayed in the table does the politicians' order not agree with the voters'. Three of these exhibit very small differences—Sanguinetti, Partido Nacional, and Democracia Avanzada—in the sense that they are just one place out of line; only one, Lacalle, would have to jump over four positions to fit in line. At the voters' level it is also true that the Colorados are to the right, the Frentistas at the left, and the Blancos in between. In fact, the difference between Colorados and Blancos somewhat surprisingly appears more clear at the voters' level. The Frentistas still appear isolated at the left of the scale. Finally, the average self-placement of Montevideans in the left-right scale, 4.8, is almost the same found in Madrid in the 1977 survey quoted above, 4.7. The Spanish total average stabilized later around 4.8. Montevidean voters thus self-place themselves very close to Italians and Spaniards and to the left of the electorates of the Western European democracies Linz compared with Spain (Linz 1980, p. 129).

Table 6.1 is adequate to examine the congruence of elite's and electors' views because it probes with considerable detail the composition of the main political forces and because on this matter the central question concerns the relative position of parties and fractions along the spectrum; as Table 5.1 showed, at the elite level these relative positions do not vary with the defining criterion—be it self-placements, explicit "members only" judgments, or the judgments of the whole legislature. Nevertheless, it seems prudent to compare the distributions resulting from the same defining criterion as well.

Table 6.2 presents self-placement in the left-right scale at both levels; it summarizes the data in the more compact manner of Table 5.1. This format shows even more clearly than Table 6.1 that elites and voters have the same picture of the party system. Concerning the order each distribution assigns to parties and fractions, there is now only one discrepancy between elites and voters, as it might be expected, on the placement of the Blanco right wing. Besides the by now familiar configuration of Colorados to the right, Frentistas at the left and Blancos in between, the tables confirm that the distance between Colorados and Blancos is much shorter than the one which separates them from the Frentistas. Both at elite and mass-public levels the distance between the *lema* averages of the Partido Nacional and the Frente Amplio is 2.2 units; the corresponding distance between Blancos and Colorados is just one half of that at the mass-public level, and less than one fourth at the elite level.

TABLE 6.2
Self-Placement in the Left-Right Scale of Elites and Voters

	Legislators			Voters		
	Self-placement	standard deviation	(N)	Self-placement	standard deviation	(N)
Rightmost possible position: 10						
PC right wing	6.2	.75	(5)	7.9	2.24	(39)
Partido Colorado	4.8	1.12	(33)	6.4	1.80	(267)
PC left wing	4.5	.97	(28)	6.1	1.64	(228)
PN right wing	5.7	1.55	(6)	5.9	1.62	(42)
Partido Nacional	4.3	1.49	(40)	5.3	1.35	(214)
PN left wing	4.1	1.34	(34)	5.1	1.23	(161)
FA right wing	2.4	.72	(16)	3.6	1.45	(157)
Frente Amplio	2.1	.83	(25)	3.1	1.61	(310)
FA left wing	1.7	.87	(9)	2.6	1.63	(147)
Leftmost possible position: 1						
All	4.1	1.58	(100)	4.8	2.12	(855)

Entries are average self-placements and their standard deviations. Legislators' self-placements weighted according to main fractions. *Lemas'* wings defined on the basis of voters' self-placements presented in Table 6.1. Regarding voters' Ns, small differences between the sum of the wings and the *lema* total are due to votes "to the *lema*" but not for any particular fraction and—within the Partido Nacional—a few votes for Paysée, the military's ally who was not able to obtain parliamentary seats.

A second, particularly interesting finding of Table 6.2 is that legislators are not a competitive elite in Putnam's sense, that is, inter-party distances are smaller at the elite level than at the mass level. The mass-elite "displacement pattern" is comparable to the Italian or Swedish pattern (according to data gathered in 1968): the elites are always to the left of their voters. Nevertheless, both the Italian and Swedish elites are competitive, whereas in Uruguay they are either consensual or, more likely, coalescent, as in post-World War II Austria.[4] Unfortunately there are no comparable precoup data, and we cannot know whether this "noncompetitiveness" is new. It might well be a result of the learning process political elites experienced during the last two decades.

Table 6.2 exhibits at least one relevant difference with respect to the findings of Table 5.1. According to all the elite-based criteria for assigning positions to parties and fractions in the left-right sale, the Frente Amplio—in spite of being a coalition—covered a shorter space on the left-right axis than the traditional parties. The Blancos were, on average, the most extended *lema* along the scale. Table 5.2 shows that at the voters' level this is not true. The distance between the Blanco wings is .8 units; the distance between the

Frentista wings is 1.0, and between the Colorado wings is 1.8. The Blancos are the least extended *lema*. The mere space between wings is admittedly a rather crude indicator, but the same conclusion is reached by comparing the standard deviations reported in the table: the Blancos are the least dispersed set of voters, and the Colorados the most dispersed, with the Frentistas in between. These are not token differences: the standard deviation of the Blancos as a whole is smaller than those of the other *lemas* and all of their wings.[5] In this regard, then, at the voters' level the Blancos are by far the most cohesive party in Montevideo. This seems a particularly notable conclusion, for at the elite level exactly the opposite is true. Honoring their long-standing reputation for unruliness, the Blanco legislators are the politicians who disagree most about the position of their own party in the left-right spectrum. This is what the standard deviations presented in Table 6.2 mean.[6] The most striking result, however, is not that Blanco leaders and voters position themselves, in relative terms, at the opposite ends—at their own levels, i.e., at the parliament and mass-public levels respectively—but that the disagreement among the former is simply higher, in absolute terms, than among the latter; the standard deviations are 1.49 and 1.35, as shown in Table 6.2. This runs definitely against the theoretical expectations and comparative evidence available. In France, elites

> show much greater agreement as to party locations than is found among the lay public. The standard deviations of their assignments are always less, and often much less: on an average, the reduction in such dispersion is about 40 percent. (Converse and Pierce 1986, p. 123)

What is more, even though Converse and Pierce's 40 percent does not need to be a somewhat magic conversion factor, the corresponding figures among Frentistas and Colorados—computed on the basis of the standard deviations presented in Table 6.2—are 47 and 38 percent respectively, very close to the average they reported.

Needless to say, assuming that the unruliness of Blanco leadership explains these results does not lead us very far. In fact, for all their unruliness Table 6.2 shows that the self-placement of Blanco elites on the left-right scale is as good a predictor of their voters' self-placement as is the case among the Frentistas, and that both perform in this regard far better than the Colorados. The most reasonable explanation of this and other findings reported is of course very simple: the profile of the Blanco electorate in Montevideo is changing, displacing itself leftwards. This displacement may be due to a combination of several factors, but at least one thing is sure: the conservative Blanco voters in Montevideo have almost disappeared, either because they are voting the Colorados or the Unión Cívica, or because they are changing ideologically, or even because Blancos are incapable of recruiting new conservative voters and thus replacing older voters. Table 6.2 proves this disappearance.[7]

The leftward drift of the Blancos, and their leapfrogging the Colorados, has been one of the central points so far. What these results add is, first, the suggestion that the changes are still in progress, and second, a strong, unexpected reminder about how extensive those changes already are. With regard to the last remark, after decades of seeing—correctly—the traditional *lemas* as catch-all parties, and of marvelling at the propensity of the left for atomizing itself within a very short ideological space, the discovery that Blanco voters are now more cohesive than Frentistas comes as a real surprise. The same may be said about the more clear distinction between Blancos and Colorados at the voters level than at the elites' level. The suggestion that the changes are still in progress is also strong. In fact, it seems that changes are proceeding more quickly than the capability of the elites to grasp them. This seems to be true in general terms for all legislators, and in particular for the Blanco elite. Even though it has been common to assign the extent of the Blanco defeat to the loss of their right-wing voters, this did not prevent legislators from badly mistaking the ideological nature of Lacalle's fraction.[8] The Blanco elites' average judgments were better estimates of the position of their voters than was the case among the Colorados with regard to theirs or among all their political rivals with respect to the Blanco voters themselves. Nevertheless, those more precise judgments exhibited a very high degree of disagreement, even higher than among their own voters. This suggests a still fluid situation the nature of which the elite has not yet been able to agree upon.

Finally, which is the "true" position of parties and fractions on the left-right dimension? This does not seem a very useful question. It is clear that what matters most is their relative position, i.e., their order in the scale. At the elite level it has been shown that the three indicators of those positions lead to the same orderings, even though the actual distributions changed— their range was shortened and the whole distribution drifted to the left when changing the defining criterion from the judgment of all the legislature to the "members only" views to the self-placement of members. The same indicators may be used at the mass-public level as well. What happens there? As Linz summarized it, the Spanish data

> show a pattern that is already familiar from studies in other countries, that the electorate as a whole tends to place parties more distant from each other, and those on the extremes farther out on the spectrum, than the supporters of each of those parties. The voters themselves show an even greater reluctance to place themselves toward the extremes. (Linz 1980, p. 130)

Converse and Pierce found the same pattern of centrist preference in France: "in nine of ten possible party comparisons, identifiers with a given party fix their personal locations closer to the center of the left-right continuum than the positions they assign to their preferred parties."[9] The comparative evidence, then, leads us to expect that at the mass-public level the range of the distribution should also be shortest when measured by the self-placement of the voters, as at the elite's level, but compressed towards the center, not displaced towards the left as among the elites. The compression itself, obviously, should not alter the order of the distribution.

The public opinion survey on which this research is based does not provide data to check these expectations. Nevertheless, Table 6.3 summarizes available evidence that handsomely confirms—different origins and sample sizes notwithstanding—Linz's description and the unchanging character of the orderings produced by the different criteria.

TABLE 6.3
Left and Right in the Party System according to Voters

Average position of the three *lemas* in the left-right scale

	Position according to . . .		Ideological self-placement
	All voters	Voters of evaluated *lemas*	of voters of evaluated *lemas*
Rightmost possible position: 10			
Partido Colorado	7.7	6.8	6.4
Partido Nacional	6.9	6.4	5.3
Frente Amplio	2.6	3.0	3.1
Leftmost possible position: 1			
Maximum difference:	5.1	3.8	3.3

The data presented in the last column are those already reported in Table 6.2. The remaining data are from three different surveys of about 400 interviews each conducted by Equipos Consultores in Montevideo during 1985 in early May (Partido Colorado), late May (Partido Nacional), and early June (Frente Amplio). Averages computed on the distributions as presented in *Informes* #7 and #8 (Equipos Consultores, Montevideo, 1985).

Some findings of the surveys reported in Table 6.3 deserve further mention. First, the percentage of interviewees who do not answer the questions concerning the position of parties is far greater than the percentage of those who do not answer the question of self-placement in the left-right scale. About 40 percent of the interviewees in all three smaller samples do not place the *lemas* in the scale; this figure is more than double that of those who do not place themselves in the scale. Second, there are significant differences between the voters of the different *lemas*. About half of the Colorados, a third of the Blancos, and a fifth of the Frentista voters, on average, do not answer the questions concerning the position of the parties. Thus, the Blancos and particularly the Frentistas are far more attentive than the Colorados to the left-right dimension.

Within all the *lemas* the effective answers share a common, systematic bias: in all cases the voters of each *lema* are more willing to place the other *lemas* in the scale than their own. This pattern may involve a more cautious approach towards one's own party.[10] Blancos and Frentistas share another revealing pattern: when answering the questions concerning the position of the fractions belonging to their own *lema* the proportion of nonrespondents is lower than for the *lema* itself.[11] The differences are not small: 6 points, on average, among the Frentista voters, and 10 points among the Blancos. These differences do not exist among the Colorados. Besides being more attentive to the left-right dimension, then, Blancos and Frentistas exhibit a truly discriminating attention. They are more willing to evaluate the position of the fractions, which have better defined ideological profiles, than the *lemas* within which the fractions coalesce.[12]

Insofar as the most important characteristic of the distribution of political objects within the left-right dimension is simply the order assigned to them, the question about the "true" position of parties and fractions—or, more properly, about the best indicator for such positions—is indeed scarcely relevant. All the available indicators, both at elite and mass-public levels, lead to essentially the same arrangement of the three main *lemas* and their wings. Nevertheless, even granting that the central point is that of order, it seems clear that it is not the only point. When using averages we are accepting that order is not all that matters, since averages cannot be computed on a purely ordinal scale. Furthermore, there are important issues which cannot be studied merely on the basis of central tendency measures such as means or medians; rather we need to look at the whole distributions that produce them. In particular, it is not possible to compare parties by simply analyzing their average position in the left-right dimension. What is, then, the best map of the left-right dimension?

In the preceding discussion two possible approaches have been presented, elite or mass-public level perceptions, and three possible indicators within each level were documented—judgment of all legislators/voters, judgments of legislators/voters of the evaluated parties, and self-placement of the legislators/voters of the evaluated parties. With regard to the first distinction, elite vs. mass-public levels, in general terms the question itself is wrong: "each map is 'right' for the population that generated it. If the mass view of the party system differs from a more informed elite view, this is already an important political datum" (Converse and Pierce 1986, pp. 116–117). Thus, the real question does not ask for any "true" map, but rather asks which is the most appropriate given the nature of the problem to be studied. When the polarization of the party system—in Sartori's terms—is a central concern, as is the case of the present study, a reasonable starting point is this:

> polarization among mass publics is an important component element of the tensions (or non-tensions) that characterize democracies, and . . . elites are, to say the least, conditioned by the extent of polarization that they detect at the mass level. (Sani and Sartori 1983, p. 308)

It should be added that this general argument is particularly well-suited to Uruguayan conditions. Beginning in 1980 Uruguayan electors exhibited a considerable autonomy in the sense that—pressures and bias of the mass media notwithstanding—they rejected the institutionalization of a nondemocratic order, penalized the military's political allies, and selected the leadership who actually conducted the transition. Therefore the discussion in the following section will be based on the mass-public view of the positions of parties and fractions in the left-right dimension. More precisely, it will be based on the view implicit in the self-placement of voters in the left-right scale. This choice does not assume that the remaining indicators, the explicit judgments either of the whole electorate or of the voters of the evaluated party are not relevant. They are, and to improve our understanding of the left-right dimension it is necessary to compare the results of those different indicators.[13] Nevertheless, having to choose just one of the three indicators, several reasons point out the self-placement criterion as most adequate for the present purposes. First, besides the minimum knowledge about the left-right continuum itself that all three indicators require, the self-placement question involves a judgment on what interviewees know best—their own views. Second, when the goal is analyzing polarization the self-placement criterion is a rather prudent starting point, for as a result of the centrist preference effect it will avoid a perhaps artificial overestimation of the polarization of the system. Finally, the self-placement criterion will allow systematic comparisons with other party systems; it has been the indicator chosen by most of the relevant literature so far.

2. The Parties in Comparative Perspective

How do Uruguayan parties look in comparative perspective? Such an exercise has never been attempted in a systematic manner, even though isolated comparisons are relatively common in everyday political argument. The data source for the following comparisons is Sani and Sartori's essay on polarization in Western democracies (1983). They analyzed the self-locations of the voters of the 44 relevant parties of 11 countries in the left-right ten-point scale.[14] Their discussion was based on three measures, two of which will be presented below: (i) *overlap*, "the extent to which the electorates of different parties occupy the same spatial (left-right) locations," and (ii) *distance* between any two groups of partisans.[15] The *distance* between two parties is simply the absolute difference of the average self-placement of their voters divided by the theoretical maximum of that difference, which in the ten-point scale is 9. It varies between 0 and 1. *Overlap* is computed on the reduced version of the scale: five segments, each including two consecutive positions of the original scale. The percentages of cases falling in the same segments are subtracted, and then the measure is computed "by dividing the (absolute) sum of these differences by the theoretical maximum (which is 200, since each row adds to 100), and subtracting this figure from 1." (Sani and Sartori 1983, p. 321).

These measures were used essentially to compare parties within nations. They contributed to define properties at the party system level; the party systems were then compared across nations. The only assumption needed to give substance to those comparisons is the capability of the left-right dimension to summarize the amount of political conflict present in the different party systems. The conflicts themselves might well be different also, specific to the party systems. Thus, such comparisons would make sense even if the left-right continuum had no contents common to all systems. Nevertheless, this is an unnecessarily restrictive assumption. As Sartori summarized the point, in any specific historical period the left-right dimension is associated with a long series of common contents (Sartori 1982, p. 256), some of which—egalitarianism, role of the state in the economy—were discussed in Chapter 5. It is possible, then, to directly compare parties across nations in a meaningful way. Parties close enough in the left-right dimension should behave in relatively similar ways in issues related to the common contents of the dimension.

The direct cross-national comparison of political parties on the basis of their positions in the left-right dimension may be carried out in different ways. The present approach is centered in the concept of *political families* of parties. In order to define such "families" a second concept is needed, that of *closeness* of parties, which is in turn based on Sani and Sartori's definitions of distance and overlap.

From a formal point of view these definitions should satisfy two basic requisites. First, given a reasonable definition of *closeness*, then *political families* of parties should be formed by parties all of which are "close" to each other. This means that (i) if party A is "close" to party B, then party B must be "close" to party A as well, and that (ii) if party A is "close" to party B, and party B is "close" to party C, then all three parties belong to a family if and only if party A is also "close" to party C. On formal terms this means that *closeness* is a relationship of equivalence, and that all the parties belonging to a family are "equals" in this sense.[16]

Second, a "reasonable" definition of *closeness* cannot be arbitrarily elastic. This problem may be confronted as follows. We know that most party systems may be considered as unidimensional—in the sense that political competition is conducted essentially in a single space, which is the left-right dimension—at least when we consider only truly relevant parties in Sartori's terms. Very few other dimensions have been recognized in the literature as really significant, and very few polities have been recognized as actually needing a multidimensional space in order to analyze political competition within them. The most important "other dimensions" are the religious, ethnic, and/or linguistic, sometimes but not always accompanied by regional divisions; in extreme cases there may be a question of nationalities, as in Spain. Hence a reasonable definition of *closeness* should not find "close" parties—at least in most cases—when comparing the parties of any given party system, for, in what sense could we say they compete? If there are "close" relevant parties within a single party system then that situation, besides being exceptional, should belong to any of the few cases where the literature has recognized truly multidimensional spaces of political competition. This requisite may be called "uniqueness condition."

It is time then to define *closeness*. The first element of such a definition is obviously the above defined *distance*: "close" parties should be very close in this regard. This is not enough, however, because distributions that differ considerably may share the same average, and those differences may be very relevant politically. To avoid this possibility it suffices to require simultaneously a large *overlap*. A look at the data suggests that distances of .05 or less—that is, 5 percent of the scale or less, according to the definition of distance—and overlaps of .85 or more are sensible thresholds. Parties as close as this should look very much like the same party as far as the left-right continuum is concerned. With this definition, if party A is "close" to party B, then B is "close" to A as well, for the distances and overlaps are, according to their definitions, the same.

Does this definition satisfy our "uniqueness condition"? Sani and Sartori's essay allows a control of that criterion. From their data seventy-five within-country comparisons may be checked. Just six of those comparisons show pairs of different parties coexisting within a country while fulfilling both conditions of closeness at the same time. But all of these exceptional situations may be accounted for in terms of other relevant dimensions. Four of the six cases occur in one country, the Netherlands, and three of these involve the same party, the Liberals. The Liberals are difficult to distinguish from the Catholics on the one hand, and from the two Protestant parties (ARP and CHU) on the other. The fourth pair involves the ARP and the CHU themselves. In all four cases, then, the religious dimension appears overcrowding the left-right continuum. This is also true in one of the two remaining cases:

the Finnish LKP (Liberal-People) and KES (Center or Agrarian) parties. According to Sartori, Finland—-like the Netherlands—is a country of medium religious polarization. The voters of the Agrarian party, in particular, are far more appreciative of religion that the voters of the Liberal, who rank close to the socialists in this matter. In Finland too, therefore, the religious dimension allows us to explain the existence of parties which are very close on the left-right dimension.[17] As a result, five of the six pairs of parties whose separate existence as political rivals could not be explained in terms of the left-right dimension are successfully accounted for by a single additional dimension, religion. This is not the case of the last pair, the Swiss Farmers and Radicals. The additional dimensions that explain the survival of these parties as separate entities are region and language: the Farmers are a French-speaking Berne-based party, whereas the Radicals are a national, German-speaking party—for decades Switzerland's main party.[18]

All in all, then, the proposed definition of *closeness* does seem reasonable in the light of the available evidence; hence "families" of political parties are well defined as well—at least from a logical point of view. In order to put these definitions to work it is thus necessary to compare each of the Uruguayan parties to those of Sani and Sartori.

Table 6.4 presents all the parties of Sani and Sartori's data which are "close" to the Partido Colorado. They do not form a single political "family" in the sense defined above, but they do form two such families both of which include the Colorados; the two parts of Table 6.4 show their respective compositions and structures. Each part of the table has a central body and two separate columns. The two last columns present the position of each party in the left-right scale—i.e., the average of their voters' self-placements—and the number of cases upon which those means were computed. Each central body is formed by two halves (triangles): the upper-right triangle presents the distances between all the parties considered; the opposite half presents the overlaps between the same parties.

A few examples may help to read the data. The first number of the first row of Part A of the table (.01) is the distance between the Swiss Radical Democrats (RD) and the Italian Liberals (PLI), that is, the difference between their means (6.6 and 6.5) divided by the maximum theoretical difference—which is 9, the difference between two parties such as all the voters of the first self-place themselves at 1, the leftmost possible position, and all the voters of the second self-place themselves at 10, the rightmost possible position. The overlap between the same two parties (RD and PLI), which is .91, may be read in the other half of the table. That .91 means, according to Sani and Sartori's definition of overlap quoted above, that 91 percent of the voters of each of the two parties place themselves in the same positions in the reduced, five-step version of the left-right scale. To compute overlaps following Sani

TABLE 6.4
The Partido Colorado in Comparative Perspective

Overlapping and distance between parties along the left-right dimension

A. The rightward-leaning Colorado political family

	RD	PLI	PAB	Rep.	Col.	LKP	Mean	(N)
Swiss Rad. Dem. (RD)	—	.01	.02	.02	.02	.03	6.6	(175)
Italian Liberals (PLI)	.91	—	.01	.01	.01	.02	6.5	(30)
Swiss Farmers (PAB)	.97	.93	—	.00	.00	.01	6.4	(77)
U.S. Republicans	.97	.91	.96	—	.00	.01	6.4	(368)
P. Colorado	.86	.92	.86	.87	—	.01	6.4	(267)
Finnish Liberal-P. (LKP)	.92	.93	.94	.91	.87	—	6.3	(45)

Overlap

B. The center-leaning Colorado political family

	Col.	KES	DCI	UCD	Mean	(N)
P. Colorado	—	.01	.05	.05	6.4	(267)
Finnish Center-Agr. (KES)	.91	—	.04	.04	6.3	(199)
Italian DC (DCI)	.87	.94	—	.00	5.9	(333)
Spanish UCD	.86	.93	.92	—	5.9	(1387)

Overlap

Computed on Sani and Sartori's (1983) data on self-placement of the voters of each party in the left-right scale except for the Partido Colorado. All means computed on the full ten-point left-right scale. Overlaps computed on the collapsed five-point version of the scale.

and Sartori's definition the distributions of each party's voters in the left-right scale are needed—that of the Colorados is shown below; those of the other parties are not shown here for reasons of space (they may be seen in Sani and Sartori's paper). It is clear that all the parties of Part A of Table 6.4 do form a "family" as defined above, for all the distances are of .05 or less (in fact, the largest is .03), and all overlaps are of .85 or more (in fact, the smallest is .86).

As seen in the table, the Colorados, with a mean of 6.4, are a party of the center just on the borderline of becoming a party of the center-right—at least according to the labelling of the collapsed form of the left-right scale chosen by Sani and Sartori.[19] Two-tenths of a point would suffice to enroll them in the center-right. They belong thus to an overcrowded region of the left-right continuum, which is reflected in the fact that eight of the forty-four parties of this data set are close to the Colorados. Four of these are the two Swiss and the two Finnish parties mentioned above; the remaining four are the Spanish UCD (as of 1979), the U.S. Republicans, and the Italian Christian Democrats and Liberals. The nine parties (including the Colorados) form the two families shown in the table.[20]

The two Colorado families differ in several respects, the most interesting of which is perhaps the role of religion. Religion is far more relevant to the parties of the second group than to those of the first. The Spanish UCD is not a Catholic party, and Linz has argued that it was a functional equivalent of the Italian DCI (Linz 1980, p. 171). But there was a Christian Democratic component among the founding group of leaders, and it received a disproportionately large share of the Catholic vote at least in 1979, the same date of the data reported above (Linz 1980, pp. 139 and 171). The importance of religion to KES's voters was already noted, and the DCI certainly does not need explanations on this matter. Nothing comparable to this appears in the first group of parties.[21] The interesting point is that these configurations do not exist merely because it happens, by chance, that the more religion-influenced parties are to the center and the other parties to the right of the Colorados. The data show that the Finnish LKP and KES have the same mean—i.e., the distance between them is zero—and a high overlap of .88. But while the LKP is close neither to the DCI nor to the UCD and is a member of the first family, the KES, to the contrary, is close neither to the Swiss Radicals nor to the U.S. Republicans and is a member of the second family. Thus, the two parties tied on the borderline seem to "choose" family according to their religious inclinations. In short, the two families look like the secular and religious relatives of the Colorados. According to the distance and overlap averages the Colorados are slightly closer to the lay, rightmost family. Nevertheless, religion is not necessarily the only or even the most important elective affinity among the members of each family. In formal terms the distinguishing characteristic between the two families is that the members of the second have a higher, more neatly distinguished mode in the center of the distribution. To what extent this is or is not related to other substantive matters is an open question.

The Blancos are definitely to the left of the Colorados–1.1 units–but they still are a party of the center. In fact, at least in arithmetic terms they are more so than the Colorados. Their companions look quite different from the Colorados'. Four parties are close to them: the Swiss Independents, the West German and British Liberals, and the Italian Social Democrats-Republicans (which Sani and Sartori count as a single party). Table 6.5 presents the complete matrix of distances and overlaps among the five parties. It may be easily seen that leaving aside the PSDI/PRI they form a political family in the sense defined above. The Blancos are at the left end of this family; the Italian party, even more to the left, is close to no member of the family other than the Blancos themselves. The three other members of the family belong to the left wing of European liberalism: they are secular, cosmopolitan parties, sometimes engaged in coalitions with parties to the left of their own positions.[22] The presence of the Italian PSDI/PRI close to the Blancos points to the same direction. All the European political parties close to the Blancos are relatively small.

TABLE 6.5

The Partido Nacional in Comparative Perspective

Overlapping and distance between parties along the left-right dimension

Distance

	W.G. Lib.	U.K. Lib.	S. Ind.	P. Nac.	Ital. SD/R	Mean	(N)
W. German Liberals	—	.02	.03	.05	.11	5.8	(111)
U.K. Liberals	.96	—	.01	.03	.09	5.6	(164)
Swiss Independents	.93	.91	—	.02	.08	5.5	(58)
Partido Nacional	.90	.91	.90	—	.05	5.3	(214)
Italian PSDI/PRI	.82	.83	.87	.85	—	4.8	(79)

Overlap

Computed on Sani and Sartori's (1983) data on self-placement of the voters of each party in the left-right scale except for the Partido Nacional. All means computed on the full ten-point left-right scale. Overlaps computed on the collapsed five-point version of the scale.

With regard to the left, it makes little sense to consider the Frente Amplio of 1984–85 as a single party. It was not, and it is not going to become so in any foreseeable future. This was simply an almost impossible event for a coalition which included a Christian Democratic Party and a Marxist-Leninist Communist Party, both proud of their own traditions. What must be decided is whether its five members are considered separately or rather clustered in the two wings discussed above. In strictly formal terms the first course should perhaps be chosen. A more substantive perspective points to the latter. Applying the criterion of closeness, as will be seen below, there are good reasons to consider only the wings. This will be the course followed here.

To put it bluntly, the Frente right wing is European socialism. Four parties among Sani and Sartori's data are close to it. They are the Spanish socialists (PSOE), the Finnish Social Democrats and the French and Italian socialists (PSF, PSI). They do not form a family because, as Table 6.6 shows, the PSOE and the PSI "repel" each other—they are almost close, but they do not satisfy the definition because their overlap is .83. Suppressing either, the four remaining parties do form a family. According to both criteria—overlap and distance—the PSI is slightly closer to the FA right wing than the PSOE, but the most closely knit together family is obtained by dropping the PSI. Within this family a particularly tightly tied subfamily is formed by the Finnish social democrats, the PSOE and the PSF. As in the case of the Blancos, the FA right wing is at the left end of its own family.

TABLE 6.6
The Frente Amplio Right Wing in Comparative Perspective

Overlapping and distance between parties along the left-right dimension

Distance

	Finn. S.D.	PSOE	PSF	PSI	FA r.w.	Mean	(N)
Finnish Soc. Dem.	—	.00	.01	.02	.03	3.9	(360)
Spanish Soc. (PSOE)	.96	—	.01	.02	.03	3.9	(1040)
French Soc. (PSF)	.99	.96	—	.01	.02	3.8	(420)
Italian Soc. (PSI)	.86	.83	.86	—	.01	3.7	(181)
FA right wing	.94	.91	.94	.92	—	3.6	(157)

Overlap

Computed on Sani and Sartori's (1983) data on self-placement of the voters of each party in the left-right scale except for the Frente Amplio right wing. All means computed on the full ten-point left-right scale. Overlaps computed on the collapsed five-point version of the scale.

If the right wing of the coalition of the left is European socialism, then Table 6.7 shows that its left wing is European communism—more properly, Eurocommunism. Three parties of those reported by Sani and Sartori are close to it: the Italian, Finnish, and French Communist parties. The four parties do form a political family which is in turn composed of two pairs of tightly tied parties: the Italians and the FA left wing on the one hand, and the Finnish and French parties on the other. Thus the label *Eurocommunist*. Nevertheless, this is a direct consequence of counting together the votes of

TABLE 6.7
The Frente Amplio Left Wing in Comparative Perspective

Overlapping and distance between parties along the left-right dimension

Distance

	FA l.w.	PCI	Finn. CP	PCF	Mean	(N)
FA left wing	—	.01	.03	.04	2.6	(147)
Italian C.P. (PCI)	.95	—	.02	.03	2.5	(356)
Finnish C.P.	.86	.87	—	.01	2.3	(129)
French C.P. (PCF)	.86	.87	.96	—	2.2	(82)

Overlap

Computed on Sani and Sartori's (1983) data on self-placement of the voters of each party in the left-right scale except for the frente Amplio left wing. All means computed on the full ten-point left-right scale. Overlaps computed on the collapsed five-point version of the scale.

Democracia Avanzada plus IDI's plus the socialists'. The Communists per se are still close to the PCI, but they are closest to the PCF and the Finnish Communists, in this order.[23] The Spanish Communists stand out of the group: they are close to neither.[24]

3. A Polarized Party System

Which conclusions follow from this rather sketchy analysis? The systematic comparisons did find clusters of parties close to each of the relevant Uruguayan parties, and most if not all the parties of those clusters formed political *families* in the strict sense defined above. The Uruguayan party system does not have a large, truly conservative party like the British Tories or the German CDU-CSU. Its rightmost party, the Colorados, also the largest in the 1984 election, has a position and a profile comparable to those of the relatively small members of the right wing of European liberal parties or to the U.S. Republicans; more towards the center of the spectrum, it is comparable to the Italian DCI as well. The Blanco profile is comparable to those of the left wing of European liberal parties. Both parties are thus parties of the center, though the Colorados are close to the center-right. Towards the left of the Uruguayan spectrum, the niche of the large labor and social democratic parties, as in Britain and West Germany, is also empty. This absence is symmetrical to that of a conservative party. The Uruguayan left has two wings: the moderate wing is comparable to Southern European socialisms (and Finnish social democracy), and the radical wing to Eurocommunism.[25]

Looking in the opposite direction two facts stand out. The first is simply that there is nothing comparable to the Frente Amplio in the countries Sani and Sartori classify as of low polarization. The second is that only one country included in their study has parties close to each of Uruguay's: Italy. Two countries have parties belonging to three of the four families (counting the two Colorado families as only one) associated to the Uruguayan parties: Italy and Finland. They are the most polarized polities analyzed by Sani and Sartori. All of this, obviously, strongly suggests that Uruguay's level of polarization cannot be low.

Sartori's formal definition of *polarization* of a party system is simply the distance between the rightmost and leftmost relevant parties of the system. His definition of *relevant* parties was stated initially for parliamentary regimes. Even though it may be translated into terms suitable to presidential regimes, the details of such a translation are unnecessary to study the Uruguayan system. The traditional parties are relevant simply because they are the major parties, either the government party or the one which expects to become so in the next election—as they were in the past. Each of the two

Frente Amplio wings are relevant at a minimum because of what Sartori calls "potential of intimidation." They control the relatively strong urban unions, they have high levels of militant participation, and each of them alone has about 10 percent of the national vote. The only remaining party, the small, Catholic Unión Cívica, clearly does not fulfill any of Sartori's "counting rules"; it is not, then, a relevant party from the system's point of view.[26] Any reasonable version of Sartori's rules would lead to the same conclusion: these are the four relevant actors of the Uruguayan party system.

Accordingly, the polarization of the system is .42, as Table 6.8 shows. This distance and its associated overlap of only .17 put the Uruguayan party system—at least as it is in Montevideo—together with the most polarized systems. The eleven systems studied by Sani and Sartori may be ordered in three groups. The first includes the U.S. alone, which in comparative perspective exhibits an extremely low polarization. The second group includes six countries of low polarization, from .27 to .32, coupled with still moderately high overlaps, from .56 to .45. The countries of this group are West Germany, Austria, Belgium, United Kingdom, and The Netherlands. The last group includes the countries of high polarization: Spain, France, Italy, and Finland. Within this group polarizations vary from .44 to .64. The difference between the two groups is particularly striking when the overlaps among the

TABLE 6.8
Polarization of the Uruguayan Party System

A. Profiles

	Left	C-L	Center	C-R	Right	Mean	(N)
P. Colorado	.4	4.5	57.5	21.9	15.8	6.4	(267)
P. Nacional	.5	21.0	63.6	11.6	3.2	5.3	(214)
FA right wing	17.8	55.4	24.2	2.6	—	3.6	(157)
FA left wing	52.4	35.4	7.5	4.8	—	2.6	(147)

B. Overlapping and distance

Distance

	P. Colorado	P. Nacional	FA right wing	FA left wing
P. Colorado	—	.12	.31	.42
P. Nacional	.77	—	.19	.30
FA right wing	.32	.48	—	.11
FA left wing	.17	.34	.63	—

Overlap

The profiles show the self-placement of the voters of each party in the left-right scale (percentages). All means computed on the full ten-point left-right scale. Overlaps computed on the collapsed five-point version of the scale (1,2: Left; 3,4: Center-left; 5,6: Center; 7,8: Center-right; and 9,10: Right).

most extreme relevant parties of each nation are compared: in the low polarization group those overlaps vary from .56 to .45, whereas among the highly polarized systems they vary from just .15 to .06. The Uruguayan results—polarization of .42 coupled to an overlap of .17—clearly belong to the last group; in particular, they are close to Spain's in 1979, .47 and .15 respectively. The data also show that Uruguay is the least polarized of the highly polarized systems. In short: in comparative terms Uruguay has a relatively highly polarized party system.

4. A Glance within the Parties

It might be observed, not without some reason, that the present argument still has two somewhat loose ends. First, how do the major parties look if their composing fractions are analyzed as autonomous political forces, as the parties themselves were analyzed in the preceding sections? Is the idea that they are indeed parties capable of surviving such a test? Second, in a similar vein, what if the members of the Frente Amplio coalition are subjected to the same type of analysis? How does the Frente's dichotomization into two relevant political actors discussed above stand that scrutiny?

These are important questions. In order to answer them let us begin by establishing a few preliminary points. First, fractions of a party that are close in the formal sense defined above may be reasonably considered as parts of the same whole (i.e., party). We have found that at least in the party systems studied by Sani and Sartori no different parties are "close" in the ideological dimension except when there are other relevant dimensions that disentangle their ideological closeness. There were very few exceptions, and even fewer additional relevant dimensions, *none of which is significant in Uruguay*. It is natural, then, to consider "close" fractions as parts of a single party. They may exist as separate entities simply because the institutional framework does not penalize party fractionalization but rather encourages it. Some of them may be fractions in the pejorative sense of the term; others may reflect no more than a genuine clash of personalties between leaders; still others may reflect changes in progress that are not yet clearly perceived or defined.

Second, fractions of a party separated by a greater distance than that accepted as "normal" between the different parties of a coalition should clearly be exceptional occurrences. If it is not very common for different parties which are as distant as that to form coalitions, it should be even more exceptional to establish the still closer and more stable relationship involved in being parts of the same party. Such a distance may be easily—though somewhat crudely—estimated. In parliamentary systems coalitions including parties belonging to adjacent positions in the five-point collapsed version of the left-right scale are relatively common. As each position in the collapsed scale includes two points in the original version, the theoretical average distance in the sense defined above between such parties is thus .22 (dividing 2 by the maximum, 9). Parties separated by a distance of .22 or less are then potential candidates for "normal" alliances or coalitions. Hence, fractions of a party separated by a distance of .22 or more are not normal occurrences.

Third, there is a grey area in between the two situations just described, that is, when the distance between the two fractions of a party is more than .05 but less than .22. It is reasonable to admit that fractions that are not strictly "close" but that are not very distant may coexist within the same party. But where are we to draw the line? This final question poses a difficult problem. It may be prudent to check the data before dealing with it.

We may begin analyzing the most difficult case, as will be seen below. Table 6.9 shows that the Colorado fractions do not form a political family in the sense defined above. The Tarigo and Sanguinetti fractions, however, are very close, strictly speaking, and together they form the core of the party—they obtained about 60 percent of the party's votes. The Colorado left wing, Flores Silva's fraction, does not form a family with that core, but it is close to its next fraction, Sanguinetti's. The distance and overlap of Flores Silva's fraction with respect to Tarigo's—.08 an .80 respectively—fall

TABLE 6.9
Colorado Fractions in the Left-Right Scale

A. Profiles

	Left	C-L	Center	C-R	Right	Mean	(N)
Pacheco	—	5.2	28.3	18.0	48.7	7.9	(39)
Tarigo	1.1	4.3	56.0	23.7	15.1	6.3	(93)
Sanguinetti	1.1	3.3	63.8	22.0	9.9	6.1	(91)
Flores Silva	—	8.3	72.2	19.4	—	5.6	(36)

B. Overlapping and distance

		Distance		
	Pacheco	Tarigo	Sanguinetti	Flores Silva
Pacheco	—	.18	.20	.26
Tarigo	.65	—	.02	.08
Sanguinetti	.59	.92	—	.05
Flores Silva	.51	.80	.86	—
		Overlap		

The profiles show the self-placement of the voters of each fraction in the left-right scale (percentages). All means computed on the full ten-point left-right scale. Overlaps computed on the collapsed five-point version of the scale (1,2: Left; 3,4: Center-left; 5,6: Center; 7,8: Center-right; and 9,10: Right).

within the "grey zone" just mentioned, but they are very near to the formal definition of closeness. Thus the only real problem appears with the right wing, Pacheco's fraction. It looks different even with respect to the party's center; with regard to the left wing it is beyond the limits of normal alliances or coalitions between different parties. All in all, then, the mainstream Colorados do constitute a reasonably compact party in spite of their fractions, a party that includes a left wing which is a recognizable part of it. The Colorado right wing, however, is far from the party's main body.

In comparative perspective the closest party to Pacheco's fraction is the MSI, the Italian Neo-Fascists—a distance of .04 and an overlap of .83; this falls a hairbreadth short of the formal definition of closeness. It is even less distant from the Finnish conservatives, although they overlap less. Its nearest parties are thus the two rightmost parties of Sani and Sartori's data set. Since we assumed at the beginning of this analysis that distances as large as those found within the Pachequistas and the left wing of the party are not normal occurrences, should we then conclude that the Partido Colorado is a fiction? If this were so, the Uruguayan party system would have a right wing party, and its polarization would be pretty much like that of Italy or Finland.

I do not think, however, that this is the right answer. Each of the eight parties belonging to the two Colorado families includes a subset of electors very similar to the Pachequistas—and all of them are considered parties. This is so because of the nature of the definition of *closeness*: being close requires a very high overlap, which in turn assures the existence of such subsets. What is specifically Colorado, or rather Uruguayan, is the ease with which the party's internal currents may become full-fledged, independently organized fractions. Hence the final question concerning the identity of parties still is: does the eventual party actually constitute a meaningful unit? We have thus returned to the question already posed in Chapter 2, and the strength of the historical arguments presented there seems overwhelming to me. Besides, the discussion of this chapter has contributed some additional considerations. Pachequista voters are a captive electorate: to the right of the Partido Colorado they have nowhere to go. Pachequista leaders may decide they are "captive" as well because of their own self-interest: they are more powerful as a strong minority within the party than as a small independent party. In fact, in 1984 they carried about a quarter of the party's votes, without which the Colorados would have lost to the Blancos; this gave them real leverage within the party and the government, as has always been the norm of Uruguayan politics. Furthermore, if, as seems reasonable, the particular political conditions of the 1984 election and its aftermath included a strong though probably short-lived antimilitary backlash, the wise decision for the Colorado right wing was simply to wait: when the wind changed again, they would still be there to reap the benefits.

Summing up: though certainly not in a "normal" situation, the Colorados may still be seen as a single party with a captive, distant right wing. That exceptional situation may be explained through a combination of historical roots—as seen in Chapter 2—and present circumstances—mainly the relative positions of the remaining political actors. It should be noted that those "positional" or contextual considerations do not hold for the party's left wing, which is not "captive" in any meaningful sense.[27]

We may turn now to the Blancos. If we are willing to accept—as I think we should—that Flores Silva's short distance from, and large overlap with, mainstream Colorados allow us to consider his fraction as part of an actual party, then the Blanco situation in Montevideo is clear. As Table 6.10 shows, within the Blancos there is no left wing; the main body of the party—about two-thirds of its national vote—is formed by two fractions very "close" to each other. The Blanco right wing (Lacale-Ortiz) is not "close" to the core of the party (distance of .08 and overlap of .78), but it is very near to Pereyra's fraction—as near to it as Flores Silva's fraction to Tarigo's. The Montevidean Blancos are thus a real party, though fractionalized.

TABLE 6.10
Blanco Fractions in the Left-Right Scale

A. Profiles

	Left	C-L	Center	C-R	Right	Mean	(N)
Lacalle-Ortiz	—	9.6	59.5	23.8	7.2	5.9	(42)
Pereyra	—	20.5	70.6	7.3	1.5	5.2	(68)
Ferreira	1.1	26.9	61.3	7.6	3.3	5.1	(93)

B. Overlapping and distance

Distance

	Lacalle-Ortiz	Pereyra	Ferreira
Lacalle-Ortiz	—	.08	.09
Pereyra	.78	—	.01
Ferreira	.80	.91	—

Overlap

The profiles show the self-placement of the voters of each fraction in the left-right scale (percentages). All means computed on the full ten-point left-right scale. Overlaps computed on the collapsed five-point version of the scale (1,2: Left; 3,4: Center-left; 5,6: Center; 7,8: Center-right; and 9,10: Right).

Finally, let us analyze simultaneously the distances and overlaps between the five members of the Frente Amplio coalition as of 1984. Table 6.11 shows that there are two well-defined political "families" at the two extremes of the Frente. To the right, Batalla's fraction is very close—as defined above—to the Christian Democrats. To the left, the Izquierda Democrática Independiente (IDI) is also very close to the Communists and its electoral associates (Democracia Avanzada, DA). The Partido Socialista is midway in between the two families, close—strictly speaking—to neither of its immediate companions, but very near to any of them: distances of .07 and .05 with regard to Christian Democrats and IDI, and overlaps of .81 and .77 respectively. It is as near to them as Flores Silva's fraction to Tarigo's among the Colorados, or Lacalle-Ortiz to Pereyra among the Blancos.

TABLE 6.11
The Members of the Frente Amplio in the Left-Right Scale

A. Profiles

	Left	C-L	Center	C-R	Right	Mean	(N)
Batalla	17.0	57.0	23.0	3.0	—	3.6	(135)
Dem. Cristiana	22.7	45.5	31.7	—	—	3.6	(22)
P. Socialista	37.1	46.3	13.0	3.7	—	3.0	(54)
Izq. D. Indep.	59.1	31.8	4.5	4.5	—	2.5	(22)
Democ. Avanzada	62.0	28.1	4.2	5.6	—	2.3	(71)

B. Overlapping and distance

			Distance		
	Batalla	DC	PS	IDI	DA
Batalla	—	.00	.07	.12	.14
Dem. Cristiana	.86	—	.07	.12	.14
P. Socialista	.79	.81	—	.05	.08
Izq. D. Indep.	.56	.59	.77	—	.02
Democ. Avanzada	.52	.55	.73	.96	—

Overlap

The profiles show the self-placement of the voters of each member of the coalition in the left-right scale (percentages). All means computed on the full ten-point left-right scale. Overlaps computed on the collapsed five-point version of the scale (1,2: Left; 3,4: Center-left; 5,6: Center; 7,8: Center-right; and 9,10: Right).

These results are very clear and, when added to the political histories of the members of the coalition, conclusive. The Frente is essentially an alliance of just two relevant political actors, the two "families" reported above. At least theoretically the PS could be considered as a separate actor, but this makes little sense when considering its size and the very small "breathing space" it has in between the two families reported above.[28] From a purely formal point of view—positions in the left-right scale—the PS could be considered as part of either of those two actors, but as an avowedly Marxist-Leninist organization it clearly belongs to the Frente's left wing. This was the line of reasoning followed since the preceding chapter. The

Frente Amplio at the time of the 1984 national election was thus an alliance of two relevant political actors, though the whole of it still made sense as a coalition: Table 6.11 shows that the maximum distance among members (Batalla and DA) was .14, well below the upper limit (.22) for "normal" coalitions.[29]

5. Relatively High Polarization and Moderate Pluralism

The data analyzed in this chapter add considerable precision to the polemics on the fractionalization of the major parties and on their status as real parties. In comparative perspective the traditional parties do not appear as the ideological patchwork critics have repeatedly described. At the voters' level, according to the standard deviations of self-placements in the left-right scale, the Blancos were the most homogeneous political actor in Montevideo, even more so than any of the Frente wings. The analysis at the level of fractions conducted in the previous section showed clearly a single party as well. Subjected to the same analysis, the Colorados exhibited a solid central core associated with a distant right wing. The whole polemics thus boils down to the nature of the relationship between the Colorado right wing, the Pachequismo, and the mainstream Colorados. That relationship, in turn, may be considered as a rather exceptional case of party fractionalization—not without negative consequences for the party itself—on the basis of historical roots, shared political identities, and current, contextual considerations.

The Frente Amplio, when subjected to the same type of analysis, appeared also clearly as an alliance of two relevant political actors. Those actors would be called, for the sake of brevity, radical socialists (the Frente's left wing) and social democrats (the right wing).[30]

According to Sartori's "counting rules" we have thus four relevant political actors: Colorados, Blancos, social-democrats, and radical socialists. The consequences of the birth of the Frente Amplio in 1971 were described above with the expression "two-and-a-half" party system. This was a reasonable label for the logic of the system by 1971, and perhaps still in 1984,[31] but not for its format and structure. In Sartori's terms the Uruguayan party system, with its four relevant actors, is a moderate pluralism system.

The present structure and format of the party system were born thus in the 1971 election. Two-partyism itself began to change probably in 1966, when the Communists—under the Fidel banner—obtained 5.7 percent of the national vote and, perhaps more important, the unions unified as Convención Nacional de Trabajadores (CNT). In political terms that unification benefitted the Communists in the first place, even though it was also fostered by other sectors of the left and undoubtedly strengthened the unions themselves. The

Communists controlled more than half of the CNT through a truly Leninist organization, and the remaining part was politically divided. All of this means, I think, that by 1966 the Communists had become a relevant political party. As their voters were very few by comparison with those of the traditional parties, contemporary witnesses saw as merely incremental what was, at least theoretically, a significant change. The Communists were indeed anticipating the direction of the wind, and the barrier that only in 1971 appeared clearly surpassed—i.e., the seemingly unmovable two-partyism—had in fact been broken in 1966.

In ideological terms, or at least in those aspects of ideology which appear reflected in the left-right dimension, this chapter has shown that Uruguay has a relatively highly polarized party system. For it belongs unequivocally to the small group of the most polarized democratic polities, but is the least polarized system of that group. At first sight it might appear that a system of moderate pluralism could not be relatively highly polarized, but there is no contradiction between those characteristics. The first refers to the *structure* of the system (number of relevant parties), whereas the second refers to the *ideological tension* of the system (its polarization, i.e., the distance between its two most extreme relevant parties in the ideological dimension).[32] The two conditions tend to be directly associated (the higher the one, the higher the other), but there is no perfect correlation. A truly multiparty system is not necessarily highly polarized, as when there are other politically meaningful dimensions in the system besides the left-right space, for example religion.[33] When a party system appears as essentially unidimensional in this regard as Uruguay's, the number of relevant parties beyond which it is unlikely to find anything but high polarization is "around five (or six)" (Sartori 1976, p. 132). Uruguay is thus a perfect borderline case: in fragmentation terms (four relevant actors) it is next to the frontier, and in ideological terms (polarization) in is on the border as well (the least highly polarized system of those analyzed above).

On historical grounds there is little doubt that Uruguayan polarization increased as the number of relevant actors within the system expanded. The best guess about the level of polarization thirty years before the 1984 election is that it was very low, perhaps almost as low as in the U.S. Things began to change in 1966, as a third relevant actor emerged from the left, and went on increasing till 1971, this time because of the consolidation of the Colorado right wing as the majority of its party. It is difficult to assess the position of the main fractions before 1971, in part because the left-right continuum itself was probably less visible to all participants, elite and voters alike. As long as a two-party system remained in place this was a natural state of affairs: it has been often noted that the relevance of the ideological dimension is greater the larger the number of relevant parties of the system.[34] Nevertheless, it seems clear to me that the Colorado majority in 1966 was very different from that of 1971—a difference reflected in their respective leaders, the late President Gestido, a respected man even within the left, and his successor, former President Pacheco, an extremely controversial politician. Thus, polarization increased in 1966 "to the left" and again in 1971, this time "to the right." Even though there are no comparable data, the discussion of the preceding chapter strongly suggests that polarization was lower in 1984 than in 1971. Assuming that the position of the Frentista and Colorado wings in 1971 was the same as in 1984 (a rather conservative assumption, as probably the Frentistas were more to the left, and perhaps the Pachequistas more to the right as well; it cannot be forgotten that the Tupamaros were then at the apex of their political influence) it is easy to estimate Montevideo's polarization in 1971: the left-most position does not change, but the rightmost (the Colorados') is displaced to the right because the Pachequistas were then the majority. The estimate of the Colorados' average position in 1971—taking into account each wing's relative size—is 7.2, which in turn leads to a polarization of .51. According to this estimate, then, polarization decreased 18 percent from 1971 to 1984—from .51 to .42. The 1973 coup suggests that Uruguayan democracy could not absorb a level of polarization perhaps comparable to that of Finland, France, or Italy around the same years—though the Uruguayan figure is an educated guess which most probably underestimates actual polarization at the time.

7. Voters and the Changing Party System

1. The Social Bases of the Parties in the Past

Some aspects of the historical description of the traditional parties presented in Chapter 2 are still controversial, but not those concerning their social bases. They were catch-all, multiclass-based parties. Even if there were some differences among them, they were comparatively minor; the traditional parties were supported by similar cross-sections of Uruguayan society. The other parties, the Marxian left and the Catholic party, were very small, led by intellectual elites; they were, as it has been noted, the "parties of ideas." At least in electoral terms they looked essentially as middle-class parties, even though the Unión Cívica was more upper-middle-class based than the rest.

It is widely accepted that this picture was still true in 1971. Some studies were conducted with special emphasis on the social bases of the left, leading to common conclusions. The left remained middle-class based, even though it had a working class component—most of the leadership and part of the rank-and-file of unions. The analyses did not necessarily agree on the explanation, but the did agree on the essential point: the left was no less multiclass based than the traditional parties. This did not imply that class or sectoral-based cleavages were irrelevant in Uruguayan politics. But it implied that, whatever their importance in everyday life, they were not decisive at the polls.[1] In fact, if any difference existed at all between the voters of the traditional parties and those of the left—besides the obvious one that the left was purely urban—it was that the left was more middle-class based. Since in 1971 the Frente obtained only 10 percent of the vote in the Interior, it was clear that the left had little popular appeal outside the capital. The eventual discussion was thus restricted to the sources of the left vote in Montevideo. In this regard, Ures reported that considering four strata defined in occupational terms, the left was most often voted within what he called upper-middle class, followed by the white-collar workers. The blue-collar vote for the left came in third place. Considering the social composition of the electorate of each *lema*, working-class vote was highest for the Colorados, second for the Blancos, and then, again in third place, for the left. Even though the differences concerning social composition of the electorate were not large,

113

the party of the working class, if any, was the Partido Colorado.[2] In the same vein, summarizing the evidence provided by Ures and two other independent studies (Biles 1972, Graceras 1977), Aguiar concluded that the left obtained its votes essentially among middle strata (Aguiar 1984, p. 25).

The only differences within this consensual picture appeared in relation to the role of age and education. Biles found "very little association between age and voting choice" (Biles 1972, p. 10), and a weak relationship between education and vote. The most important conclusion for him concerned

> the flatness of the curves. There is really very little difference in party choice between age, sex or educational groupings in Uruguay. Without exception, all of the demographic groups show the same basic pattern: a Colorado majority or occasional plurality, the Blancos second, and the parties of the left third. (Biles 1972, p. 114)

Biles's conclusions were based on Gallup poll information on voting choices in the 1966 election and on data on party identifiers gathered in 1970. Analyzing a survey conducted one year later—close to the 1971 election—Graceras agreed that social class was not related to party preferences or party identification "except for the left coalition, which receives relatively *more* support from the upper and upper middle classes than it does from the other strata" (Graceras 1977, p. 151; emphasis added). Nevertheless, he found, contra Biles, that "political value orientations" could be predicted on the basis of "generational and educational statuses" (ibid., p. 158).

Gillespie's examination of Gallup polls conducted before and after the 1982 *elecciones internas* supported Graceras's views against Biles's and, more generally, reaffirmed the picture described above.[3] The "radical opposition to the regime" was "young, urban, intellectual, and upper-class"; in particular, this was the profile of the blank vote, the vote the left had promoted (Gillespie 1986b, pp. 223–224). After reviewing opinion data from different sources on the 1984 election be concluded that

> voting in Uruguay is not at all class based, at least in the traditional sense. Although the Frente Amplio claims to have advanced in working-class neighborhoods, they did not do well among the very poor, who live in outlying suburbs and shantytowns and work in the informal sector. (Gillespie 1986b, p. 243)

Finally, an analysis of the Montevidean voters published a week before election day in 1984 remarked that the Frente Amplio voters were in particular (*en especial*) young middle-class males, and concluded that in spite of some moderate differences, the electorates of all the parties represented fairly well "all social classes, educational levels, occupations and age groups."[4] The overall impression, then, is similar to the accepted views concerning the 1971 election, which in turn agreed with the long-established characterization of the Uruguayan party system just summarized.

For reasons which Chapter 2 left—I hope—clear, the first third of the present century may be considered the stage of consolidation of two-partyism under democratic rules. Two-partyism, as well as the identity of the dominant parties, remained unchanged from the 1942 reequilibration till the 1960s. The classical view on the social bases of the parties is consistent with the available information on both periods and with some theoretical expectations derived from the stability of the party system.

Concerning the consolidation period it must be noted in the first place that, since there were no clearly defined social cleavages associated with the birth of the traditional parties, they were multiclass-based parties during all of their extended predemocratic life; they began democratic life as catch-all parties. Even though they were fractionalized parties of notables they also had ample mass followings. Their continued dominance during the first third of this century may be explained simply on the basis of the historical accidents of their birth first and then of their own impulse. Other characteristics of the Uruguayan polity during the period reinforced that dominance, however.

First, the confrontation of two large catch-all parties which were already "traditional"—i.e., they had deep historical roots—at the beginning of democratic life left little or no room for the emergence of competing parties of similar structure and social basis. Second, the competing parties that actually emerged—the parties of ideas—were indeed very different in those regards, but the differences themselves further limited their eventual growth. On the one hand, the Catholic party was severely constrained: the Church had never been an important social force in Uruguay, and since the past century the prevailing social practice had made religion women's business, and not even all women, but rather middle- or upper-middle-class women (Real de Azúa 1971). On the other hand, the socialists, and later the Communists as well, were also severely constrained for different reasons. To begin with, the working class which theoretically should have provided their social basis was comparatively small. Furthermore, not even that small base proved willing to turn socialist or Communist; many of them voted the traditional parties, and at least some influential union leaders became Batllistas.

The history of socialism in Uruguay is a textbook example of Lipset's theory on the conditions that promote or prevent the formation of working-class-based revolutionary parties. In his view, two central factors shaping the character of working-class movements are "the nature of the social-class system before industrialization" and "the way in which the economic and political elites responded to the demands of workers for the right to participate in the polity and the economy" (Lipset 1983b, p. 1). With regard to the first factor, the rigidity of status differences favored the emergence of radical working-class-based parties because it provided the social cement capable of keeping together a radical political movement. As for the second factor, the greater "the duration and intensity of state repression of working-class economic and political rights, the more likely workers were to respond favorably to revolutionary doctrines" (ibid., p. 6). On both counts Uruguay was exceptional in Latin America. It is a well-known fact that the Southern Cone countries, especially Argentina and Uruguay, the bulk of whose population is the result of comparatively very late European migrations, were far more open societies than the rest of Latin America, and these differences also indicated that Uruguay was a less status-conscious society, if only because its elites were much less rich and powerful—not merely in absolute terms, but in relative terms as well.[5] Concerning the political and economic participation of the workers, finally, it has already been noted that Uruguay's was the only real, enduring process of democratization in Latin America during the first quarter of the century.[6] On both counts, then, Uruguayan conditions contributed to preventing the development of significant revolutionary working-class-based parties. This did not eventually exclude reformist, social-democratic movements; but, of course, this niche was already occupied by the Batllistas.

The preservation of two-partyism and the continuing dominant role of Blancos and Colorados during the quarter of a century which followed the 1942 democratic reequilibration also preserved the previous state of affairs concerning the social bases of the parties. As Kirchheimer observed, denominational and class-based parties could, and in many cases did become catch-all parties, but the opposite transformation seems extremely unlikely, and no important examples of such transformation have actually occurred.[7] Electoral law, as shown in Chapter 2, was a central mechanism preserving two-partyism; other factors contributed to maintaining the dominant position of the traditional parties in the system.

The first factor is the strength of party identifications. From a purely theoretical point of view Uruguay fulfilled Converse's requisites for a mature rate of party identification (Converse 1969) more than any other Latin American party system—because of the sheer age of the parties and their relatively extended democratic experience. The available evidence shows that Uruguay fared well in this regard even by comparison with other well-established non-Latin American polities. Biles found that the level of party identification of Montevideans in the 1960s was slightly lower than in the U.S., very similar to that of Norway, and definitely higher than in France (Biles 1972, p. 40). The regional comparison is consistent with all of the above: Kalman Silvert contrasted the strength of Uruguayan party identifications to the weaker Chilean pattern (Silvert 1961, pp. 145–146), and Snow pointed out "the low level of party identification" in Argentina (Snow 1979, p. 49).

Other, more impressionistic evidence further confirms this picture: the word *correligionario* (i.e., "of the same religion") is still used in Uruguay to refer to other supporters of one's own party. The consequences of party identification were particularly significant: "Uruguayans show an even stronger tendency than do North Americans to remain with their party throughout their lives and to vote consistently for it" (Biles 1972, p. 121).

Second, and obviously related to the previous point, family political socialization processes seem to have been important in Uruguay, resulting in relatively high intra-family common patterns of party identification and voting behavior.[8] Third, and finally, it has been suggested that when party identifications are directly linked to parties, as in the U.S. and Uruguay, the capability of parties to resist change is greater than when this is not the case, i.e., when the prior identification is towards other formal organizations—as unions or churches, for example—or is based in informal, extrapolitical group identities. This is so because in the latter case the party's appeal among its followers depends on processes the party itself does not control. Thus,

> If we term parties that receive support on the basis of prior loyalties to party-associated groups or organizations "derived parties," and parties that receive their support directly rather than through such intermediaries "direct parties," then we can suggest that party systems characterized by direct parties are more likely to be in a position to maintain themselves than those characterized by derived parties. (Mair 1983, p. 424)

In the end, the classical view on the social bases of the parties is consistent with the available data and with the theoretical expectations relevant to the Uruguayan case until at least the mid-1960s. From the mid-1950s to the mid-1960s, however, a deep social and economic crisis affected the country, a crisis which also had notorious political consequences—most notably the behavior of the voters, who from 1954 through 1966 always voted the "outs" into office, either in party or fractional terms. Such results had no precedents in Uruguayan democratic political history. The preceding chapters have also shown that after the 1966 election the party system experienced deep changes as a result of the very crisis the traditional parties proved unable to solve.

It seems to me, then, that the classical approach on the social bases of the parties has become increasingly misleading. If the social bases of the traditional parties and the growing left did not change, it would follow that the party system experienced a purely ideological transformation. What is more, if the social bases of the parties remain, in relative terms, as they were in the past, then those ideological transformations occurred roughly in the same proportions throughout all social groups, irrespective of the ways and intensity with which the crisis struck them. But this seems unlikely. The responses to the crisis, even with regard to similar stimulus, differ according to the context and resources of the actors, which in turn vary systematically among the different social groups. Emigration was also a response to the crisis, and a large number of Uruguayans relative to the population emigrated; but those migrants, as is well-known, were a definitely biased sample of the population: relatively well-educated young men were overrepresented. The simple fact that the political response to the crisis in the Interior was slower and more muted than in Montevideo is enough to show that the political reactions to the crisis were not identical across the social spectrum.[9] In short, the real questions do not ask whether there have been changes, but what changes actually occurred, what was their intensity, and why precisely those changes occurred.

2. The Montevidean Voter in 1984

A somewhat narrow but useful definition of catch-all party is simply the extent to which the distribution of a party's voters according to any given attribute is similar to the distribution of that attribute within the voting population (Sani 1984, p. 35). "Similarity" may be assessed by means of percent differences; the average of the absolute values of those differences[10] is an easily computed summary measure of how much catch-all the party is with regard to that attribute. The higher the average, the less catch-all the party is. These definitions will be repeatedly used in the rest of this chapter.

Men are definitely underrepresented among Colorado voters and overrepresented among the Frente's left wing: the percent differences between the men's share of the vote of each party and the percentage of men in the whole sample are -6 and +12 respectively. The distribution by sex of the electorate of the four relevant parties exhibits a pattern which reappears in all the cases discussed below: the party whose electorate is most similar to the population as a whole is always the Partido Nacional; in the opposite extreme, the least catch-all is always the Frente Amplio's left wing. The Partido Colorado and the Frente's right wing fall in between, sometimes with one of them more catch-all, sometimes the other way around. With regard to sex in particular, the Colorados are less catch-all than the Frente's right wing.[11]

Table 7.1 probes the links between age and voting behavior. It presents the age profiles of the voters of each of the relevant parties (Part A) and the voting patterns of different age groups (Part B). The age profiles of voters reported in Part A are percent differences between the distribution of all the voters of each party according to age and the age distribution of the whole sample, which is presented in the last column. For example, Colorado voters of 18–29 years old are 11.6 percent of all Colorado voters, hence the corresponding figure in Part A of the table is 11.6 less 24.0 (percentage of persons of 18–29 years old in the sample), i.e., -12.4. In other words, 24.0 plus -12.4—which is the reported data—gives 11.6, the percentage of Colorado voters who are 18–29 years old. It is thus easy to reconstruct the original Colorado percentages, and those of the other parties, if it is so wished. The total Ns of the last row do not add up to the grand total of 996 because this last figure includes all the sample—that is, voters of the four relevant parties (reported in the table) plus voters of non-relevant parties (the Unión Cívica) and nonvoters. The voting patterns of age groups reported in Part B are also percent differences, this time between the voting behavior of each age group and that of the whole sample. For example, 15.5 percent of the persons who are 18–29 years old voted Colorado, hence the corresponding figure in the table is 15.5 less 31.9 (percentage of Colorado voters in the sample), i.e., -16.4. Original percentages can also be easily reconstructed here following a similar procedure to that of Part A. The last row of Part B of the table does not add up to 100 because it includes the voters of relevant parties alone, leaving aside other voters and nonvoters.

TABLE 7.1
Age and Voting Behavior

Age	Partido Colorado	Partido Nacional	FA right wing	FA left wing	
A. Age profiles of voters					
					Sample (%)
18–29	-12.4	-5.1	11.4	20.6	24.0
30–49	-5.0	-1.9	6.4	9.0	33.0
50–59	2.8	3.4	-3.0	-9.1	16.7
60 and over	14.6	3.6	-14.9	-20.6	26.3
(N)	(318)	(244)	(175)	(157)	(996)
B. Voting patterns of age groups					
					(N)
18–29	-16.4	-5.3	8.3	13.6	(239)
30–49	-4.9	-1.4	3.4	4.4	(329)
50–59	5.4	5.0	-3.1	-8.5	(166)
60 and over	17.7	3.4	-10.0	-12.3	(262)
Sample (%)	31.9	24.5	17.6	15.7	(996)

Entries are percent differences with respect to the sample's distributions, which are presented in the last column (Part A) and in the last row (Part B).

The first age group (18–29) reached voting age (18 years) during the authoritarian regime; the second (30–49) during the period of high competitiveness of the party system (1954–73); the third (50–59) during the period of Colorado predominance, and the last (60 and over) around the 1942 democratic reequilibration or before.

As Table 7.1 shows, age is strongly associated to voting patterns. Colorado voters are disproportionately old, and Frentistas—particularly the left-wing voters—disproportionately young. There is a relatively smooth transition between the two extremes of the political spectrum, the less biased electorate being that of the Blancos. Colorados and right-wing Frentistas are similarly biased, but in opposite directions; the bias of the leftmost voters is even greater. When considering the distribution of the vote within each age group it is found that 50 percent of those over 60 years old voted Colorado, whereas 55 percent of those under 30 voted the FA. These are comparatively large differences. The Uruguayan pattern is similar to that of Spain in 1979—except for an interesting difference. Focusing, for simplicity, on the two extreme Uruguayan political actors (the Colorados and the FA left wing; their Spanish terms of comparison are the UCD and the Communists) and on the two extreme age groups, the percent differences with regard to their respective populations show that old voters were six points more overrepresented among the Colorados than in the UCD, and fifteen points more underrepresented in the FA left wing than in the PCE; young voters were about equally underrepresented to the right, but eleven points more overrepresented in the FA left wing than in the PCE. Although the pattern is the same, it appears more marked in Uruguay than in Spain, with the difference increasing from the right to the left and from young to old age. The gap is widest for old voters of the left and it disappears at the opposite extreme. This picture is confirmed comparing the FA right wing and the PSOE.[12]

Education is strongly associated with voting patterns as well. Both traditional parties receive a disproportionately large share of their votes from citizens with a low educational level. Voters with a medium educational level are considerably underrepresented in their electorates, and the highly educated voters, though still underrepresented, are closer to the relative size they have in the population. Within the left the picture is symmetrical: the low-educated voters are underrepresented, particularly in the FA left wing. The voters the left attracts most are those of medium education; highly-educated voters are overrepresented as well, but to a lesser extent. The differences are more marked within the FA left wing. These unbalances may be summarized as follows: 42 percent of the low-educated citizens voted the Colorados, whereas about the same proportion of the medium-educated and of the highly-educated voted the FA. The Blancos remain the most catch-all party in Sani's terms.

What is atypical here is not any particular aspect of the pattern, as in the case of the age-vote relationship, but the pattern itself. It did not exist in Spain in 1979; the three parties discussed above showed no definite pattern in this regard.[13] The opposite picture is true for the Italian left. In the early 1950s a full 90 percent of the PCI voters and more than two thirds of the PSI's were low-educated in the sense defined in Table 7.2; thirty years later the effects of the expansion of the educational system were clearly visible, but the education of Communist and socialist voters still was below the national average. In 1982 56 percent of the Communist voters were low-educated (Sani 1984, pp. 38, 41); the corresponding figure in the FA left wing was 18 percent, less than a third.

TABLE 7.2

Education and Voting Behavior

Education	Partido Colorado	Partido Nacional	FA right wing	FA left wing	
A. Educational profiles of voters					
					Sample (%)
Low	12.4	9.4	-15.5	-21.1	39.6
Medium	-9.3	-6.1	11.1	15.1	43.5
High	-3.1	-3.3	4.4	6.0	16.9
(N)	(319)	(243)	(174)	(157)	(994)
B. Voting patterns of different educational levels					
					(N)
Low	10.0	5.8	-6.8	-8.4	(394)
Medium	-6.9	-3.3	4.5	5.5	(432)
High	-5.9	-4.8	4.5	5.6	(168)
Sample (%)	32.1	24.4	17.5	15.8	(994)

Entries are percent differences with respect to the sample's distributions, which are presented in the last column (Part A) and in the last row (Part B).

Low education: primary or less (up to 6 years of formal education); Medium: at least some secondary but no higher education (at most 12 years), and High: at least some higher education (Technical, University; no less than 13 years).

Measured by an admittedly rather crude indicator—interviewers' judgments on the quality of interviewees' homes—socio-economic status is less associated with voting choices than age or education. This seems to be a relatively normal pattern within the systems referred to above. Both traditional parties are catch-all in this regard. The two FA wings are less catch-all,[14] and there is an important qualitative difference between them: the right wing is, in relative terms, particularly attractive for the lower-middle stratum but quite unpopular within the lowest one; the left wing, while doing about average among the voters of the lower-middle stratum, is most popular in the lowest. Thus, the FA wins a plurality in the lower half of the social pyramid, but its wings specialize in different quarters of that half, those of lowest socio-economic status being the most radical.

TABLE 7.3
Socio-economic Status and Voting Behavior

SE status	Partido Colorado	Partido Nacional	FA right wing	FA left wing	
		A. Socio-economic profiles of voters			
					Sample (%)
High	.7	.7	-1.0	-1.6	2.2
Upper-middle	.7	-1.1	.3	-.7	13.7
Middle	-1.4	-2.6	3.4	-8.8	27.0
Lower-middle	-2.7	-.5	7.2	1.7	30.8
Low	2.8	3.5	-9.9	9.4	26.3
(N)	(313)	(238)	(171)	(154)	(976)
		B. Voting patterns of socio-economic strata			
					(N)
High	10.8	8.9	-8.0	-11.0	(21)
Upper-middle	1.7	-1.8	.5	-.8	(133)
Middle	-1.8	-2.4	2.2	-5.2	(264)
Lower-middle	-2.9	-.5	4.1	.8	(301)
Low	3.3	3.2	-6.6	5.6	(257)
Sample (%)	32.1	24.4	17.5	15.8	(976)

Entries are percent differences with respect to the sample's distributions, which are presented in the last column (Part A) and in the last row (Part B).

Socio-economic strata defined according to interviewer's judgment of the quality of the interviewee's home.

The most striking result of the analysis of the voting behavior of the economically active population lies perhaps in its marginal distribution: the four political actors exhibit similar strength. This implies, of course, that among the noneconomically active citizens there is a heavy pro-Colorado bias. This is indeed so: 49 percent of the retired and 41 percent of housewives voted Colorado, and together they make 82 percent of the nonactive adults. Students do not share that pattern, but they are a small minority of the nonactive. Their voting behavior is even more biased than that of housewives and senior citizens, but in the opposite direction: 55 percent of them voted the FA, and just 10 percent voted Colorado. All in all, 40 percent of the nonactive voted the Partido Colorado. Needless to say, this result is consistent with, and should have been expected on the basis of, the voting behavior of the population according to sex, age, and education reported above. Once more, this is not an exceptional state of affairs; the electorate of the Italian DC exhibits the same traits as the Colorados in this regard (Sani 1984, pp. 43–44).

Table 7.4 shows contrasting patterns in the parties' electorates within the economically active population. The Blancos are the most catch-all party, as in the previous results. Among the Colorado voters the residual category "other occupations" and the managers are overrepresented, whereas blue-collar workers and technicians are underrepresented. The white-collar occupations are slightly below their share of the sample. The residual category "other occupations" is not amorphous: 90 percent are personal services workers, 87 percent of which, in turn, are women. Most of those women are low-educated—60 percent, doubling the share of low-educated workers in the economically active population as a whole—and two-thirds are self-employed. Most of those having "other occupations," then, are in the margins of the modern economy. The left has a profile exactly opposite to the Colorados'. Both FA wings were least successful, in relative terms, with managers and "other occupations," and did best among technicians and blue-collar workers. Similar differences to those observed with regard to the left's support within the lowest socio-economic strata reappear here: the right

TABLE 7.4
Occupation and Voting Behavior

Occupation	Partido Colorado	Partido Nacional	FA right wing	FA left wing	
A. Occupational profiles of voters					
					Sample (%)
Managers	3.3	1.5	-1.1	-2.5	4.7
Technicians	-3.0	-2.5	3.3	1.8	16.0
White collar	-1.2	1.2	1.7	-2.1	33.2
Blue collar	-7.5	-.4	2.8	11.5	28.5
Other occupations*	8.3	.1	-6.9	-8.8	17.7
(N)	(100)	(96)	(83)	(90)	(407)
B. Voting patterns of different occupations					
					(N)
Managers	17.5	8.0	-4.6	-11.6	(19)
Technicians	-4.6	-3.6	4.2	2.5	(65)
White collar	-.9	.8	1.1	-1.4	(135)
Blue collar	-6.5	-.3	2.0	8.9	(116)
Other occupations*	11.5	.0	-7.9	-11.0	(72)
Sample (%)	24.6	23.6	20.4	22.1	(407)

*Mostly personal services.

Includes all members of the economically active population except unemployed. Entries are percent differences with respect to the sample's distributions, which are presented in the last column (Part A) and in the last row (Part B).

wing did best among the technicians, and the left wing—by far—among the blue-collar workers. There is a difference in the relative size of the white-collar vote within each wing's electorate as well: although the white-collar vote does not present important biases, its weight within the FA's right wing is the highest, and within the left wing the lowest, of all four political actors (Table 7.4, Part B).

The left as a whole is the strongest political force among the workers. Leaving aside technicians and managers, 42 percent of the economically active population voted for the left, with each of the traditional parties obtaining the vote of about one fourth of the workers. These global results obscure important sectorial differences: more than half of blue-collar workers voted for the left, whereas less than one-fourth of the more marginal workers did so.

Table 7.5, showing the occupational category of the voters, presents again the by now familiar picture of the Blancos as the most, and the FA left wing as the least, catch-all parties of the system. It also adds some further details to an already clear picture. Even though employers obviously cannot be the electoral basis of any major party, they amount to 11 and 9 percent

TABLE 7.5
Occupational Category and Voting Behavior

	Partido Colorado	Partido Nacional	FA right wing	FA left wing	
A. Voters' profiles according to occupational category					
					Sample (%)
Employer	3.2	1.3	-3.8	-6.4	7.5
Self-employed	7.1	1.3	-6.2	-4.0	28.4
Public worker	-2.8	1.9	5.4	-3.5	16.8
Private worker	-7.5	-4.5	4.6	13.8	47.3
(N)	(93)	(91)	(81)	(90)	(387)
B. Voting patterns of different occupational categories					
					(N)
Employer	10.5	4.1	-10.6	-19.8	(29)
Self-employed	6.0	1.0	-4.5	-3.2	(110)
Public worker	-4.0	2.7	6.8	-4.7	(65)
Private worker	-3.8	-2.2	2.0	6.9	(183)
Sample (%)	24.0	23.5	20.9	23.2	(387)

Includes all members of the economically active population except unemployed and a few active interviewees whose occupational category was not identified. Entries are percent differences with respect to the sample's distributions, which are presented in the last column (Part A) and in the last row (Part B).

of the Colorado and Blanco electorates respectively. Thirty-five percent of them voted Colorado, and only 3 percent voted for the FA left wing. The self-employed are an important part of the Colorado electorate, as of the Spanish UCD in 1979; the left did poorly among them. The most successful competitor for the vote of those who work in the public sector is the FA right wing alone; the left taken together obtained as many votes as the two traditional parties jointly considered. If providing jobs has been a central piece of clientelist politics, as the literature has indicated, it is clear that in the present such practice no longer returns in votes the past favors of the parties, at least not in a significant manner. The left has never been in a position which allowed it to provide such services—assuming it would have been wiling to do so. The private sector has been even more propitious for the left: 53 percent of private-sector workers voted for the Frente Amplio.

On the whole, the Uruguayan party system is not a class-based system. In this general appraisal the classical view on the nature of Uruguayan parties remains true. A class-based system is characterized by at least two parties or blocs, one "bourgeois" and the other "working class," with the eventual presence of a third, agrarian party or bloc of parties, each of them recruiting its voters mostly in its specific constituency. The models in this regard are the four Scandinavian party systems, the most class-based among contemporary democracies. In all of them, for example, more than two-thirds of working-class voters consistently vote the left (Worre 1980). Neither of these traits apply to the Uruguayan system.

This corroboration does not lead us very far. After all, this is true for most contemporary party systems in democratic polities. Beyond this rather obvious generalization, the central aspects of the classical view no longer apply, at least in Montevideo. The parties are definitely not equally catch-all. There is one truly catch-all party in Sani's sense, the Partido Nacional. The Partido Colorado's electorate adds pluralities from both extremes of the social spectrum: on the one hand, 43 percent of those of highest socio-economic status, 42 percent of managers and 35 percent of employers voted Colorado; on the other hand, 36 percent of those working in personal services—mostly low-educated women—and 35 percent of those of lowest socio-economic status voted Colorado as well. *All* of these percentages are pluralities, even considering the two FA wings as a single unit. The largest part of this electorate, of course, comes from the basis of the social pyramid, not from its apex. Fifteen-seven percent of Colorado voters belong to the lower-middle and low socio-economic strata—a percentage equal to their share in the population. The Colorado's appeal within the lowest strata, however, is strongly biased: they attract mainly old, low-educated, nonactive citizens.

The left as a whole—i.e., both FA wings—is, first and foremost, the choice of those who are employed. An absolute majority of those employed in the private and public sectors voted the left. There are significant differences according to the nature of the jobs: 53 percent of blue-collar workers voted the left, whereas it did poorly among the most marginal jobs—24 percent of personal services workers voted the FA. The left was more voted by the economically active than by the nonactive; by the young more than by the old; by men more than by women; and by those with at least some secondary education more than by those with little or no formal education.

Thus, considering only the three main *lemas* it is true, as many have argued from 1971 onwards, that age and education are strongly associated with voting behavior. Ure's findings concerning the behavior of occupational strata in the 1971 election, however, are definitely not true in 1984. The party of the working class, if any, is not the Partido Colorado but the Frente Amplio instead. The workers' vote for the left almost doubles their Colorado or Blanco vote. Still, this is a misleading way of analyzing the data, useful only for purposes of direct comparison with the existing literature. The left has two well-defined wings, as Chapter 6 showed, and the system has four relevant political actors. It is at this level—that of the information presented in Tables 7.1 through 7.5—that the data must be assessed. When this is done a fuller picture appears.

The two wings of the left have different electorates. The middle and lower-middle socio-economic strata add up to 58 percent of the population; they amount to 68 percent of the FA right wing's electorate but only 51 percent of the left wing's. There is a seventeen-point difference between them, larger than that existing between any of the two wings and any of the traditional parties. In fact, these strata's share of the Colorado and Blanco electorates lies between the figures of the left: 54 percent among the Colorados, and 55 percent among the Blancos. A similar picture, but in the opposite direction, appears when the lowest socio-economic stratum is considered. It amounts to 26 percent of the population, but it accounts for 36 percent of the FA left wing's electorate and for only 16 percent of the right wing's. The gap is now even larger, 20 points, and, again, the figures corresponding to the traditional parties lie between those of the left: 29 percent among the Colorados and 30 percent among the Blancos. In this regard, then, the FA right wing is indeed more middle-class based than the traditional parties, and the left wing is less so than any of the other parties. This result is confirmed by the data on voters' occupation presented in Table 7.4. White-collar voters add to 35 percent of the electorate of the FA right wing, their largest share in the four electorates, and to 31 percent of the left wing's—their smallest. These are small differences, but they are considerably more marked for blue-collar workers: they add to 40 percent of the electorate of the FA left wing, but only 31 percent of the right wing's. In fact, the left wing alone wins a plurality among blue collar workers: almost a third of them voted the FA left wing; the right wing and the Blancos obtained less than a fourth each, and the Colorados less than a fifth. The working class's most preferred party is the FA left wing—the Communists and their ideologically closest allies.

This state of affairs is similar to that existing in two of the four highly polarized European polities mentioned in Chapter 6—Italy and Spain. According to Sani, who presents data for British, French, German, Italian, and Spanish parties directly comparable to those of Table 7.4, the percent difference measuring the overrepresentation of blue-collar vote in the FA left wing's electorate is similar to those corresponding to the Italian and Spanish Communists and to the Spanish PSOE, lower than those of the French Communists and the British Labour, and higher than those of all the other relevant parties in the five countries. The Blancos and the FA right wing are in a position similar to that of Italian socialists in this regard, and the Colorados, once more, to the DCI and the Spanish UCD in 1979 (Sani 1984, p. 36). The other two highly polarized polities discussed in the previous chapter, France and particularly Finland, are considerably more class-based systems. Nevertheless, if the present level of association between social strata and voting choices is neither particularly high nor atypical, the trend itself is atypical. The available evidence suggests that since the beginning of the 1960s there has been a discernable decline in class-linked voting in democratic polities (Lipset 1983a, pp. 503–504). Even in the Scandinavian countries the working-class vote for the left, although "fluctuating from election to election," has "declined during the past two decades" (Sainsbury 1985, p. 1).

This quick review of the evidence allows a simple conclusion. In comparative terms the Uruguayan party system is not particularly class-based, but the accepted views on the social bases of the parties are no longer true. The parties—at least some of them—are definitely less catch-all than it has been assumed so far. The left, in particular, is not as middle-class-based as the traditional parties or even more so, as has been the usual contention; exactly the opposite is true. The direction of the change has been from a party system very little affected by class divisions towards a more class-based system. The intensity of those changes is, to a certain extent, a debatable matter. It might be argued that they have not been very important, since the present state of the system is very different from that of the most class-based systems, such as the Scandinavian. But this amounts to assessing the changes with regard to what they could be, not with regard to what they have actually been in the past. According to the latter criterion, the changes have been significant: first, parties which initially had no specific social bases of their own have become clearly different; second, these intrinsically important changes have gone against the contemporary dominant trend within democratic polities.

When did the classical view on the social bases of the parties begin to diverge from the facts, and why did it survive after that point? The studies mentioned in the previous section, taken together, provide a strong feeling of gradual change. Biles's conclusions, based mainly on data gathered in 1966 and 1970, confirmed the central points of the traditional vision. Graceras's findings concerning the relationship between age, education, and voting behavior in the 1971 election were not so easily accounted for in that tradition. Some reports from independent sources based in 1984 pre-election surveys, finally, further confirmed Graceras's results—which had reappeared in Gallup polls conducted in 1982, before the parties' *elecciones internas*—and presented information on the relationship of occupation, socio-economic status, and voting which went against the grain of the classical view.[15]

Thus, at least some of the facts summarized in Tables 7.1 to 7.5 were already beginning to emerge by the time of the 1984 election. This was not enough to affect the prevailing views for several reasons. First, the discussions published close to the election were rather hurried, and there was no further research later. Second, the changes themselves were not extreme, and they did not make evident the need to review old schemes. Third, the extent of the changes was obscured by the customary ways of presenting and discussing the information—most notably by considering the FA as a whole, thus allowing the opposite trends of its wings to partially cancel each other out.[16] A fourth factor whose importance is more difficult to assess concerns the circumstances surrounding the surveys which supported most of those analyses. The political climate of the 1971 election was more akin to that of a pre-civil war environment than to that of a normal election—it was perhaps comparable to that of the Chilean election Allende had just won. During the 1982 *elecciones internas* the FA was outlawed; the blank vote, which was promoted only by the FA, identified the interviewees who favored it as Frentistas. At the time, being a Frentista had some risks, and these risks varied according to the different groups within the FA. Nevertheless, in the 1984 election, which certainly was not a standard election, the results of the different pre-election surveys suggest that those effects were no longer significant.[17]

These remarks may explain the survival of the classical view, but they leave unanswered the most important issue, i.e., *when* that view began to fail. I think that the starting point may be dated with considerable precision: the 1966 election. This date also marked the beginning of the structural transformation of the party system, and the coincidence, needless to say, is not fortuitous. The initial stages of both processes resulted from common causes, which will be discussed in the following section. Whatever the weight of the remarks of the previous paragraph, if this argument is right analysts have been rather slow in recognizing the nature of the transformations the party system underwent. What is more, the results of the present analysis on the social bases of the left are perfectly consistent with all the available evidence based on aggregate data. A pioneer compilation of data at the level of the 19 *Departamentos* discovered a consistent, stable pattern of high correlations between vote for the left—especially for the Communists and their allies, now the organizational and electoral bulk of the FA left wing—and the proportion of industrial workers in the economically active population and other indicators of development of the secondary sector of the economy throughout the 1962, 1966, and 1971 elections (Filgueira 1976). A more elaborate model regressed vote for the FA in 1971 on three variables: urbanization, proportion of urban middle and upper-middle class occupations, and proportion of blue-collar workers in the economically active population. This model attained a remarkable fit to the data: it explained almost 90 percent of the variation of the FA vote, and it showed that the strongest impact on that vote, measured by the unstandardized coefficients of the regression line, was that of the proportion of blue collar workers in the economically active population—its coefficient more than doubled, and tripled, respectively, those of the other variables (González 1983). The same model was later applied to the 1982 *elecciones internas*, obtaining similar results (Gillespie 1986b).

The conclusions of this analysis open a new set of questions. Some of the most important are the following: First, why did the system experience a transformation towards more class-based electorates which runs against the contemporary prevailing trends? Second, how can some very atypical characteristics of that transformation, most notably the effects of education, be explained? Third, how can the role of each party in those changes, that is, the Blancos remaining a truly catch-all party and the Colorados and the left, particularly the FA left wing, acquiring the opposite biases which altered the whole system, be accounted for?

3. A Party System in Transition

The first and most important cause of the transformation of the party system was of course the crisis the major parties could not solve. The crisis was deep, as Chapter 3 showed, and proved enduring as well: it began in the mid-fifties and was still there in 1973 when the coup finally came—in fact, its social and economic dimensions remain even now essentially untouched. It was also a Uruguayan crisis: in spite of its external component it was evident that most comparable countries were not experiencing problems of similar order of magnitude. Uruguayans who are now middle-aged were educated thinking of Spain as a backward country whose citizens still were looking for opportunities outside their homeland, and of Brazil as a very backward country. Now Spain looks like an extremely desirable goal, and many Uruguayans migrate to Brazil. In short, the major parties no longer delivered the goods, and they had had time enough to change course. This suggested that they did not wish to do so—or perhaps that they could not. Under this light the resilience of the party system is remarkable. The first symptom of change, the 1966 election, came ten years after the onset of the crisis, and the Frente Amplio was born five years later, in 1971.

Still, this explains the *why*, not the *how* of the changes of the party system. Besides, the crisis struck all Uruguayans. Those at the bottom of the social ladder were the most affected in absolute terms, but in relative terms not a single social group large enough as to have some electoral weight of its own consistently benefitted from the crisis. In other words, socio-economic status alone will not help to understand the political erosion of the traditional parties, because the whole social spectrum was affected by the crisis. For this reason the socio-economic profiles of the voters of the traditional parties (Table 7.3, Part A) are the least biased of those presented in the previous section. In this regard the Colorados remain a truly catch-all party. We may thus turn to the reasons that explained the preservation of the dominance of the traditional parties until the 1960s. In the first place, the central mechanisms that maintained two-partyism—the combination of electoral law and institutional framework—are useless for the present purpose, for they were constants before 1973 (and after 1984) and they were in fact obstacles to the transformations the party system actually experienced. We have to look instead to the factors that specifically contributed to support the dominant role of the traditional parties. How did they become less effective?

The most important of those factors was the strength of party identifications. Party identifications are acquired: their acquisition is a time-consuming process, and as a result older voters tend to develop stronger party identifications. Besides, the initial, formative political experiences by means of which party identifications are acquired tend to produce a generational effect: cohorts are marked by the events occurring at the time of their political coming of age.[18] All of this means that we should expect the following results: (i) older voters should be less likely defectors from the traditional parties because of their stronger party identifications, and (ii) older cohorts should be more definitely Colorado, since before 1958 the Blancos had never won Montevideo. This is exactly what Table 7.1 shows. The older the age group, the better the performance of the two traditional parties, and the opposite is true of the two FA wings. On the other hand, the Colorado performance is dismal among those who reached voting age during the authoritarian regime, but crushing among those who reached voting age when the Colorados were a predominant party, that is, those over 50 years old.

The observed differences between the two traditional parties as well as those between the two FA wings also suggest that the effect of age on voting

behavior adds two different components: the effects linked to party identifications and a life-cycle effect according to which voters tend to become
more conservative as they grow older.[19] As Lipset pointed out, it is not necessarily true that conservatism increases with age (Lipset 1983a, pp. 282 and
ff.), but it seems true that times of social instability affect younger and older
people in different ways because of their different positions in the social
structure: youth reacts turning left, while their elders tend to choose deliberately the status quo over a potentially better future at the cost of an even
greater actual instability. The comparison with the Spanish pattern in the
discussion of Table 7.1 also suggests the same conclusion. Spain should reasonably exhibit a life-cycle effect perhaps not very different from Uruguay's,
but Uruguayan figures add a generational effect stronger than, and different
from, any such effect eventually existing in Spain—because of four decades
of Franquismo and the different history of its party system. The latter factor
helps to understand why the PSOE and the PCE fared so much better than
their ideologically similar FA wings among the eldest voters. The distinctiveness of the Uruguayan generational effect leads to the pattern according to
which the differences between the age profiles of ideologically similar parties in the two countries increase systematically from young to old age and
from the right to the left—being zero at the "initial" corner (young voters
of the right) and reaching its maximum at the opposite corner (old voters
of the left). On the basis of the present survey life-cycle effects cannot be
estimated. Nevertheless, some tentative manipulations of the data suggest
that a life cycle effect could have been at work from the 1971 to the 1984
elections, hurting the left, leaving the Blancos unchanged, and favoring the
Colorados.[20]

The remaining factors favoring the continuing dominant role of the
traditional parties, although most probably influential, are considerably less
documented. They are, first, the role of family political socialization, and
second, the direct nature of the link between the traditional parties and their
voters—that is, the link was independent from social collective identities
and/or organizations. Little can be said regarding the latter. In the past the
clubes políticos of the neighborhoods probably played a more important role
than in the present, but it is difficult to assess the effects of their relative decay. The first—family political socialization—is perhaps the most traditional
of the mechanisms of political recruitment, and as such it is vulnerable to
all agents capable of corroding traditional patterns of authority and behavior,
most notably formal education. That corrosive effect of education was further enhanced in Uruguay for two reasons. First, Uruguay had a reasonably
extended network of primary schools since the beginning of democratic life,
particularly by Latin American standards, but the real expansion of secondary
education began in the fifties.[21] This means that many voters during the late

sixties and seventies—and still now—had received more formal education than their parents, thus opening ample room for the potentially disruptive effects of education. Parents themselves regarded education as a highly desirable goal, partly because it was seen as a channel for upward mobility. Second, those expectations were not fulfilled. The net effect of a massive educational expansion in a country whose economy was stagnating since the mid-1950s was an equally massive devaluation of education.[22] An extreme example of this devaluation is that nowadays many highly educated job-seekers understate their educational level because the distance between it and the job they are looking for becomes an obstacle. Thus, besides its potential for corroding traditional patterns, education generated expectations that could not be fulfilled. The net result is what may be seen in Table 7.2: the educational profiles of the voters of the two traditional parties—most successful among the least educated voters—are very similar to each other, and opposite to those of the two wings of the left, which in turn are very similar to each other. The trend appears weakened among the highest educated voters simply because that is the place, after all, of the most favored strata of the population—those who most benefit from the status quo.

Thus far I have examined the weak points of the mechanisms that contributed to maintain the dominant role of the traditional parties—that is, the sites where the discourse of the challengers could be most effective. But the challengers were not undiscriminating actors disseminating their message evenly among the whole electorate. They had a strategy, which aimed at a space largely ignored by the traditional parties. Until the very times in which the challengers began to gain force, the family and the neighborhood were territories belonging mostly to the traditional parties—out of the sheer volume of their followers and out of tradition. Nevertheless, a third and potentially very important political arena, the workplace, was systematically ignored by Blancos and Colorados.[23] What is more, that indifference was not merely political laziness: it reflected the view that unions should not do "politics," and accordingly political parties should not disturb union matters. The left, needless to say, had exactly the opposite view. Uruguayan unions were created by the left, which was able to develop and consolidate a relatively strong labor movement, though essentially restricted to urban workers. The bulk of those organizations were created during the peak of the import-substitution industrialization process—that is, the "second" Batllismo, that of Luis Batlle—or even earlier. Most of the now largest unions were already important during the forties.[24] Since electoral support for the left was low before the birth of the Frente Amplio, that relatively extended history of left-controlled unions implies that to some extent workers had a divided political personality: most of them followed the leftist leadership of the unions in everyday business but not at the polls. On election day they voted for the traditional parties instead.

In other words, the efforts of the left did not bear fruit, at least in electoral terms, for a long time.[25]

The patience of the left, however, was finally recompensed. When the successive failures of the efforts of the traditional parties to reverse the crisis began to look like a permanent inability, the unionized workers already knew alternative proposals and were familiar with some of the politicians who sustained those ideas, who were, or had been, union leaders. Unions became a primary source of political socialization and recruitment for the left. The main steps of this process have already been mentioned. First came the coalescence of the bulk of labor organizations into a single federation, the Convención Nacional de Trabajadores (1964–1965). Then the Communists became quietly a relevant party of the system, in 1966, and five years later the Frente Amplio was born. This does not mean that the birth of the FA was a consequence of those events, but the unity of the labor movement probably was a necessary condition, if only because without that social precedent the political unity of the left would have appeared as a process controlled by the Communists for their own benefit. The Communists certainly spearheaded the process, partly because they sensed the opportunities and since the mid-1950s they developed a consistent strategy and worked hard for it, but they never controlled the whole left.[26] They had strong competition first from their left and then from their right, as attested by the electoral success of the FA right wing in 1984. In relative terms they have always been more powerful within labor than in the broader context of the left; even regarding labor, however, it cannot be said that they control it—though Communists are by far the single most important political actor therein.

The role of the unions as political socialization agents for the left appeared clearly in several polls conducted in 1985 and 1986 which produced consistent, stable results. In particular, a survey conducted in March, 1985, in Montevideo showed that 44 percent of the workers had voted the FA, and that each of the traditional parties had obtained about a quarter of the workers' votes; these results confirm those of the survey reported in the previous section. But this survey included several questions on unionization, and it was found that among nonunionized workers the three main *lemas* obtained a relatively similar proportion of the workers' votes—33, 30, and 26 percent for the FA, the Colorados, and the Blancos respectively—the corresponding figures for each of the three *lemas*, in the same order, were 58, 15, and 23 percent.[27] The percentage difference in the vote for the left is very large indeed: it doubles that found in the Scandinavian countries, for example, though the difference is probably due to the much higher vote for the left in those countries at both levels; the leftist vote of union members in Uruguay is close to, but slightly below that of the Scandinavian nonunion members (Worre 1980). In short, unionization almost doubles the working-class vote for the left, and halves that of the Colorados. If we consider the relative size of the economically active population of Montevideo with regard to its total adult population, according to the results just summarized one out of twelve Colorado voters, one out of seven Blancos, and one out of just three Frentistas were unionized workers.[28] From a comparative perspective this effect of unionization is scarcely surprising: in Western European countries, for example, the level of union density is strongly associated with class voting: "about one half of the variance in class voting is related to the level of unionization" (Korpi 1983, pp. 35–36).

We may return now to the questions that closed the preceding section. Why did the system experience a transformation towards more class-based electorates, running against contemporary prevailing trends in democracies? Insofar as Uruguayan politics was dominated by two old catch-all parties there was no room for another party of the same kind: the cost of organization-building would have precluded any such attempt, since it was far easier to work from within the traditional parties. More single-issue or single-constituency oriented movements could and did appear, and whether they became and remained autonomous parties—though small ones—depended partly on the reaction of the old parties and partly on the nature of the new movement itself. The small parties of ideas survived for a long time because they had strong identifications rooted in Catholic thinking or in socialist tradition; almost by definition they could hardly fit within traditionally catch-all parties. But the important *Ruralista* movement of the 1950s, on the other hand, was finally absorbed by the major parties. By the 1960s the inability of Blancos and Colorados to cope with the crisis strengthened the position of those who had the "right" mix of resources: the Communists, in particular, had a definite strategy and an organizational base—the unions—which were becoming more important precisely as a result of the crisis itself. Communists, socialists, and the Catholic left wing, who also had links with labor, became the organizational core of the FA. The most important splinter group from the traditional parties that joined the FA, the former Colorado Lista 99, was born within the more labor-oriented of Batllista groups, Luis Batlle's so-called "neo-populist" Lista 15.

When the FA was born it benefitted from the then recent success of the Chilean Unidad Popular; its huge mobilization capability, inherited from the militant parties of ideas, also contributed to offset the perennial "wasted vote" problem. In this manner, since one of the most important resources of the challenger was organized labor, its improved performance among workers debilitated that of the traditional parties, hence the party system as a whole evolved towards more class-based electorates. The losses of the traditional parties, however, followed other fracture lines as well, most notably age and education: the first because of combined life-cycle and generational

effects, and the second because it provided resources for antitraditional political behavior while at the same time generating relative deprivation—since
the educational expansion created expectations that the stagnant Uruguayan
society and economy could not fulfill. Hence the atypical role of education
in particular in contemporary Uruguayan politics.[29]

The political discourse of the two Frente Amplio wings is the classical
discourse of the left: egalitarian, prolabor, prostate interventionism, and akin
to socialism—when not directly socialist. Thus, in ideological terms as well
as according to the social bases of the main political actors, the trend the
Uruguayan party system followed from the 1960s through 1984 was from
a two-party system dominated by two catch-all parties towards a moderate
pluralism—a relatively highly polarized system, whose extremes tended to
appear as a "bourgeois" party to the right and a "labor bloc" to the left. The
Blancos appeared consistently—from 1971 on—in an intermediate position.
These are the processes which explain why the Colorados and the Frentistas
evolved in opposite directions as the least catch-all members of the system,
and the Blancos remained somewhere in between as the most catch-all party.

8. Political Elites and Democratic Stability

1. Elites and Democracy

The Uruguayan political elite led a democratic restoration and was backed in its endeavor by a substantial majority of the electorate. This was one of the main conclusions of the analysis carried out in Chapters 4 and 5, and it is a particularly important result with regard to the prospects for democracy in Uruguay. Such a conclusion obviously involved a judgment on the goals of those political elites. The survey addressed to Uruguayan legislators allows a closer look on these matters.

At first sight Uruguayan political elites are overwhelmingly democratic. A full 99 percent of legislators agreed that "democracy is the best political system for a country like this," although consensus on the efficacy of the system was not so widespread.[1] Such a level of agreement on the essentials, however, might have little substantive meaning; that depends on whether the elites share a common view on the nature of democracy. A set of indicators derived from Dahl's two dimensions of polyarchy—which from the legislators' point of view becomes an external but "shared" definition of democracy—allows an assessment of the elite's views on the nature of democracy. The particular approach chosen in this study is a simplified version of the procedure followed by Aberbach, Putnam, and Rockman in their study of bureaucrats and politicians in Western polyarchies. This will make possible a cross-national check of the Uruguayan findings.

As these authors pointed out, Dahl's dimensions of polyarchy—participation and opposition—are closely linked to the "basic elements of the democratic creed" considered from a more philosophical perspective, equality and liberty:

> liberty refers to those freedoms of political thought and action that had been broadly proclaimed in the West by the nineteenth century, though not universally implemented. Political equality, by contrast, refers to the distribution of access to these political freedoms, the sharing of political influence among all citizens . . . important steps towards equality in this sense have been taken over the last century, although the

political systems studied here remain far from fully egalitarian except in the formalistic sense of voting rights. (Aberbach et al. 1981, p. 172)

A democratic order is such because oppositions enjoy a broad spectrum of freedoms and because all citizens are entitled to participate as political equals. Political elites of countries with democratic traditions will surely exhibit, and probably will sincerely share, some basic agreements concerning both dimensions. Nevertheless, "as democrats have always recognized, the real test of freedom of political expression comes when the views in question are substantively repugnant or provocatively expressed"; analogously, political equality may be a commendable ideal, but the opinions of the elites "about the practicality and even the desirability of political equality beyond the ballot box" will differ (ibid., pp. 175 and 185 respectively). In other words, probing the limits of the two ideas allows an estimation of the depth of the commitment of the elites towards liberalization and egalitarianism.

Table 8.1 presents four agreement-disagreement questions concerning political freedoms asked to MPs from several European countries during the 1970s and also asked to Uruguayan legislators in 1986. The table ex-hibits averages for three countries (Britain, West Germany, and Italy) and singles out the Italian data—since the Italian and Uruguayan party systems, as shown in Chapters 5, 6, and 7, share several common traits on matters that might be linked to this subject. The rationale underlying the selection of the items—and their relationships to political liberty—is obvious in the case of the item on political propaganda ("the freedom of political propa-ganda is not an absolute freedom, and the state should carefully regulate its use"), more indirect in the items on parties and interest groups ("although parties play an important role in a democracy, often they uselessly exacer-bate political conflicts" and "the general welfare of the country is seriously endangered by the continual clash of particularistic interest groups"), which tap the disposition to assume eventual costs in order to assure political lib-erties, and, finally, is based on a contemporary variation of the theme of the wise philosopher-autocrat in the term on technical considerations ("in contemporary social and economic affairs it is essential that technical con-siderations be given more weight than political factors"). Definite absolute majorities of Uruguayan legislators answer favoring political liberties in all cases except that concerning the clashes of interest groups; perhaps those an-swers were particularly influenced by the upsurge of labor conflict following democratic restoration and during the field work of this research. Whatever the case, considering all four items the attitudes of Uruguayan politicians towards political liberties do not seem qualitatively different to those of the Europeans. The comparison with the Italian MPs—though for one of the items I was not able to find the data from the Italian sample in the sources quoted in the table—is particularly enlightening. First, the Uruguayan results show an antiliberty absolute majority in only one of four items, whereas among the Italians two such majorities obtain from just three items; second, the ranking of the items according to the percentage of liberty-supporting answers is the same in the two countries; and third, the average proliberty score is 55 percent for the Uruguayan legislators and 52 percent for the Italians. In short, Uruguayan legislators do not look less proliberty than the Italians.

TABLE 8.1
Support for Political Liberty

	Legislators		
Agreement-disagreement items	Uruguayan	Western European	Italian
(i) In contemporary social and economic affairs it is essential that technical considerations be given more weight than political factors	74	71	67
(ii) Although parties play an important role in a democracy, often they uselessly exacerbate political conflicts	62	57	46
(iii) The freedom of political propaganda is not an absolute freedom, and the state should carefully regulate its use	57	73	n.a.
(iv) The general welfare of the country is seriously endangered by the continual clash of particularistic interest groups	27	66	44

Entries are percentages disagreeing with the statements (i.e., the most liberty-supporting answers). Western Europe data are averages based on equally weighted samples from Britain, West Germany, and Italy; data for (iii) from Aberbach et al. (1981, p. 177), and all others from Eldersveld et al. (1975, pp. 149, 150, and 155). Ns are over 250 for the European data, about a third of that for the Italian sample, and 104 or more for the Uruguayan data. Uruguayan answers weighted according to main fractions.

Table 8.2 presents four agreement-disagreement questions concerning political equality based on the same studies reported in Table 8.1. In this case the logic supporting the selection of the items and their links to political egalitarianism is obvious for the first item ("all citizens should have the same chance of influencing governmental policy"), is based on the reactions to cautiously worded elitist statements of the meritocratic and aristocratic varieties in the second and third items respectively ("in a world as complicated as the modern one, it doesn't make sense to speak of increased control by ordinary citizens over governmental affairs" and "certain people are better qualified to lead this country because of their traditions and family background"), and in the last item, finally, is based on a "rather vague, but somewhat authoritarian assertion" (Aberbach et al. 1981, p. 185) that in fact establishes the permanent need for strong leadership from exceptional individuals ("it will always be necessary to have a few strong, able individuals who know how to take charge"). Most Uruguayan politicians hold pro-egalitarian views with respect to three of the four issues raised, the exception being the majority which believes that firm leadership from the top will always be necessary—but European legislators are equally elitist in that matter. In fact, the table allows a straightforward conclusion: the overall Uruguayan pattern of answers concerning egalitarianism is very close to the European one reported in the table.

TABLE 8.2

Support for Political Equality

| | Legislators | | |
Agreement-disagreement items	Uruguayan	Western European	Italian
(i) All citizens should have the same chance of influencing governmental policy	93	92	95
(ii) In a world as complicated as the modern one, it doesn't make sense to speak of increased control by ordinary citizens over governmental affairs	68	68	52
(iii) Certain people are better qualified to lead this country because of their traditions and family background	63	76	80
(iv) It will always be necessary to have a few strong, able individuals who know how to take charge	40	37	52

Entries are percentages of answers agreeing with item (i) and disagreeing with all other items—i.e., the most equality-supporting answers. Western European data are averages based on equally weighted samples from Britain, West Germany, and Italy (Eldersveld et al. 1975, p. 153). European Ns not reported by Eldersveld et al., but should be close to those mentioned in Table 8.1 from Aberbach et al. (1981, p. 177); Uruguayan Ns are 105 or more. Uruguayan answers weighted according to main fractions.

More generally, taking into account the two dimensions and all eight indicators, the attitudes of Uruguayan legislators towards democracy are similar to those of their European peers. In fact, not only do the general pictures look similar; the other subpatterns reported by Aberbach et al. that can be tested on the Uruguayan data lead to identical conclusions as well. Support for the two dimensions "is higher among leftists than among rightists, [and] higher among younger elite members than among their older colleagues" (Aberbach et al. 1981, p. 205). It may be discussed how democratic those views are, but if we use the attitudes of European legislators as a standard, then Uruguayan politicians are also democratic.

Within the limits defined by that global conclusion, however, the single most important Uruguayan deviation from the European pattern—particularly high distrust of social conflict among Uruguayan legislators—is related to a theoretically significant point. Consider the two sets of items presented in Tables 8.1 and 8.2: on those bases two simple additive indexes may be easily computed. These indexes may be called, for obvious reasons, indexes of liberalism and of egalitarianism respectively. The cross-classification of the legislators according to the two indexes produces a matrix of democratic attitudes; let us call "authoritarians" those ranking low in the two indexes, "democrats" those in middle or higher positions in both indexes, and "elitist liberals" and "populists" the two remaining, unbalanced configurations—where "elitist liberals" stands for liberals of nonegalitarian views, and "populists" are those of egalitarian but illiberal views.[2] That matrix may be compared to a similar arrangement of European legislators presented by Aberbach et al. (1981, p. 204). The comparison is far from perfect, for the European indexes were built on the basis of more elaborate techniques applied to twice as many indicators; Uruguayan indexes may be thus considered as rather crude estimators of those presented by Aberbach et al.

In spite of the caveats above, Table 8.3 suggests two conclusions. First, the general similarity of the two maps of democratic attitudes is once more remarkable. Second, the single most important difference between the two arrangements concerns the relative size of the respective populist groups. In the three remaining cells the differences between European and Uruguayan legislators are far smaller, and they all favor the European group; hence all those differences reappear added, and in the opposite direction, in the populist cell. Whereas the ratio between the two "unbalanced" groups—populists and liberals—is 1.4 among Europeans, it more than doubles this figure among the Uruguayans. For each old-fashioned Uruguayan liberal there are three populists. It seems to me that the difference is genuine—neither an artifact of the imperfect Uruguayan measuring instrument nor a consequence of exceptional circumstances. Furthermore, I suspect that what we may see now in Table 8.3 is a considerably eroded image—eroded by half a century of democratic experience—of the past weight of populists among Uruguayan political elites. Aberbach and his colleagues had noted that freedom of political expression "is the *oldest* strand in the skein of democratic values" (ibid., p.175; emphasis added). More generally, Dahl had observed in the same vein that the path to polyarchy followed by most, if not all, established democracies had been from rather closed hegemonies to competitive oligarchies and then to polyarchies (Dahl 1971). That is, progress was made following the liberalism axis first and later on the egalitarian axis. But this was not the path of Uruguayan democratization; for several reasons, including the absence of a rigid social stratification in the past, the important proportion of recent European migrants in the population and the channeling of political conflicts through two mass-based, catch-all parties, some basic principles of political equality had been already established when the idea of an organized political opposition becoming government by peaceful means was still in the making. As Barrán pointed out, universal male franchise had been accepted without discussion by the parties and the press—even the conservative press—at least since 1910 (Barrán 1986, pp. 63–64),[3] when the Colorados were a quasi-hegemonic party and the idea of the Blancos winning government peacefully was almost unthinkable—irrespective of their actual electoral support. If egalitarian ideas had become common before the acceptance of a truly competitive polity—and with it, necessarily, respected and unrestricted political liberties—the present relative weight of the populists appears as a reasonable inheritance of the path to democracy the country followed. Populists are now a relatively small minority because they have been losing ground to democrats during half a century of democratic learning.

TABLE 8.3
Matrix of Democratic Attitudes

Liberalism and egalitarianism of European and Uruguayan legislators

Liberalism	Egalitarianism	
	Low	Moderate or high
Low	"Authoritarians" Europ.: 6 Urug.: 4	"Populists" Europ.: 15 Urug.: 27
Moderate or high	"Elitist Liberals" Europ.: 11 Urug.: 9	"Democrats" Europ.: 67 Urug.: 60

Entries are percentages of the total N for each group (Europeans: 365; Uruguayans: 98). Uruguayan data are additive indexes of liberalism and egalitarianism built on the basis of the items presented in Tables 8.1 and 8 .2 respectively. European data—which include equally weighted samples from Britain, West Germany, Italy, and the Netherlands—are based on more complex indexes; in particular, the items used in Uruguay are part of the larger set of items used in the European samples (Aberbach et al. 1981, especially pp. 189 and 204). Uruguayan data are weighted according to main fractions.

This argument cannot be directly tested, but at least one of its important consequences may be easily checked. Most of the egalitarian but illiberal elites obviously had to be Colorados, because they had the upper hand: being illiberal was suicidal for the opposition—essentially the Blancos, but also the smaller parties—for it amounted to conceding the de facto dominant position of the Colorados. If the ideas we have been discussing have real substance and are an important part of political culture and traditions, then most contemporary populists should be Colorados. This is indeed the case. The Colorados are 44 percent of the legislators on whom we have information on these matters, but amount to 79 percent of the populists; the rest are Blancos. A full 48 percent of Colorado legislators are populists; only 16 percent of the Blancos are so, and there is not a single populist in the left. In relative terms, then, there are three Colorado populists for each Blanco populist.

2. Past Errors and Present Agenda

The views of the Uruguayan legislators are thus democratic, at least from a comparative point of view. The survey also showed that they think that the political elite—to the upper stratum of which they belong—has to bear part of the responsibility for the 1973 breakdown. They believe that the three most important factors that led to the coup, out of a listing of seven which included a wide variety of themes, were the military's view of their own role, the long stagnation of the economy, and the inadequacies of the political parties and the antagonisms among their leaders: 85, 82, and 79 percent respectively of the legislators think these factors were important. Overwhelming majorities within each of the three main *lemas* share these views; these are not partisan opinions. The last of the three factors ("the inadequacies of the political parties and the antagonisms among their leaders," as stated in the question) does not need further comment: it is a direct failure of the political elite. As for the stagnation of the economy, its single most important cause for all the legislators and within every *lema* considered separately, this time out of a listing of fourteen items also covering a wide variety of themes, was the lack of adequate policies which, of course, is again a failure of the political elite. Hence the only important factor leading to the coup for which they were not directly responsible is the first, the military's view of its own role. In short, legislators think that the political elite deserves a considerable part of the blame for the 1973 coup.

A democratically-minded political class was thus able to lead a real democratic restoration, but democracy had to be restored because of the failures of this elite in the first place. Since this is not merely what actually happened, but the way the elites perceive those past events as well, it might be expected that legislators would have some definite views about how to avoid or to overcome the obstacles that burdened and finally broke down democracy. Nevertheless, the answers they gave to an open question that asked: "If you think about the problems that could be discussed and eventually solved during the present legislature [i.e., 1985–1989], what would you say is the most important of them?" produced a rather fragmented, blurred picture. The single most important group of answers included political problems: 41 percent of the legislators gave such answers, but they covered a wide spectrum of themes. The most common answer—17 percent—referred to the human rights question,[4] followed by 9 percent of answers that pointed, in very generic terms, to the consolidation of democracy as the most important problem. Another group of answers—15 percent—also mentioned more specific political problems, none of them obtaining more than 3 percent of the answers. Nineteen percent of the interviewees mentioned specifically economic problems, but only one clearly defined area emerged among these answers—8 percent that focused on agro-industrial matters. The same pattern, dispersion of themes and rather generic contents, appear in the 18 percent of answers that mentioned social problems. The remaining answers were more imprecise: 13 percent mentioned general socio-economic problems; 3 percent pointed out political and economic issues; and 5 percent stated that, given the nature of Uruguayan problems, all of them had to be tackled at the same time. A skeptical and lonely legislator said that the question had no real answer, since the political composition of the legislature virtually assured that none of the really important problems of the country could be successfully dealt with. Finally, this picture also emerges within each of the major *lemas*. The global result just described is not the seemingly disordered set obtained by adding up several well focused but different smaller units; the same description holds for the legislature as a whole and for its main actors separately considered. It is perhaps unfair, however, to criticize the legislators because of the fragmented image produced by their answers to that question. Legislatures are not expected to provide political leadership, and similar pictures would probably obtain if the same question were asked in other legislatures. But it should be noted that this is not a "normal" legislature conducting regular business; it is the first democratic legislature confronting the results of the worst crisis the country experienced since the end of the last civil war in 1904.

Whatever the case, on the specific focus of this research the legislators as a group do not perceive any politico-structural issue as central or at least as deserving special attention within the set of national problems. Just 3 percent of the answers to the previous question mentioned electoral law; the other politico-structural matters discussed in the preceding chapters received even less mentions or none at all. This means that, at least implicitly, legislators see the political failure of the elites as a sum of personal failures—added to the intrinsic complexity of the substantive problems that had to be solved. For if in the face of democratic breakdown no rules have to be changed, then it follows that those who applied the rules did not do their job. This "personalization" of political problems has some consequences. First, it is at least consistent with the extreme dispersion of projects just reviewed, even within party lines, for a successful performance in all those tasks should be enough to achieve democratic consolidation. And second, even if it makes somewhat uncertain the prospects for Uruguayan democracy—because those prospects depend on unpredictable personal qualities—at the same time it allows perhaps a cautious optimism, if only because it would seem unlikely that the same errors will be repeated soon. In the absence of objective constraints, appropriate behavior following a business-as-usual line should be enough to avoid past mistakes; politicians can learn from experience.[5]

Nevertheless, granting that there is no collective perception of political constraints as obstacles to democracy, more legislators than those detected by that open question may think that some political reforms would improve the chances of democracy. That particular question may fail to detect them simply because they might think that such reforms are not the most pressing in the present circumstances or that the reforms that would be necessary have no chance to pass in the present legislature.

3. On Political Structures

In the first place, irrespective of their beliefs on the convenience of political reforms, legislators do think that there are important politico-structural changes in the making. After the 1984 election there was some controversy about what was the most likely future of the party system, and three main theses were discussed. The first argued that the party system was going to remain essentially as in the past: two dominant parties, Colorados and Blancos, with the Frente losing ground and perhaps breaking down into its component parts. This idea, not surprisingly, came from the traditional parties. The second thesis argued that the system would retain a two-party format as in the past, but that one of the dominant actors would change: the Blancos would lose their place to the Frente. This idea, whose source is obvious, was partly a forecast and partly a goal based on the perception that the closest competitor of the left was the Blancos and that, as a result, the best strategy for the left vis-à-vis the Blancos was plain confrontation. This has been, and still is, a conflictive issue in the left. According to the third thesis, which was not so partisan, the party system was heading towards a three-party format whose members would have roughly comparable electoral strength. The legislators were asked their opinions on this; the question mentioned explicitly the three alternatives.[6] One hundred three out of the 107 interviewees answered the question, though two of them said that they thought the party system would change but that the direction of the change was unpredictable.

Table 8.4 shows the legislators' answers to that question and allows some conclusions. First, an absolute majority of the legislature thinks that the party system is changing in enduring ways—a full 60 percent. Second, a plurality—close to half of the interviewees—thinks that the trend is towards a stable increase in the number of relevant actors of the system: 46 percent forecast a three-party system whose members would have "comparable electoral weight," as stated in the question. This does not imply three equal parties, but does suggest more parity of forces than is the case at present. Finally, in line with their past preponderance, the Colorados exhibit by far the greatest self-confidence. The answers confirm eloquently that in the legislators' views the eventual "nontraditional" two-partyism would be born at the expense of the Blancos; what is more, half of the Blancos see their own party losing ground—becoming a third instead of a half of the electorate—whereas only one in four Colorados foresee the same future for their own party. In fact, with the same or a new partner, two-thirds of the Colorados see themselves remaining as a half of the system.

TABLE 8.4

The Future of the Party System according to Legislators

10–15 years ahead the party system will be	Legislators' parties				
	Partido Colorado	Partido Nacional	FA right wing	FA left wing	Legislature
Two-party (traditional)	53	46	—	—	40
Different (unpredictable)	5	—	—	—	2
Two-party (nontraditional)	14	—	31	25	12
Three-party	27	54	69	75	46
(N)	(35)	(42)	(16)	(8)	(103)

Entries are percentages. "Traditional" two-partyism means continued dominance of the traditional parties; "nontraditional" means that one of them is replaced by a third party. The question was: "Assuming that electoral law does not change in significant ways, which do you think would be the most likely evolution of the party system during the next ten to fifteen years?" Answers weighted according to main fractions.

Partly because of those winds of change, partly as a reaction to the events that led to the authoritarian regime, discussions on eventual changes of electoral law began to resurface after the democratic restoration. The best known proposal suggested a second round ("ballotage") in the presidential election if no candidate obtained absolute majority in the first round. The second round would be restricted to the most voted candidates within each of the two most voted *lemas*. The idea was based on the arguments favoring the present French constitution; in more national terms, it could spare the country another president like Bordaberry, The weak point of the proposal, however, was not theoretical. The Blancos backed the idea, and it was clear that, given the composition of the electorate in 1971 and 1984, ballotage most probably would result in a Blanco president, since most of the left would likely choose what, from its perspective, would appear as the lesser evil. This argument was well known among political elites, and the findings of the preceding chapters concerning the ideological composition of the electorates suggest it is right. The discussion, accordingly, was tainted by the suspicion that "the reform of the Blancos" was not inspired by national interest but by the presidential ambition of the Blanco leader, Wilson Ferreira. Other reform proposals have circulated as well, but only at the elite level. Some of them suggested a cap on the number of presidential candidacies of each *lema*, eventually allowing only one presidential candidate per *lema*. Most of those ideas also suggested certain limits on the multiplication of *listas*—which had reached rather absurd levels, as shown in Chapter 2. Still others proposed the abolition of the double simultaneous vote (DSV) device.

The legislators were asked their views on these matters with the help of a card that ordered the different reforms in a systematic way; Table 8.5 summarizes their answers following the main lines of the discussions mentioned above. The first three alternatives presented in the table ("current system," "limits on the number of presidential candidacies," and "only one presidential candidate per *lema*") are variations on the status quo, and together obtain an absolute majority of favorable judgments. The third alternative describes the actual structure of the candidacies of the Frente in the 1971 and 1984 elections—it used the DSV at the legislative level but presented only one presidential candidacy. It is the only reform, according to these data, that has any chance to pass.[7] Some influential Colorado politicians favor that reform, and from the point of view of the Blancos it may appear as second best, not as effective as ballotage but having some of its effects. According to the table part of the left will sincerely agree, and the rest cannot oppose the blueprint of its own present structure; hence such a reform would most probably pass if pushed by the Colorados. Ballotage has considerably less chances to pass: it is supported by little more than one-third of the legislators, and it has few potential allies among the rest, for most Colorados and part of the left are not interested in contributing to produce a Blanco president—which is the way they see ballotage. The suppression of DSV fares even worse—just one-fifth of the legislature supports the idea. This has its logic too. For Blancos and Colorados the DSV device ruled the game they played so successfully for a long time; changing it just now could risk adding even greater dangers to those they already perceive as shown by Table 8.4. For the left, the DSV allows them to have the Frente Amplio and retain their different political identities at the same time. The end of the DSV would be the end of the Frente such as it now exists as well.

TABLE 8.5
Models of Electoral Law Favored by Legislators

Electoral law	Legislators' parties				
	Partido Colorado	Partido Nacional	FA right wing	FA left wing	Legislature
Current system	38	10	—	—	19
Limits on the no. of candidacies	35	10	—	—	18
Only one presidential candidate per *lema*	17	7	18	70	18
Ballotage maintaining double s. vote	6	51	23	10	25
Ballotage suppressing double s. vote	—	14	35	—	10
Suppression of double s. vote, no ballotage	3	7	23	20	10
(N)	(34)	(41)	(17)	(10)	(104)

Entries are percentages. The question was: "The double simultaneous vote is a distinctive trait of Uruguayan electoral law. Its pros and cons have been discussed, and several changes have been proposed. Assuming that the main characteristics of the 1966 Constitution remain in force, which of the following alternatives do you prefer?" Answers weighted according to main fractions.

Besides suggesting the limits for electoral reform, Table 8.5 shows neatly different approaches to it within the left. On the one hand, an absolute majority of the Frente right wing is willing to suppress the DSV—in relative terms, three times more than in the left wing: 58 to 20 percent. This indicates that the present Frente is much more important for its left than for its right wing; at least their respective legislators see things in that way. On the other hand, an absolute majority of the legislators of the FA right wing supported ballotage, whereas just one among ten legislators of the left wing did so. This means that for the right wing it is reasonable to avoid a Colorado president even if this requires helping elect a Blanco president, whereas the left wing prefers a confrontational approach towards the Blancos. Those differences have some implications for the alliances that can be formed within the present system.

The questionnaire addressed to legislators also included several questions to probe the presidentialism issue. The approach was double: on the one hand a battery of agreement-disagreement items was designed in order to construct an index of support for presidentialism on a rather conceptual basis; on the other hand, that battery was followed by a direct question on which system was preferable for Uruguay "leaving aside the issue of which system is theoretically desirable." Table 8.6 presents the results obtained for the index of support for presidentialism. Since the limits of the categories

TABLE 8.6
Index of Support for Presidential Systems

Support for presidentialism	Legislators' parties				
	Partido Colorado	Partido Nacional	FA right wing	FA left wing	Legislature
High	42	12	—	—	21
Medium	58	37	12	12	41
Low	–	51	88	88	38
(N)	(30)	(40)	(16)	(8)	(96)

Entries are percentages. The index of support for presidential systems is a simple additive index that results from adding the pro-presidential answers to the six items listed below. The resulting values were labelled as follows: 0,1,2: low; 3,4: medium; and 5,6: high. The items are:

(i) In principle, presidentialism assures a stable and popularly supported government for a full period. A parliamentary system does not allow that certainty.

(ii) Parliamentary systems give too much power to political parties and lead to unstable coalitions and frequent changes of government.

(iii) Presidentialism introduces two different democratic legitimacies (a directly elected president and the chambers also popularly elected) that may engage in insolvable conflict, which doesn't happen in a parliamentary system;

(iv) In a presidential system a candidate with a plurality short of an absolute majority may feel entitled to enact changes for which he doesn't really have majority support.

(v) The most democratic method to select a chief of government is the direct election, as in presidential systems. That quality is more important than the eventual shortcomings attributable to presidential systems.

(vi) A parliamentary system allows the substitution of chiefs of governments and governing coalitions without special difficulties for the majority party. That flexibility is preferable to the rigidity of presidential systems, which choose chief of governments for a full period.

Answers weighted according to main fractions.

are arbitrarily fixed the marginal distribution has little intrinsic interest; the significant data is the very high association between political affiliation and attitude towards presidentialism.[8] None of the other politically significant variables considered in this study come close to that level of association.[9] The two wings of the left react in the same way, and the Blancos, even though in a somewhat intermediate position, are closer to the left than to the Colorados, as may be seen considering percentage differences. In other words, the significant fracture is Colorados vs. opposition. It seems to me that perhaps the best way of making sense of this finding involves the Colorados' self-confidence mentioned above and their historical position in the system. The Colorados do not depict themselves as "the party of government" as a mere propagandistic discourse; they actually feel that way. That feeling, in turn, has deep historical roots. They were at least a quasi-hegemonic party during the last third of the past century, and became a dominant party after World War II—until 1958. Their record within the system is unique. Nevertheless, they cannot ignore the steady weakening of the position of the party within the system since the early 1950s. Starting from being something like "the bigger half" of the system they have become at best a plurality—that is, they may still think that they remain "essentially" a plurality, even though they lost a couple of elections in the recent past. Accordingly, pure presidentialism in the Uruguayan tradition—ballotage—is the best institutional solution for the Colorados in order to retain their preeminence within the system and a Colorado government for the country. They may well see these solutions as the best for themselves and for the country. From an institutional point of view, then, "the best" for the Colorados is essentially the status quo, which does not exclude some adjustments as, for example, changes in the electoral law concerning the number of candidacies as discussed above. Conversely, the opposition has no historical reasons to feel that way; if anything they may still fear the Colorados may be right in their self-diagnosis as the "normal" plurality within the system. Accordingly, reasonable institutional solutions against the grain of Uruguayan presidentialism, whether ballotage or a truly parliamentary system, may look like interesting alternatives from the opposition's point of view. Whether the Colorado self-diagnosis is true is, then, an important question in several ways; I will return to it in the next chapter.

Table 8.7, finally, shows that the Colorados and the left follow nicely the expectations of the preceding argument, i.e., Colorados are massively pro-presidency and the left equally massively in favor of a parliamentary system. The Blancos appear in an intermediate position: a robust three-fifths of them

TABLE 8.7
The Uruguayan Polity: Parliamentary vs. Presidential

	Legislators' parties				
Preferred system	Partido Colorado	Partido Nacional	FA right wing	FA left wing	Legislature
Presidential	92	59	6	10	56
Parliamentary	8	41	94	90	44
(N)	(35)	(41)	(17)	(10)	(105)

Entries are percentages. The question was of the agreement-disagreement type: "Leaving aside the issue of which system is theoretically desirable, a parliamentary system offers better prospects for the consolidation and stability of Uruguayan democracy." Answers weighted according to main fractions.

remain true to Uruguayan presidentialism, though not necessarily in its traditional form; part of these Blancos also favor ballotage. This pattern has its logic: the left is at the same time the nontraditional and the smallest opposition—in the short run it has the least expectations of becoming a plurality. But the most important result of Table 8.7 concerns the eventual chances of an institutional reform: there is a propresidential absolute majority, but the difference is not as large as could have been expected on the basis of Uruguayan political traditions.

9. Political Structures and the Prospects for Democracy

1. A Summary of the Argument

Uruguayan democracy was born during the two first decades of the century, partly as an intentional result of the action of political elites, partly as a result of a certain equilibrium of forces amidst intense political conflict. With democracy was born an early welfare state which resulted from the action of the Colorado Batllista elite. Both processes were made possible, or at least encouraged, by a steady, export-led economic growth.

From the rather chaotic republic of the nineteenth century the new democracy inherited a strong presidential tradition and two catch-all, fractionalized dominant parties. When polyarchy itself was still in the making a peculiar electoral system was created whose core, together with what may be called quasi-presidential institutions, remained stable from then on, under the turbulent surface of several constitutional reforms which affected many aspects of the Uruguayan institutional framework. The combined effect of electoral law and quasi-presidentialism powerfully contributed to maintaining two-partyism, whereas electoral law not only maintained, but actually increased the fractionalization of the dominant parties.

In the late 1920s the young democracy was in an early stage of its process of consolidation. Although the man who has been called its guarantor— José Batlle y Ordóñez—died in 1929, the generation of the builders of Uruguayan democracy was still in charge. In such conditions it had to absorb the destabilizing impact of the Great Depression, which proved too much. The relative frailty of the new political order, the peculiar combination of power resources and pressures Uruguayan quasi-presidentialism deposited on the shoulders of the president, and the complexities of "party government" with a highly fractionalized party in charge created a particularly vulnerable situation. To those structural weaknesses were added the accidents of the incumbent president's personality, scarcely democratic, and of his political situation, weak and increasingly isolated within his own party, leading to the 1933 coup.

Uruguayan democracy had not been born by chance, however, and the factors which had produced democracy in the first place were still there,

153

probably even strengthened by the first, though rather brief, experience with democratic government. Hence, as the more circumstantial factors receded, the comparatively mild *dictablanda* was followed by the 1942 democratic reequilibration. During the ensuing quarter of a century Uruguayan democracy was at its best.

Forty years after that first crisis Uruguayan democracy was a far stronger and consolidated political order. It had successfully tried the rotation of the major parties in government. Its party system had been strengthened by the steady action of the political structures described above. But from the mid-1950s onwards a new crisis, that of the import-substituting industrialization process, began to affect the country. As the crisis dragged on and the traditional parties failed to contain the damage, increasing social tensions began to affect the party system itself, though in a slow manner, for the system had very strong structural defenses. The protracted character of the crisis and the growing feeling of hopelessness of ever widening strata of the population finally created disloyal, organized political minorities— first to the left and then to the right—which began to feed on each other in a classical scenario, and ended up involving the army in the conflict. All of this proved too much, once more, for Uruguayan democracy. On the one hand, the old, peculiar combination of power resources and pressures Uruguayan quasi-presidentialism deposited on the shoulders of the president had been reinforced by the 1966 constitutional reform; on the other hand, the complexities of party government with a highly fractionalized governing party had been aggravated because the increasing fragmentation of the party system had transformed the incumbent, "major" parties into bare legislative pluralities. Chances of reaching a parliamentary majority within the existing rules became rather remote. When these structural factors were coupled with a scarcely democratic president, politically weak and increasingly isolated within his own party, the 1973 coup finally came.

The general argument is thus the following. Uruguayan democracy has been characterized since its birth by two central traits, quasi-presidentialism and the fractionalization of the major parties. The origins of the two traits lie deep in the nineteenth-century roots of the Uruguayan polity; their persistence is the result, in the first case, of direct decisions of the political elite, and in the second, of their allegiance to an electoral system which inevitably produces fractionalization. Both traits played an important role in the two breakdowns of Uruguayan democracy, in 1933 and 1973, though it cannot be said that they caused those breakdowns. The second crisis was compounded by the increasing fragmentation of the party system from 1966 on, which occurred in a way that also increased its polarization. In 1973 Uruguay could not withstand a level of polarization probably similar to that absorbed by Finland, France, and Italy at the time.

This combination of presidential rule on the one hand and fractional-ization of the major parties—and eventually increasing fragmentation and polarization of the party system—on the other contributed to destabilize democratic regimes which already were under stress because of difficult so-cial and economic problems. The bad times of the late 1920s and early 1930s, and again those of the sixties, proved lethal to democracy when coupled to these politico-structural factors.

2. The 1989 Election: Confirming the Trends

The record of the first government of the democratic restoration was mixed. Its main successes were essentially political: it managed to consolidate democracy and it solved the particularly intractable problem of the violations of human rights during the military government. Those successes, not inciden-tally, occurred when clear political majorities backing the involved policies emerged—almost a national consensus regarding the consolidation of democ-racy or the country's foreign affairs, and at least a Colorado-Blanco majority regarding the violation of human rights during the military government. The solution of this especially difficulty problem—a law granting amnesty to the military—was really final, since it was legitimated via a national referen-dum in early 1989 and all parties agreed that the people's choice closed the issue.[1]

On socio-economic matters President Sanguinetti's record was good if compared to those of Alfonsín in Argentina and Sarney in Brazil, but it was not enough to recover positions lost in the previous years. GNP per capita increased steadily during Sanguinetti's five-year term, but it did not recover the levels attained in 1980—the year of the political defeat of the military—and 1981. Real wages increased during the initial years of the period (1985–87), remained essentially stagnant later (1987–89), and never recovered the levels of 1980–81. Inflation rose in 1985, fell during the two following years, and rose again in 1988 and 1989, the worst year of Sanguinetti's term in this regard, when it reached 90 percent.[2]

Longer-term prospects did not improve either, for investment remained very low throughout the whole period. By the end of 1987, more than halfway through Sanguinetti's term, the vice president, Enrique Tarigo, could re-joice that investment had increased in two years—1985 and 1986—more than during the previous fifteen, although he acknowledged that the ac-tual levels of investment were low. Uruguayans were reminded how low by a well-known economist, Ramón Díaz: the level of net investment was close to zero. Total investment was just enough to cover capital depre-ciation; during the preceding years net investment had been negative.[3]

Those low levels of investment did not improve during the rest of Sanguinetti's term.

In a nutshell, Sanguinetti's term was the second half of the Uruguayan
version of the so-called "lost decade" for development in Latin America.
Though it is true that his administration recovered part of the ground lost
during the first half of the "lost decade," these gains were only partial, and
they occurred essentially during the first part of Sanguinetti's term. The second part of the term suggested that the initial impulse had run out of steam.
Inflation on the rise again and a rapidly increasing fiscal deficit added further
signals of danger.

Whatever judgment the record of the Colorado government might deserve on objective grounds, it did not satisfy the expectations of voters; when
the national election of November, 1989, came, the population's mood was
of *desencanto*, as in the Spain of Suárez. That disenchantment was partly a
result of the very high expectations associated with the new democracy, as in
Spain, but it was also a result of more objective and specifically Uruguayan
conditions. In comparative terms the economy of the country has been essentially stagnant since the mid-fifties, more than a full generation ago,[4] and
Uruguayans are well aware of this. By the end of 1988 just 13 percent of
Montevideans thought the country's situation was improving; 55 percent believed it was *estancado* (stagnant), and 31 percent said it was *en decadencia*
(decaying). A majority of the voters of each of all four major parties thought
the country was stagnant. The judgments on the president's handling of his
job and his personal popularity fell from 1986 onwards; less than 20 percent
of Montevideans had positive opinions on the president and his performance
by 1989.[5] The fate of the Colorados, confronted with such a disenchanted
mood among voters, was the same as Suárez, Alfonsín, and Sarney in the
elections at the end of their respective terms. As Table 9.1 shows, the Blancos
obtained a wide victory over the Colorados—though the Blanco share of the
vote was slightly lower than that of the Colorados in 1984—and Luis Alberto
Lacalle, grandson of Herrera, became president for the period 1990–94.[6]

The political events of 1989 confirmed the essentials of the analysis of
the transformation of the party system carried out in Chapters 5 through 7.
The most striking of those events was the breakdown of the Frente Amplio: in
early 1989 the Frente broke down because of internal disagreements exactly
following the lines described in Chapter 6. The left wing retained the name
"Frente Amplio," and the moderate wing took the name "Nuevo Espacio"
(New Space). This breakdown and the electoral results themselves confirmed
that the party system is now a "moderate pluralism" system of four relevant
actors. In spite of the division the new, reduced Frente got the same proportion
of the vote as its broader predecessor in 1984, which this time was enough—
because of the greater fragmentation of the electorate—to win the election

TABLE 9.1
Popular Vote in Presidential Elections:
The "Moderate Pluralism" Party System, 1971–? (Percent)

	1971	1984	1989
Colorado Party	40.9	41.2	30.3
Blanco Party	40.2	35.0	38.9
Subtotal, "traditional" parties	81.1	76.2	69.2
Nuevo Espacio	(5.8)	(10.4)	9.0
Frente Amplio	(12.5)	(10.8)	21.2
Subtotal, other relevant parties (the "Left")	18.3	21.3	30.2
Subtotal, all nonrelevant parties	.6	2.5	.6
TOTAL	100	100	100
N (millions)	1.7	1.9	2.0

The Frente Amplio right wing (the alliance between the Christian Democrats and the Partido por el Gobierno del Pueblo, the former Lista 99 Colorado splinter group), which had voted under a single common *lema* with the Frente's left wing in 1971 and 1984, in 1989 became the Nuevo Espacio (New Space) and voted separately under its own *lema*.

in the capital city, Montevideo. Together, the two halves of the left polled 30 percent of the national vote and 48 percent in Montevideo.

That moderate pluralism party system has become ever more fragmented since it was born in 1971; in other words, the dispersion of voters among the available alternatives has been increasing steadily. Any standard measure of fragmentation leads to that conclusion, as a simple look at Table 9.1 suggests. More generally, the dominant trend during the past fifty years has been towards an increasing fragmentation of the party system. Table 9.2 shows the average share of the vote obtained by all relevant parties during each of the three stages of the party system from 1942 onwards. Using election dates to limit the periods, those stages are, as discussed above: Colorado predominance, 1942–54; return to two-partyism, 1958–66; and moderate pluralism, 1971–89. Fragmentation increased when Colorado predominance ended and two-partyism returned, and it increased again when two-partyism was in turn replaced by the moderate pluralism system.

The fractionalization of the traditional parties, measured by the number of *listas*, reached an all-time high in 1989. In the 1984 election the number of lists of the major parties had been smaller than in 1971, prompting several politicians and observers to declare that the fractionalization of the parties was finally decreasing. Those comments took mistakenly short-term events as signals of deeper changes. The very peculiar conditions preceding the 1984 election pushed naturally towards a certain unification within the major currents of the parties. Doing politics was difficult until close to election

TABLE 9.2
Popular Vote in Presidential Elections:
A Changing Party System, 1942–1989
(Average Percent Share of the Vote for Each Period)

	1942–1954	1958–1966	1971–1989
Colorado Party	52.1	44.7	37.5
Blanco Party	38.4	45.5	38.0
Subtotal, "traditional" parties	90.5	90.2	75.5
Subtotal, other relevant parties (the "Left")	—	—	23.2
Subtotal, all nonrelevant parties	9.5	9.8	1.2
TOTAL	100	100	100
N (millions)	.7	1.1	1.8

The columns show the average results of the following national elections: (i) the elections of the Colorado predominance period, i.e., those of 1942, 1946, 1950, and 1954; (ii) the elections of the Return to two-partyism period, i.e., those of 1958, 1962, and 1966, and (iii) the elections of the Moderate pluralism period, i.e., those of 1971, 1984, and 1989. "The Left" includes the Frente's right and left wings and—in 1989—their respective successors, the New Space and the Broad Front.

day, and most of those major currents had been acting united in a common front against the military government anyway. After the successful democratic restoration, though, electoral politics returned to its business-as-usual patterns, which led to a record number of *listas* in the 1989 election. Blancos and Colorados together ran 601 lists, well above the previous historical record of 1971, 561. The total number of lists of all parties, 816, also toppled the previous record of 1971, 719 *listas*. This was a further confirmation of the strong link between electoral law and the fractionalization of the parties.[7]

The party system remains relatively highly polarized, as discussed in Chapter 6. Table 9.3 shows that the polarization of the system increased very slightly, from .42 in early 1985 (Table 6.8) to .44 in late 1989. The overlapping between the two most distant parties of the system also increased slightly, from .17 to .24, but this change goes in the opposite direction—more overlap implies that in a certain sense the parties are closer in 1989 than in 1984, not more distant. We can thus conclude that the situation remains essentially unchanged.

Still, Table 9.3 shows some intriguing changes. On the one hand, the ideological profile of voters is the same: the average self-placement of Montevideans in the left-right scale was 4.8 in 1984 and 5.1 in 1989, a small difference indeed.[8] On the other hand, in 1989 the means of the self-placements of the voters of *all four parties* are, on average, 1.1 units of the scale to the right of their positions in 1984. The pattern of the displacements is interesting as well: the Frentistas are now .7 units to the right of the position they

TABLE 9.3
Polarization of the Uruguayan Party System, 1989

A. Profiles

	Left	C-L	Center	C-R	Right	Mean	(N)
P. Colorado	—	1.9	31.1	40.8	26.2	7.3	(103)
P. Nacional	—	6.1	44.8	26.1	23.0	6.8	(165)
Nuevo Espacio	4.1	32.0	54.6	7.2	2.1	4.9	(97)
Frente Amplio	32.9	45.2	21.3	.7	—	3.3	(301)

B. Overlapping and distance

Distance

	P. Colorado	P. Nacional	Nuevo Espacio	Frente Amplio
P. Colorado	—	.06	.27	.44
P. Nacional	.82	—	.21	.39
Nuevo Espacio	.42	.60	—	.18
Frente Amplio	.24	.28	.58	—

Overlap

Montevidean data from a survey by Equipos Consultores Asociados in November, 1989. The format of the table is identical to that of Table 6.8. The profiles show the self-placement of the voters of each party in the left-right scale (percentages). Distances and overlaps as defined in Chapter 6, Section 6.2.

occupied in 1984; the voters of the New Space (the former Frente's right wing) moved 1.3 units to the right; the Blancos 1.5 units, and the Colorados .9 units. The ideological profiles of the parties are thus changing rapidly; the pace of those changes as well as their simultaneity are very peculiar from a comparative point of view.[9]

The feeling of change resulting from the displaced spectra of the parties along the left-right continuum is further reinforced by other aspects of the 1989 election. Net electoral volatility 1984–89 measured by Pedersen's index of aggregate volatility was 14.3, the highest by far since 1942 (Table 4.1). It was higher than those of the two critical elections of the period, that of 1958 (11.5), which ended Colorado predominance and returned the country to two-partyism and the Blancos to power, and that of 1971 (8.6), in which both the Frente Amplio and a moderate pluralism, a relatively highly polarized party system, were born. Accordingly, legislative turnover, as defined in Chapter 4, was also high. Global turnover of the whole legislature was 55 percent, above the 1950–71 average (50 percent); it was highest for the biggest winner—in relative terms—of the election, the Frente (66 percent).[10]

Nevertheless, these changes are very different from those that occurred in the late sixties and early seventies. Twenty years ago there was a process of politico-ideological polarization which changed the field of political competition: its size—that is, the distances between competitors—increased, and the number of competitors itself also increased—from two-partyism to moderate pluralism. The present processes do not alter the field of political competition; they reflect rather the characteristics of the competition within that space. They are thus more akin to the competition that occurred during the period of recovered two-partyism, not to the changes which ended that period. The difference between the two periods lies simply in the number of competitors, four instead of two.

The peculiarities of the 1989 election pointed out above resulted from the combination of three processes: first, the short-term anti-Colorado *desencanto*; second, the longer-term reaction against both traditional parties, which are seen by an increasing part of the population as the main culprits of a deeply unsatisfactory state of affairs; and third, the relative success of the Frente within the left, partly because of reasons already discussed in the last section of Chapter 7 and partly because of its successful handling of the campaign.[11] All three processes "pushed" voters towards their left. The aggregate, final result was a series of musical chairs: all parties lost voters to their left, except the leftmost, the Frente, and all parties won voters to their right, except the Colorados, the rightmost. Voters "went shopping," so to speak, to their left, though without changing, on average, their own ideological positions. As a result, on the one hand the ideological profile of voters did not change, but those of the parties did, all of them towards the right. On the other hand, the parties of the middle ground—Blancos and Nuevo Espacio—experienced the biggest changes in the ideological profile of their voters (respectively 1.5 and 1.3 units of the left-right scale, as seen above), for they experienced both gains from their right and losses to their left, whereas the parties of the extremes—Colorados and Frente—changed less (.9 and .7 units respectively), since they experienced a single, one-sided gain (the Frente) or loss (the Colorados).[12]

After the first two national elections of the democratic restoration, then, what can be said on the political structures we have been discussing throughout this book? First, the return to the legal status quo ante restored both the strongest presidential system the country has had during all of its democratic life—that of the 1966 Constitution—and a peculiar electoral law which fosters fractionalization to uncommon extremes. Second, the party system keeps the "moderate pluralism" format it acquired in 1971, and still is relatively highly polarized, though polarization during democratic restoration has been definitely lower than in the precoup years. From a purely theoretical point of view we should perhaps consider this party system as a transitional stage, since the institutional-legal framework favors two-partyism. That "transitional" stage, however, has already survived three national elections (1971, 1984, and 1989), and shows no clear signs of radical, short-term change.[13]

This party system looks thus relatively stable, probably at least in part thanks to a little help from the political "freezing effect" of the authoritarian regime. But its fragmentation has increased steadily since it was born in 1971. In fact, the long-term trend during the last fifty years has been towards an increasing fragmentation: Uruguay has now the most fragmented party system it has ever had. Besides increasing fragmentation at the *system* level, finally, the fractionalization, as measured by the number of lists, of the still major *parties* has reached its highest historical values so far. In a rather perverse twist, the smaller the share of the electorate of the major parties (Tables 9.1 and 9.2), the more fractionalized they have become.

3. The Prospects for Democracy in Uruguay

What are the prospects for democracy in Uruguay if the institutional setting does not change? On the one hand, at least in the short run, there are no reasons to expect anything different from the summary that closed the preceding section. Fractionalization will remain at best at about the present levels. If the trends we have observed so far are not dramatically reversed, which is unlikely, fragmentation will probably increase.[14] In short, barring major, unexpected events, the winner of the next election, that of 1994, will not have a legislative majority. That winning party will have to govern the country until the end of the century (1999).

On the other hand, the country has not yet been able to overcome the relative decline it entered since the mid-fifties. Local and foreign observers alike share this rather somber view: "what is distinctive about Uruguay is that for nearly two generations it has experienced chronic economic stagnation and decline to an extent unknown in other nations" (McDonald 1988, p. 36). To confront successfully that state of affairs is a difficult task for any party, even assuming it has the necessary ideas and leadership; it is extremely difficult for a government lacking legislative majorities. This was the case of Sanguinetti's administration, it is now that of Lacalle's, and most probably will be that of the winning party in 1994.

All of this means that, assuming no institutional changes, the same risk-prone configuration of the years preceding the 1933 and 1973 coups remains the most likely forecast: serious substantive problems, fractionalization of the governing party, which has no legislative majority either, and presidentialism. This does not necessarily lead to democratic destabilization or breakdown, though it may lead very easily to stalemates blocking the formulation of policies.

Without political engineering there are just three ways to overcome those stalemates. The first is a government of national unity, which is almost surely impossible given the present level of polarization of the system. The second approach consists of explicit, programmatic alliances sharing governing responsibilities. This solution, as discussed in Chapter 3, is almost impossible in a presidential system like that of Uruguay, and recent experience has so far confirmed this view—both Sanguinetti and Lacalle tried, and failed, this approach. The third approach includes ad hoc agreements on a one-at-a-time basis. This is what actually happened during Sanguinetti's government. It proved enough to solve at least one difficult political problem—the amnesty for the military—and several ordinary matters. According to its results so far, however, this approach does not measure up to the tasks it should have to tackle.

Hence Uruguayans might easily find themselves facing complex political stalemates, high pressure on the president to deliver, and the president unable to deliver without circumventing parliament. Not even this situation can be said to cause democratic breakdowns, but once that point is reached, a modest amount of bad luck may be devastating. Increasing polarization, or the personalities of some of the central actors, among other factors, may be enough to produce a crisis of unpredictable consequences.

This is a less than enthusiastic picture of the prospects for democracy in Uruguay. Unfortunately, however, given the historical record this seems to be a plausible picture. It is perhaps impossible to quantify how plausible this picture is, but this is not the really interesting question. Having concluded that the assumption of no institutional changes leads to undesirable consequences, the next question must probe a different approach: Is there any institutional change which, on the whole, leads to better prospects for democracy?

An increasing number of Uruguayan politicians thinks that this is indeed the case. In the aftermath of the 1971 election it became clear that the fragmented and fractionalized Uruguayan party system makes party government—government by the party of the president—impossible, for the winning party is always far from a legislative majority of its own. In those years, however, politicians were testing for the first time the characteristics of the new system. Besides, that test proceeded under very extreme conditions which made it difficult to assess the workings of the system, for everything went wrong. After democratic restoration collective learning became easier. President Sanguinetti, the winner of the 1984 election, looked for a government of national unity, which he did not obtain. His real goal was some kind of coalition, which he could not obtain either; he had to do with a government of national "intonation" (*entonación*). It included two Blanco ministers, but their jobs were "technical" and did not impose political obligations on the Blancos. The ministers themselves were certainly not politicians—one of them was Enrique Iglesias, of ECLA and later IDB fame, in charge of foreign relations. President Lacalle, the winner of the 1989 election, also attempted to build what he himself called a coalition government. He also failed. He obtained the same kind of collaboration as Sanguinetti: a vague agreement which did not create politically binding obligations and nonpolitical Colorado ministers in his cabinet. This time the agreement was called *coincidencia nacional*, national "coincidence."

Partly as a result of that growing body of practical experience, politicians have proposed two broad directions of political reform. On the one hand there are those who favor a change towards a parliamentary system, in order to promote coalition-making and the formation of governments with real majorities; on the other hand there are those who favor presidentialism and promote changes capable of assuring, within certain limits, a legislative majority for the winning party. This means moving towards a majoritarian principle of representation; at any rate, it assumes a system far less proportional than the present one. These ideas came into the open by the end of Lacalle's first year. In late 1990 a group of young leaders from the four parties began to campaign for a constitutional reform aimed at establishing a parliamentary system, and in December, 1990, it organized a seminar on the subject in Montevideo. At the same time former President Sanguinetti–who is widely seen as a likely presidential candidate in 1994—took sides favoring the other alternative in a public speech (quoted in *Búsqueda* in December, 1990).

From a theoretical point of view those initiatives are not contradictory. In principle they combine two choices, one of them concerning regime: presidential/parliamentary; and the other concerning electoral law: proportional representation/majoritarian principle. This produces four possibilities. One of them—a PR presidential system—is the status quo to be reformed. Another possibility—a parliamentary model with some kind of majoritarian electoral law—has no public defenders so far. The remaining two options are the actually competing proposals: a kind of majoritarian presidentialism versus PR parliamentarism.

Any reform capable of assuring legislative majorities to the winners of the 1984 or 1989 elections involves a very significant departure from present electoral law. Such a reform has little chance to pass, since the present oppositions probably will not agree with an idea which involves direct loss of power for the minorities. Even if an unlikely majority could be formed favoring that reform, the minority could perceive it as a defeat for democracy, not merely for the minorities. The delegitimizing effects of that situation might well outweigh the eventual advantages of the reform.

This generic objection against the establishment of some form of majoritarian principle in Uruguay is not, however, the main objection against majoritarian presidentialism. We have seen that Uruguay has a relatively highly polarized party system. In such a system a reform allowing a modest plurality to govern alone may well end creating an Allende-like situation or even worse: a situation in which a plurality in one of the extremes of the spectrum feels, and is, rightly entitled to carry out policies strongly disliked by an ample majority. In that case the risk for democracy is probably no smaller than in the present status quo.

Which leaves us the option of a real parliamentary system. Since in a democratic order the party system cannot be modified overnight, perhaps the quickest way of attacking Uruguayan politico-structural problems consists of turning to a parliamentary system. Besides, the mere logic of coalitions would ease the problems related to the fractionalization of the parties: since the "market value" of the collaboration of the fractions would be lower because of the increased supply, the fractions themselves would probably feud less.

These considerations appear reinforced by the results presented in Chapter 8. The chances of changing DSV within the present system, as well as those of other suggested reforms like ballotage,[15] appear decidedly slim. A significant 44 percent of Sanguinetti's legislature, however, thought that a parliamentary system would be more appropriate to Uruguayan conditions than the status quo. It might appear somewhat surprising to find more agreement on reforms which would entirely change the institutional framework of the nation than on comparatively modest changes of electoral law. One of the implications of the analysis of Chapter 8, however, is that in matters of political reform Uruguayan politicians act as short-term utilitarians: they are particularly attentive to the immediate consequences on the status quo the reforms might have—and to the eventual intentions of their rivals. It should also be noted, however, that, as shown in Chapter 2, parliamentary ideas have been present in Uruguayan political thinking for no less than half a century, even if sometimes focused in rather sui generis ways.

According to these results, then, eventual political reformers who agree with the main conclusions of this study—if any—should concentrate their efforts in that direction. A parliamentary system cannot guarantee that Uruguayans will finally solve their problems, but at least its risks seem to be significantly lower than those of the other alternatives. After all those years of harsh authoritarianism, prudence should be a valued virtue.

4. Beyond Uruguay

It should be noted, finally, that the logic of the main argument of this book is not specifically Uruguayan, though it is circumscribed by the general, so-called "threshold conditions" for democracy mentioned in Chapter 1. This research is a case study of the negative effects of certain political structures on democratic stability. Chapter 3, in particular, is as much a case study as a theoretical argument illustrated by the Uruguayan experience.[16]

Consider, first, the following situation: a presidential system in which government is normally party government—a rule that when in force, though unwritten, is very important—and in which the president lacks a legislative majority. Structured party systems are usually "party government" systems as well. When the president of such a system lacks a legislative majority, the situation is uncharted and open: there are no rules capable of regulating really serious political conflict between president and legislature. This is a crucial difference with regard to parliamentary systems: a minority government is always at the mercy of the majority. That very idea does not exist in a presidential system. It should also be noted that "party government" does not necessarily exclude coalitions, but the mechanics of a presidential system makes extremely difficult what is a common state of affairs in parliamentary systems. In fact, in parliamentary regimes a coalition government is simply the standard substitute for party government when there is no party strong enough to govern alone. This is a platitude, of course, but the point is that presidential systems do not have such substitutes.

This situation described in the preceding paragraph is unbalanced: institutionally, the presidency is always a very powerful position, for the president is at the same time chief of state and chief of government. But a president without legislative majority—be it because his own party is fractionalized and/or because the party system is rather fragmented and his own party has a mere plurality—is politically weak.

Consider, second, the event of such an unbalanced situation occurring during really bad times. In that case conflict between president and legislature becomes likely. The president will have his own ideas about how to confront the crisis, and he will probably lack the necessary legislative support to enact those ideas. He has more institutional resources than a prime minister, and at the same time more pressure to deliver; he may well begin to work in those grey areas where legality is difficult to assess in order to enact his views while at the same time avoiding, if possible, a definite violation of the letter of the law. All systems have such grey areas; in Uruguay, the favourite resource was "*Medidas prontas de seguridad*," a kind of state of siege. When that point is reached, unpredictable events and conditions like the personality of the main actors may become decisive. The combination of these two factors—a substantive crisis superimposed on a political stalemate between president and legislature—does not cause democratic breakdowns, but creates a structural predisposition facilitating such a result.

Let us examine that political stalemate alone. When will it be likely to occur? A multiparty system, or even—as Uruguay in the past—a two-party system whose members are highly fractionalized may easily generate such stalemates. Thus, the combination of presidentialism and an electoral law which allows or promotes fractionalization and/or multipartyism is an intrinsically risk-prone configuration. This idea implies a further step too. There are no party systems immune to change, and when change is in the making, which in itself is a signal of difficulties, there is a transition period with, as experience shows, more actors than in more normal times. So, even the "right" electoral system does not provide immunization; it simply lowers the chances of entering a stalemate of that kind. Hence, given a presidential system the only real escape is the absence of party government.[17]

Let us consider now that rather generic category of "substantive crises." When they are deep and extended, as those typically associated with the social and economic transformations of the process of development, this factor is not really independent from political stalemates. The crises of development may actively contribute to the instability of the party system, fostering fractionalization and fragmentation which in turn create the conditions for political stalemates to appear.

It follows that the nations outside the first world which attempt to build democracies imitating the U.S. presidential model choose an unnecessarily difficult route. During the present century Latin America in particular has known several democratic failures which, in my view, share the essentials of the Uruguayan scenario I have attempted to analyze. Some of them were directed against the incumbent president, unlike in Uruguay, but this should not obscure the fact that the pattern of confrontations we have discussed above is clearly recognizable in those breakdowns as well. From Yrigoyen to Allende, more or less consolidated Latin American democracies experienced crises which, in the context of political stalemates and conflicts between presidents and legislatures, proved too much for democracy. If this were indeed so, then the institutional engineering which appears appropriate to the Uruguayan case would perhaps apply elsewhere as well.

References

Aberbach, Joel D., Robert D. Putnam, and Bert A. Rockman. 1981. *Bureaucrats and Politicians in Western Democracies*. Cambridge, Mass.: Harvard University Press.

Agor, Weston H. 1971. "Introduction: Latin American Legislative Systems," in Agor, ed., *Latin American Legislatures*.

Agor, Weston H., ed. 1971. *Latin American Legislatures: Their Role and Influence*. New York: Praeger.

Aguiar, César. 1984. "La doble escena: clivajes sociales y subsistema electoral," in Gillespie et al., eds., *Uruguay y la democracia* (vol. I).

————. 1983. "Elecciones uruguayas: un marco de análisis preliminar," CIEDUR, Montevideo.

————. 1977. "Notas sobre política y sociedad en el Uruguay, 1942–1962," CIEDUR, Montevideo.

Balbis, Jorge. 1984. "Los resultados en cifras," *Cuadernos del CLAEH* #31 (2a. serie, IX).

Barnes, Samuel H., and Max Kaase, eds. 1979. *Political Action: Mass Participation in Five Western Democracies*. Beverly Hills, Calif.: Sage.

Barrán, José P. 1986. "1916: La consolidación de la democracia," *Cuadernos de Marcha* (Tercera época) II:9.

Biles, Robert E. 1972. "Patronage Politics: Electoral Behavior in Uruguay." Ph.D. diss., The Johns Hopkins University.

Blondel, Jean. 1973. *Comparative Legislatures*. Englewood Cliffs, N.J.: Prentice-Hall.

Bobbio, Norberto, et al. 1984. *Il sistema politico italiano tra crisi e innovazione*. Milano: Franco Angeli.

Bordaberry, Juan María. 1980. *Las opciones*. Montevideo: Imprenta Rosgal.

Bruschera, Oscar H. (1986). *Las décadas infames*. Montevideo: Librería Linardi y Risso.

Budge, Ian, Ivor Crewe, and Dennis Farlie, eds. 1976. *Party Identification and Beyond*. London: Wiley.

Butler, David. 1981. "Electoral Systems," in Butler, Penniman and Ranney, eds., *Democracy at the Polls*.

Butler, David, and Dennis Kavanagh. 1984. *The British General Election of 1983*. London: Macmillan.

167

Butler, David, Howard R. Penniman, and Austin Ranney, eds. 1981. *Democracy at the Polls: A Comparative Study of Competitive National Elections*. Washington, D.C.: American Enterprise Institute.

Caetano, Gerardo, et al. 1985. *De la tradición a la crisis: pasado y presente de nuestro sistema de partidos*. Montevideo: CLAEH - Ediciones de la Banda Oriental.

Canzani, Agustín. 1990. "Restauración democrática y opinión pública en el Uruguay." *Revista Uruguaya de Ciencia Política* #3.

Castellanos, Alfredo, and Romeo Pérez. 1981. "El pluralismo: examen de la experiencia uruguaya," CLAEH, Serie *Investigaciones* #15.

Catterberg, Edgardo, and María Braun. 1989. "¿Izquierda y derecha en la opinión pública Argentina?," *Crítica y Utopía* #18.

Cavarozzi, Marcelo. 1981. "La crisis del orden oligárquico y la constitución del estado burgués en América Latina," presented at the XIV Congreso Latinoamericano de Sociología, Puerto Rico.

Cayrol, Roland, Jean-Luc Parodi, and Colette Ysmal. 1973. *Le Député Français*. Paris: Fondation Nationale des Sciences Politiques - Armand Colin.

CELADU. 1988. "Análisis de la encuesta nacional de opinión pública, 1a. parte." Centro de Estudios para la Democracia Uruguaya, Montevideo.

Cocchi, Angel, ed. 1988. *Reforma electoral y voluntad política*. Montevideo: FESUR-Ediciones de la Banda Oriental.

Converse, Philip E., and Roy Pierce. 1986. *Political Representation in France*. Cambridge, Mass.: The Belknap Press of Harvard University Press.

Converse, Philip E. 1969. "Of Time and Partisan Stability," *Comparative Political Studies* 2:2.

Cosse, Gustavo. 1985. "Clase obrera, democracia y autoritarismo," in Carlos H. Filgueira, ed., *Movimientos sociales en el Uruguay de hoy*. Montevideo: CLACSO - CIESU- Ediciones de la Banda Oriental.

Crewe, Ivor. 1987. "What's Left for Labor: An Analysis of Thatcher's Victory," *Public Opinion* 10:2.

Crewe, Ivor, and David Denver. 1985. *Electoral Change in Western Democracies: Patterns and Sources of Electoral Volatility*. New York: St. Martin's Press.

Daalder, Hans, and Peter Mair, eds. 1983. *Western European Party Systems: Continuity and Change*. London: Sage.

Dahl, Robert A. 1985. *A Preface to Economic Democracy*. Berkeley: University of Califonia Press.

————. 1971. *Polyarchy: Participation and Opposition*. New Haven, Conn.: Yale University Press.

De Riz, Liliana. 1983. "Notas para el análisis comparado de los partidos (Argentina, Chile, Uruguay y Brasil)." Buenos Aires: CEDES.

De Sierra, Gerónimo, et al. 1972. *Partidos políticos y clases sociales en el Uruguay*. Montevideo: Fundación de Cultura Universitaria.

Denver, David. 1985. "Conclusions," in Crewe and Denver, eds., *Electoral Change in Western Democracies*.

DeSwaan, Abram. 1973. *Coalition Theories and Cabinet Formations.* San Francisco: Jossey-Bass.

Downs, Anthony. 1957. *An Economic Theory of Democracy.* New York: Harper.

Drake, Paul, and Eduardo Silva, eds. 1986. *Elections and Democratization in Latin America, 1980-85.* San Diego: Center for Iberian and Latin American Studies, Center for U.S.-Mexican Studies, and Institute of the Americas.

Eldersveld, Samuel J., Sonja Hubée-Boonzaaijer, and Jan Kooiman. 1975. "Elite Perceptions of the Political Process in the Netherlands, Looked at in Comparative Perspective," in Mattei Dogan, ed., *The Mandarins of Western Europe: The Political Role of Top Civil Servants.* New York: Halsted.

Errandonea, Alfredo, and Daniel Costábile. 1969. *Sindicato y sociedad en el Uruguay.* Montevideo: Fundación de Cultura Universitaria.

Fa Robaina, Juan Carlos. 1972. *Cartas a un diputado.* Montevideo: Alfa.

Fabregat, Julio T. 1971. *Elecciones uruguayas: Plebiscito y elecciones de noviembre de 1971.* Montevideo: Cámara de Senadores.

Filgueira, Carlos, et al. 1989. "De la transición a la consolidación democrática: imágenes y cultura política en el Uruguay," CIESU, Serie *Informes* #38.

Filgueira, Carlos. 1976. "Indicadores comparativos de los departamentos del Uruguay," *Cuadernos CIESU* #13.

———. 1973. "Imbalance y movilidad en la estructura social: el caso uruguayo," *Cuadernos de Ciencias Sociales* #3.

———. 1970. "Burocracia y clientela: una política de absorción de tensiones," *Cuadernos de Ciencias Sociales* #1.

Finch, Henry. 1980. *Historia económica del Uruguay contemporáneo.* Montevideo: Ediciones de la Banda Oriental.

Franco, Rolando. 1986a. "El sistema electoral uruguayo en una perspectiva comparada," in Franco, ed., *El sistema electoral.*

———. 1986b. "Modificación o mantenimiento del régimen electoral uruguayo: conclusiones de un seminario," in Franco, ed., *El sistema electoral.*

Franco, Rolando, ed. 1986. *El sistema electoral uruguayo: peculiaridades y perspectivas* (2 vols.). Montevideo: Fundación Hanns Seidel.

Gargiulo, Martín. 1986. "El desafío de la democracia: la izquierda política y sindical en el Uruguay post-autoritario," *Cuadernos del CLAEH* #38 (2a. serie, XI).

Gillespie, Charles. 1987. "Party Strategies and Redemocratization: Theoretical and Comparative Perspectives on the Uruguayan Case." Ph.D. diss., Yale University.

———. 1986a. "Uruguay's Transition from Collegial Military-Technocratic Rule," in O'Donnell, Schmitter, and Whitehead, eds., *Transitions from Authoritarian.*

———. 1986b. "Activists and the Floating Voter: The Unheeded Lessons of Uruguay's 1982 Primaries," in Drake and Silva, eds., *Elections and Democratization.*

———. 1983. "From Suspended Animation to Animated Suspension: Political Parties and the Reconstruction of Democracy in Uruguay." Paper presented to the APSA Annual Convention.

Gillespie, Charles, and Luis E. González. 1989. "Uruguay: The Survival of Old and Autonomous Institutions," in Larry Diamond, Juan J. Linz, and Seymour M. Lipset, eds., *Democracy in Developing Countries*, vol. 4: *Latin America*. Boulder, Colo.: Lynne Rienner Publishers.

Gillespie, Charles, et al., eds. 1984–85. *Uruguay y la democracia* (3 vols.). Montevideo: The Wilson Center, Latin American Program, and Ediciones de la Banda Oriental.

Godoy Arcaya, Oscar, ed. 1990. *Hacia una democracia moderna: la opción parlamentaria*. Santiago: Ediciones Universidad Católica de Chile.

González, Ariosto D. 1922. *Los partidos tradicionales*. Montevideo: Librería Cervantes.

González, Luis E., and Andrés Rius. 1989. "La opinión pública montevideana a cuatro años de la restauración democrática," *Rivista Uruguaya de Ciencia Política* #2.

González, Luis E. 1988. "Perspectivas electorales," *Cuadernos de Marcha* (Tercera época) IV:34.

———. 1986. "Los sindicatos en la arena política," *Cuadernos de Marcha* (Tercera época) II:9.

———. 1985a. "Transición y restauración democrática," in Gillespie et al., eds., *Uruguay y la democracia* (vol. 3).

———. 1985b. "Transición y partidos en Chile y Uruguay," CIESU, Montevideo, *Documento de Trabajo*, 93/85.

———. 1984. "Uruguay: una apertura inesperada," *Cuadernos CIESU* #47, Ciesu-Ediciones de la Banda Oriental.

———. 1983. "Uruguay, 1980–1981: An Unexpected Opening," *Latin American Research Review* 18:3.

González Risotto, Rodolfo. 1990. *Elecciones nacionales de 1989*. Montevideo: CELADU - Fundación Friedrich Naumann.

Graceras, Ulises. 1977. "Inter-generational Cleavages and Political Behavior: A Survey Study of the 1971 Presidential Election in Uruguay." Ph.D. diss., Michigan State University.

Grofman, Bernard, and Arend Lijphart, eds. 1986. *Electoral Laws and Their Political Consequences*. New York: Agathon Press.

Gros Espiell, Héctor. 1956. *Las Constituciones del Uruguay*. Madrid: Ediciones Cultura Hispánica.

Guidobono, Alberto. 1986. "La clase política uruguaya y el sistema electoral," in Franco, ed., *El sistema electoral uruguayo*, vol. 2.

Heintz, Peter. 1970. *Paradigma sociológico del desarrollo*. Buenos Aires: Editorial del Instituto Di Tella.

Hofstadter, Richard. 1969. *The Idea of a Party System: The Rise of Legitimate Opposition in the United States, 1780–1840*. Berkeley: University of California Press.

Huneeus, Carlos. 1987. *Los chilenos y la política*. Santiago: CERC-ICHEH.

Inglehart, Ronald, and Dusan Sidjanski. 1976. "The Left, The Right, The Establishment and the Swiss Electorate," in Budge, Crewe, and Farlie, eds., *Party Identification*.

Inglehart, Ronald, and Hans Klingemann. 1976. "Party Identification, Ideological Preference and the Left-Right Dimension among Western Mass Publics," in Budge, Crewe, and Farlie, eds., *Party Identification*.

Jacob, Raúl. 1983. *El Uruguay de Terra*. Montevideo: Ediciones de la Banda Oriental.

Katz, Richard S. 1986. "Intraparty Preference Voting." in Grofman and Lijphart, eds., *Electoral Laws*.

Keck, Margaret. 1986. "From Movement to Politics: The Formation of the Workers' Party in Brazil." Ph.D. diss., Columbia University.

Kirchheimer, Otto. 1966. "The Transformation of the Western European Party Systems," in LaPalombara and Weiner, eds., *Political Parties*.

Klingemann, Hans D. 1979. "Measuring Ideological Conceptualizations," in Barnes and Kaase, eds., *Political Action*.

Korpi, Walter. 1983. *The Democratic Class Struggle*. London: Routledge and Kegan Paul.

LaPalombara, Joseph. 1974. *Politics within Nations*. Englewood Cliffs, N.J.: Prentice-Hall.

Lijphart, Arend. 1981. "Political Parties: Ideologies and Programs," in Butler, Penniman, and Ranney, eds., *Democracy at the Polls*.

———. 1980. "Language, Religion, Class and Party Choice: Belgium, Canada, Switzerland and South Africa Compared," in Rose, ed., *Electoral Participation*.

Lindahl, Göran G. 1962. *Uruguay's New Path*. Stockholm: Library and Institute of Ibero-American Studies.

Linz, Juan J., and Alfred Stepan, eds. 1978. *The Breakdown of Democratic Regimes*. Baltimore, Md.: The Johns Hopkins University Press.

Linz, Juan J. 1990a. "Transitions to Democracy," *The Washington Quarterly* (Summer).

———. 1990b. "Democracia: presidencialismo o parlamentarismo, ¿hace alguna diferencia?," in O. Godoy Arcaya, ed., *Hacia una democracia moderna*. An abbreviated version of this paper was published as "The Perils of Presidentialism," *Journal of Democracy* 1 (Winter 1990).

———. 1987. "La Asamblea Nacional de Primo de Rivera," in Linz et al., *Política y Sociedad: Estudios en Homenaje a Francisco Murillo Ferrol*, vol. 2. Madrid: Centro de Investigaciones Sociológicas - Centro de Estudios Constitucionales.

———. 1980. "The New Spanish Party System," in Rose, ed., *Electoral Participation*.

———. 1978. "Crisis, Breakdown and Reequilibration," in Linz and Stepan, eds., *The Breakdown*. Part I.

———. 1972. "Continuidad y Discontinuidad en la Elite Política Española: De la Restauración al Régimen Actual," in Linz et al., *Estudios de Ciencia Política y Sociología en Homenaje al Prof. Carlos Ollero*. Madrid: Carlavilla.

Lipset, Seymour M. 1983a. *Political Man: The Social Bases of Politics*, 2nd edition. London: Heinemann.

———. 1983b. "Radicalism or Reformism: The Sources of Working-class Politics," *American Political Science Review* 77:1.

————. 1977. "American 'Exceptionalism' in North American Perspective: Why the United States has Withstood the Worldwide Socialist Movement," in Elie Maynard Adams, ed., *The Idea of America: A Reassessment of the American Experiment.* Cambridge, Mass.: Ballinger.

————. 1968. "Revolution and Counterrevolution: The United States and Canada," in Lipset, *Revolution and Counterrevolution: Change and Persistence in Social Structures.* New York: Basic Books.

Lipset, Seymour M., and Stein Rokkan. 1967. "Cleavage Structures, Party Systems and Voter Alignments: An Introduction," in Lipset and Rokkan, eds., *Party Systems and Voter Alignments: Cross National Perspectives.* New York: Free Press.

Loewenberg, Gerhard, and Samuel C. Patterson. 1979. *Comparing Legislatures.* Boston: Little, Brown and Co.

Maguire, Maria. 1983. "Is There Still Persistence? Electoral Change in Western Europe, 1948–1979," in Daalder and Mair, eds., *Western European Party Systems.*

Mair, Peter. 1983. "Adaptation and Control: Towards an Understanding of Party and Party System Change," in Daalder and Mair, eds., *Western European Party Systems.*

Mainwaring, Scott. 1990a. "Presidentialism in Latin America," *Latin American Research Review,* vol. 25.

————. 1990b. "Brazil: Weak Parties, Feckless Democracy." Paper presented at the 1990 Annual Meeting of the American Political Science Association, San Francisco, August 30–September 2.

Mannheimer, Renato, and Giacomo Sani. 1987. *Il mercato elettorale: Identikit dell-'elettore italiano.* Bologna: Il Mulino.

Martínez Lamas, Julio. 1946. *Riqueza y Pobreza del Uruguay,* 2nd edition. Montevideo: Tipografía Atlántida.

McDonald, Ronald H. 1988. "The Dilemma of Normalcy in Uruguay," *Current History* vol. 87 #525 (January).

————. 1978. "Party Fractions and Modernization: A Comparative Analysis of Colombia and Uruguay," in Frank P. Belloni and Dennis C. Beller, eds., *Fraction Politics: Political Parties and Fractionalism in Comparative Perspective.* Santa Barbara, Cal.: ABC-Clio Press.

————. 1971. "Legislative Politics in Uruguay: A Preliminary Statement," in Agor, ed., *Latin American Legislatures.*

Melgar, Alicia. 1981. "Distribución del ingreso en el Uruguay," CLAEH, Montevideo, Serie *Investigaciones* #18.

Melián Lafinur, Luis. 1918. *La acción funesta de los partidos tradicionales en la reforma constitucional.* Montevideo: Claudio García.

Mieres, Pablo. 1990. "Las elecciones de 1989 en Uruguay: un sistema de partidos en transición," *Cuadernos del CLAEH* #53.

————. 1985. "Los partidos uruguayos y el sistema político: imágenes y desafíos del presente," in Caetano et al., *De la tradición a la crisis.*

Montero, José R., and Mariano Torcal. 1990. "Voters and Citizens in a New Democracy: Some Trend Data on Political Attitudes in Spain," *International Journal of Public Opinion Research* 2:2.

Nahum, Benjamín, et al. 1989. Historia uruguaya - *Tomo 7: Crisis política y recuperación económica, 1930–1958*. Montevideo: Ediciones de la Banda Oriental.

Nohlen, Dieter. 1981. *Sistemas electorales del mundo*. Madrid: Centro de Estudios Constitucionales.

Nohlen, Dieter, and Juan Rial, eds. 1986. *Reforma electoral: ¿Posible, deseable?* Montevideo: FESUR - Ediciones de la Banda Oriental.

O'Donnell, Guillermo. 1978. "State and Alliances in Argentina," *Journal of Development Studies* 15:1.

O'Donnell, Guillermo, Philippe C. Schmitter, and Lawrence Whitehead, eds. 1986. *Transitions from Authoritarian Rule: Prospects for Democracy*. Baltimore, Md.: The Johns Hopkins University Press.

Obradovic, Mileta. 1984. *Industrialisation, commerce extérieur et leur interaction: le cas des pays semi-industrialisés*. Paris: Economica.

Perelli, Carina, and Juan Rial. 1990. "El fin de la restauración: La elección del 26 de noviembre de 1989," Peitho, Montevideo, *Cuadernos de Orientación Electoral* #10.

Pérez Pérez, Alberto. 1970. *La Ley de Lemas*. Montevideo: Fundación de Cultura Universitaria.

Pedersen, Mogens N. 1983. "Changing Patterns of Electoral Volatility in European Party Systems, 1948–1977," in Daalder and Mair, eds., *Western European Party Systems*.

Przeworski, Adam. 1985. *Capitalism and Social Democracy*. Cambridge: Cambridge University Press.

Putnam, Robert D. 1976. *The Comparative Study of Political Elites*. Englewood Cliffs, N.J.: Prentice-Hall.

————. 1973. *The Beliefs of Politicians: Ideology, Conflict and Democracy in Britain and Italy*. New Haven, Conn.: Yale University Press.

Rae, Douglas W. 1971. *The Political Consequences of Electoral Laws*, revised edition. New Haven, Conn.: Yale University Press.

Rama, Germán W. 1989. "Plebiscito: primeras consideraciones," *Punto y Aparte* #21 (May).

————. 1971. *El club político*. Montevideo: Arca.

Real de Azúa, Carlos. 1984. *Uruguay: ¿una sociedad amortiguadora?* Montevideo: CIESU - Ediciones de la Banda Oriental.

————. 1971. "Política, Poder y Partidos en el Uruguay de Hoy," in Luis Benvenuto et al., *Uruguay Hoy*. Buenos Aires: Siglo XXI.

————. 1961. *El patriciado uruguayo*. Montevideo: Asir.

Regalatti, Dora. 1982. "La ampliación de la participación política en Uruguay," Report on research in progress, CLACSO.

Reyes Abadie, Washington. 1989. *Historia del Partido Nacional*. Montevideo: Ediciones de la Banda Oriental.

174 POLITICAL STRUCTURES AND DEMOCRACY IN URUGUAY

Rial, Juan. 1986a. "El movimiento sindical uruguayo ante la redemocratización," CIESU, Research Report to PREALC.

————. 1986b. "The Uruguayan Election of 1984: A Triumph of the Center," in Drake and Silva, eds., *Elections and Democratization*.

————. 1985. *Uruguay: elecciones de 1984*. Montevideo: Ediciones de la Banda Oriental.

————. 1984a. "Elecciones: reglas de juego y tendencias," *Historia y Política* - Cuaderno #3, CIEP, Montevideo.

————. 1984b. "Los partidos tradicionales: restauración o renovación," in Gillespie et al., eds., *Uruguay y la democracia* (vol. 1).

Rose, Richard, ed. 1980. *Electoral Participation: A Comparative Analysis*. London: Sage.

Rush, Michael. 1979. "The Members of Parliament," in Walkland, ed., *The House of Commons*.

Rustow, Dankwart A. 1970. "Transitions to Democracy," *Comparative Politics* 2:3.

Sainsbury, Diane. 1985. "The Electoral Difficulties of the Scandinavian Social Democrats in the 1970s: The Social Bases of the Parties and Structural Explanations of Party Decline," *Comparative Politics* 18:1.

Sanguinetti, Julio María, and Alvaro Pacheco Seré. 1971. *La nueva Constitución*. Montevideo: Alfa.

Sani, Giacomo. 1984. "Sistema dei partiti e società italiana," in Bobbio et al., *Il sistema politico italiano*.

Sani, Giacomo, and Giovanni Sartori. 1983. "Polarization, Fragmentation and Competition in Western Democracies," in Daalder and Mair, eds., *Western European Party Systems*.

Sartori, Giovanni. 1986. "The Influence of Electoral Systems: Faulty Laws or Faulty Method?," in Grofman and Lijphart, eds., *Electoral Laws*.

————. 1982. *Teoria dei partiti e caso italiano*. Milano: Sugarco Edizione.

————. 1976. *Parties and Party Systems: A framework for Analysis*. New York: Cambridge University Press.

————. 1966. "European Political Parties: The Case of Polarized Pluralism," in LaPalombara and Weiner, eds., *Political Parties*.

Sartori, Giovanni, et al. 1963. *Il Parlamento italiano 1946–1963*. Napoli: Edizioni Scientifiche Italiane.

Shugart, Matthew S. 1989. "Electoral Cycles and the Party System in Presidential Democracies," paper presented at the Research Symposium on Presidential and Parliamentary Democracy, Georgetown University, Latin American Studies Program, May 1989.

Silvert, Kalman H. 1961. *The Conflict Society: Reaction and Revolution in Latin America*. Louisiana: Hauser.

Snow, Peter G. 1979. *Political Forces in Argentina*, revised edition. New York: Praeger.

Solari, Aldo E. 1986. "El Sistema de Partidos y Régimen Electoral en el Uruguay," in Franco, ed., *El Sistema Electoral*.

————. 1967. *El desarrollo social del Uruguay en la postguerra*. Montevideo: Alfa.

————. 1964. *Estudios sobre la sociedad uruguaya*, 2 vols. Montevideo: Arca.

Somogyi, Stefano. 1963. "Costituenti e deputati 1946–1958: Analisi statistica," in Sartori et al., *Il Parlamento italiano*.

Stepan, Alfred. 1986. "Paths toward Redemocratization: Theoretical and Comparative Perspectives," in O'Donnell, Schmitter and Whitehead, eds., *Transitions from Authoritarian Rule*, part III.

Taylor, Philip B., Jr. 1960. *Government and Politics of Uruguay*. New Orleans: Tulane Studies in Political Science, Tulane University.

Ures, Jorge. 1972. "La relación clase-voto en Montevideo," in *Revista Uruguaya de Ciencias Sociales* 1:1.

Valenzuela, Arturo. 1990. "Partidos políticos y crisis presidencial en Chile: proposición para un gobierno parlamentario," in O. Godoy Arcaya, ed., *Hacia una democracia moderna*.

————. 1976. "Political Constraints to the Establishment of Socialism in Chile," in A. Valenzuela and J. S. Valenzuela, eds., *Chile: Politics and Society*. New Brunswick, N.J.: Transaction Books.

Vanger, Milton I. 1980. *The Model Country: José Batlle y Ordóñez of Uruguay, 1907–1915*, Hanover, New Hampshire: Brandeis University Press.

————. 1963. *José Batlle y Ordóñez of Uruguay: The Creator of his Times, 1902–1907*. Cambridge, Mass.: Harvard University Press.

Venturini, Angel R. 1984. *Estadísticas electorales*. Montevideo: Ediciones de la Banda Oriental.

Vernazza, Francisco. 1990. "Minoristas, mayoristas y generalistas en el sistema electoral uruguayo," *Revista Uruguaya de Ciencia Política* #3.

————. 1987. "El sistema electoral uruguayo y el descenso de la representatividad de los diputados: 1925-1984," Montevideo, Tesis de Licenciatura (Sociología), Universidad de la República.

Walkland, S. A., ed. 1979. *The House of Commons in the Twentieth Century*. Oxford: Clarendon Press.

Weinstein, Martin. 1975. *Uruguay: The Politics of Failure*. Westport, Conn.: Greenwood Press.

Weschler, Lawrence. 1990. *A Miracle, A Universe: Settling Accounts with Torturers*. New York: Pantheon Books.

World Bank. 1983. *World Development Report 1983*. New York: Oxford University Press.

Worre, Torben. 1980. "Class Parties and Class Voting in the Scandinavian Countries," *Scandinavian Political Studies* (New Series) 3:4.

Zubillaga, Carlos. 1985. "Los partidos políticos ante la crisis (1958–1983)," in Caetano et al., *De la tradición a la crisis*.

Zubillaga, Carlos, and Romeo Pérez. 1983. "Los partidos políticos," CLAEH, Montevideo, Serie *El Uruguay de nuestro tiempo* #5.

Zuckerman, Alan S. 1979. *The Politics of Faction: Christian Democratic Rule in Italy*. New Haven, Conn.: Yale University Press.

Notes

1. Introduction

1. Gillespie and González (1989) provide an ample account of the judgments found in the literature.

2. World Bank (1983), Tables 1, 25, 23, 22, and 27 respectively. The Uruguayan income distribution data are in Melgar (1981); the last statement is tentative because Uruguayan figures are only from Montevideo (about half of the country), whereas the rest are national data.

3. I believe that until the end of the 1960s most operationalizations of opposition would give Uruguay a somewhat better record (e.g., the problems the Chilean Communist Party experienced had no equivalent in Uruguay), but in the final five years preceding the 1973 coups the opposite was probably true.

4. Valenzuela (1976), p. 10. The evolution of Uruguayan early figures (before 1925) is in Regalatti (1982). The exclusion of illiterates had a strong effect in Chile.

5. A comparison of this kind is not always possible. When one regime in a given time ranks better than the other along the opposition dimension, but worse in the participation dimension, we cannot compare "polyarchical" performance unless we are willing to lose the bidimensionality of the concept by computing a single index from the two dimensions. This theoretical difficulty is compounded when the comparison is intended throughout a period, as is the present case. In such a situation the only viable comparison seems to be on Paretian terms, that is, when one of the regimes is always in as good a position as the other in all the dimensions, and better off at least part of the time in at least one dimension. This is what I attempt to do in an approximative manner.

6. Or, more generally, some form of authoritarianism.

7. This, in turn, may be interpreted in a probabilistic way: *inevitability* would mean a very high probability of occurrence.

8. This is so even with regard to party systems.

9. The survey addressed several different topics, and I was able to reprocess a small number of variables belonging to the data bank of the pollsters—the Montevideo-based consulting firm Equipos Consultores Asociados. The variables are: sex, age, education, occupation, quality of the interviewee's home assessed by the interviewer (as a proxy for socio-economic status), vote in the November 1984 election, and self-placement in the left-right continuum.

10. Fifty-four percent answered "better" and 23 percent "worse." The data were collected by Gallup International Research Institutes between December 1984 and March 1985. *World Opinion Update* IX:5 (May 1985), p. 58.

11. In particular, the samples tend to be more educated and less economically active than the population, biases that, as will be seen, lead to errors of opposite sign in the political variables. Those errors are systematic partly because the population figures used in the comparison are those of the whole *Departamento* (i.e., of the sub-national administrative unit which includes Montevideo city), including its relatively scarcely populated semi-rural areas, whereas the sample covers only the urban area. The same remarks apply to the political variables.

12. Agor (1971, p. xxvii). He presents a summary review of the literature (pp. xxiv and ff.)

13. Another reason that adds intrinsic utility to this survey is, quite simply, the lack of previous empirical work on the subject. Nothing comparable has been done in Uruguay and, as far as I am aware, the existing studies on Latin American legislators do not cover complete legislatures. The present survey thus adds to an extremely scarce literature.

14. It consists of ninety-nine representatives and thirty senators, plus the vice president, who presides over the Senate and the General Assembly, i.e., the simultaneous session of both chambers.

15. About 80 percent in Italy (Sartori et al. 1963), 84 percent in Britain and 78 percent in Italy again (Putnam 1973), and 84 percent in France (Cayrol, Parodi, and Ysmal 1973).

16. Fortunately there were no important differences in the response rates of the members of different fractions within the same party. Although the data are weighted, the totals in the tables always present the actual number of interviews used to compute the reported figures.

2. Uruguayan Political Structures: Historical Background

1. The only general overview is perhaps Taylor (1960), which also includes a useful bibliography. The crucial first third of the present century is covered in Lindahl (1962) and Vanger (1963, 1980), who also provide references. Jacob (1983) describes the de facto regime of the 1930s, and Zubillaga and Pérez (1983) update the story. The best essay on the years preceding the 1973 coup is, in my opinion, Real de Azúa 1971). Writings on the post-coup period will be quoted below in a more detailed manner.

2. It must be noted, however, that the predominant role of the Colorados was already seriously diminished in 1952, for the 1952 Constitution imposed special legislative majorities to fill several central positions in the administration, majorities which required two-party agreements (Gros Espiell 1956, p. 114). In this regard—i.e., curtailment of the predominant role of the Colorados—those majorities were perhaps more important than the more visible, mandatory two-party composition of the pluripersonal National Council of Government which replaced the president, because the minority party could do no more than oversee the work of the governing party.

3. For reasons that will become clear in later chapters, I think that under democratic governments the party system evolved in the following manner: (a) two-party, 1918–1933 and 1959–1966; (b) predominant party, the Colorados, 1943–1958, and (c) moderate pluralism, 1967–1973 and again since 1985. These judgments follow Sartori's "counting rules."

4. This was not so during the authoritarian regime (1973–1984).

5. I retain Sartori's (1976, pp. 71–74) neutral term *fraction*. His argument seems convincing to me. Besides, in Spanish, as in English, *facción* (faction) has a pejorative connotation, whereas *fracción* (fraction) does not. Uruguayans, and politicians in particular, use *fracción*, no *facción*, thus making natural Sartori's proposal. This does not deny, of course, that perhaps most of the Uruguayan historical fractions have been indeed factions (in the pejorative sense), but surely not all of them were. This is, in the end, an empirical matter, not a terminological one.

6. I can follow Sartori when he states that Uruguay has a two-party format, although the parties are in fact façade arrangements. This means, of course, that Blancos and Colorados are not really parties. Nevertheless, if this is so it is unclear to me whether the statement on the predominant role of the Colorados still makes sense.

7. It might be argued that Blancos and Colorados did not evolve from former class-mass or denominational parties, and that their followers had strong, enduring party identifications. These traits are not supposed to be typical of catch-all parties, or of the kind of parties that initiate a process of transformation in that direction; accordingly, the catch-all label would not be appropriate for the Uruguayan traditional parties. The objection is irrelevant, however, for those traits also apply to the United States, "still the classical example of an all-pervasive catch-all party system" (Kirchheimer 1966, p. 85).

8. In fact, Lindahl's emphasis on the organizational criterion is not taken for granted in later literature. Sartori may be quoted against his own conclusion on the Uruguayan case: "the distinction between party and faction has often been drawn, in the past, along organizational lines, under the assumption that the party is the organized and the faction the organizationless body. By now we know not only that the party subunits can be powerfully organized, but that the party might even compare with its subunits as the lesser organized entity" (Sartori 1976, p. 76).

9. The similarities between the Italian party and the Colorados in particular go far beyond these considerations, as Chapters 6 and 7 of the present study show.

10. Leaving aside the Institutional Acts of the 1973–1984 authoritarian regime; the democratic restoration restored the 1966 Constitution as well. Neither the 1934 nor the 1942 reforms were conducted according to the existing legality, although the 1942 reform may be described as undoing the illegitimate scenario created by the 1933 coup and in some aspects institutionalized by the 1934 Constitution. In spite of their origins, both reforms contributed in enduring ways to Uruguayan Constitutional law.

11. A nine-member National Council of Government dominated by the winning party but with three seats assigned to the runner-up; its presidency rotated yearly among the members of the majority.

12. Sartori (1982, p. 310). A distinct chief of government may exist as long as it is explicitly subordinated to the president, who has the ultimate responsibility of government. The "indirect" presidential election in the U.S. violates the form, but obviously not the substance, of this definition. Needless to say, there is an ample literature concerning the differences between parliamentary and presidential systems; the main *descriptive* points, however, are not in dispute. The disagreements appear in the evaluation of those differences.

13. This is an interesting view in more than one sense. Julio Maria Sanguinetti, one of the coauthors, a lawyer, and Colorado politician, is the president the Uruguayans elected in November 1984.

14. A special majority of two-thirds within the National Council of Administration—i.e., the pluripersonal component of the executive power—was necessary to supersede the president's veto power.

15. Between 1933 and 1942 this would have been even more difficult because of the peculiar composition of the Senate and the electoral abstention of the main opposition to the de facto regime.

16. This is a classical point, though nine persons are a small assembly.

17. At first this was also intended, at least in part, as a safeguard to the secrecy of the vote.

18. The 1918 Constitution established frequent elections; "elections affecting the whole country were held three out of every four years" (Lindahl 1962, p. 218).

19. The legal name of a party in the electoral law is *lema* (literally, "motto"). The main fractions, that is, the main subdivisions, of the *lemas* are then the *sub-lemas*. *Lema* and party are not synonyms, however, because a real coalition may become a *lema*, although the intricacies of the law establish certain restrictions on the names the *lemas* may use. The name of the Broad Front coalition ("Frente Amplio") is now a *lema*, but in the 1971 and 1984 elections the Front ran under the *lema* (legal name) "Partido Demócrata Cristiano," Christian Democratic Party. As that label was a "permanent *lema*," i.e., one that obtained seats in the legislature in the previous election, it allowed the Front to use the DSV device. In this way the members of the coalition were able to mark separately their own votes (to the legislature) while voting common candidacies to the executive positions at the national and local levels. *Lema* and *party* are often used indistinctly.

20. The DSV places Uruguay among the oldest democracies which have used uninterruptedly—except during the recent de facto regime, which did not allow elections between 1973 and 1983—some form of intraparty preference voting. The DSV idea was known in Uruguay through a book written in 1870 by Borély; Solari (1986, pp. 133–142) presents an interesting discussion of this story.

21. Suggestive summaries of those differing historical identities may be found in Real de Azúa (1971, p. 226) and Zubillaga and Pérez (1983, p. 107); none of these authors, however, agree with a purely "optimistic" approach.

22. Real de Azúa (1971, p. 302, n. 79). This is not an Uruguayan peculiarity. The argument that fractionism is a product of internal democracy is very frequent. Barnes repoerted that 90 percent of his sample of members of the Italian Socialist Party "agreed with the fact that currents are an 'instrument of democracy.'" (Sartori

1976, pp. 105 and 115, n. 73) As Sartori concluded, "those who practice fractionism are bound to justify it" (loc. cit.).

23. Weinstein (1975, p. 67). Aguiar (1983, pp. 15 and ff.) provides a more recent discussion and useful references.

24. De Riz (983, p. 5). In the same sense, and to mention only a minimal sample, McDonald (1971, p. 122) and Real de Azúa (1971, pp. 213 and ff.). More generally, diverging opoinions on the effects of Uruguayan electoral law are found in Vernazza (1987) and in three compilations: Nohlen and Rial (1986), Franco (1986), and Cocchi (1988). Authors close to the "optimistic" view tend to share Nohlen's (1981) ideas on electoral law—e.g., Franco (1986a).

25. The Indian Congress Party and the Japanese Liberals have been, and still are, predominant parties. In Italy, as in Uruuay, all major parties are fractionalized. It may be also noted that the Italian Christian Democrats and the Colorados have been predominant parties as well. The tendency of predominant parties to become fractionalized had already been asserted on theoreical grounds by Jefferson; "a party possessed of an excessively clear domination of the field, tends to 'schismatize.'" (Hofstadter 1969, pp. 248–249)

26. I suspect that the link the literature does *not* stress—i.e., between clientelistic practices and the fractionalization of parties—is far more promising than this argument, although at least in Uruguay the direction of the main causal link is probably *opposite* to those mentioned above; fractionalization promotes clientelism, not the other way round. Probing this link would require an entirely independent research, however, due to the lack of systematic studies on the subject. Interesting documents on these practices in the 1960s may be found in Fa Robaina (1972) and Rama (1971); the latter includes a brief but suggestive discussion of the interviews which compose the book. In comparative terms the link between fractions and clienteles seems obvious and very strong: among Western developed nations the most notorious cases of clientelism, Italy and Japan (Zuckerman 1979, passim) are directly linked to the most fractionalized parties—the Italian DC and the Japanese Liberals.

27. Several authars have pointed out this problem. McDonald (1978, pp. 238 and 243, n. 40) mentioned it as a "paradox"; Gillespie (1983, p. 8) wrote that the DSV exerted "moderating" effect on "the tendency of proportional representation . . . to produce a multiplication of parties." Castellanos and Pérez (1981) observed that the first Uruguayan Constitution (1830–1918) contributed to the consolidation of bipartyism because it established a plurality system. I think they are right, although it is difficult to discern what was the real importance of electoral law when elections were usually neither open nor clean.

28. A system which favors bipartyism makes more difficult the access of a third party to one of the two central positions, but once this is done one of the former main parties risks losing its position. This is not necessarily so; the challenger may be in the end defeated, but the point is that, whatever their identity, in the long run only two parties will retain a dominant position. The two perhaps best known examples— the ascent of the U.S. Republicans in the past century and of British Labor sixty years ago—concluded with the defeat of one of the previously dominant parties. The contemporary challenge to British Labor by the Alliance has been unsuccessful.

29. Solari (1986, pp. 120–121). The two-volume book edited by Franco (1986) which contains Solari's essay presents a good sample of those views.

30. This argument was proposed first by Pérez Pérez (1970), though not exactly in the same manner, Pérez Pérez shares Lindahl's position on the disguised multipartyism of the Uruguayan system. More recently he seems skeptical on his own thesis. On the general theme of the effects of electoral law on party systems his views are closer to Solari's discussed above than to those presented here—as shown in his comments in the book Franco (1986) edited, vol. I, p. 197.

31. Available evidence from other polities confirms this point. In the 1987 British general election, for example, among those "who claimed to have voted or seriously considered voting Alliance, before deciding against, the overwhelming reason given was some variation of the classic 'wasted vote' argument. Altogether, 68 percent said that the Alliance could not win or that voting Alliance would let in one of the major parties" (Crewe 1987, pp. 55–56).

32. Quoted by Lipset (1977, p. 125). Lipset provides references and a summary of the history of the argument (ibid., p. 109–110, 124 and ff., and 159, n. 48).

33. It may be underscored that although Hillquit's quote is a fine description of what happens in the Uruguayan case, the latter situation is even more rigid because ticket splitting was never allowed.

34. Italy and Japan, in particular, also are intraparty preference voting systems.

35. This, of course, is one of the main reasons suggesting a strong causal link from fractionism to clientelism.

36. Since the same reasoning applies to parties and fractions, that is, to extra- and intra-party competition, fractions should not be expected to be much more cohesive than parties —except for the fact that smaller size may make internal relationships more fluid than in the bigger unit.

37. Aguiar (1983) presents a fascinating compilation of these data.

38. Probably other factors also contributed to that multiplication of candidacies. In particular, I think that the more recent figures also reflect a context in which the opportunities to climb the social ladder for ambitious and educated young men had been quickly and steadily decreasing since the early 1950s.

3. Political Structures and Democratic Breakdowns

1. Nahum et al. (1989, pp. 13–42) describe concisely these events. Differing emphases may be found in Reyes Abadie (1989, pp. 216–225).

2. Later, he never attended the meetings of the Agrupación and "consistently ignored its recommendations" (Lindahl 1962, p. 178). The Agrupación was by far the single most important policy-making body of the Colorados, and its actions and deliberations influenced the whole party. In fact, its work gave the Batllistas considerably more influence than their actual share of the party's votes.

3. A Blanco *caudillo*, Nepomuceno Saravia, was said to be preparing an invasion from Brazilian territory. It is highly unlikely that such an invasion could have actually taken place, and even more unlikely—thirty years after the defeat of the Blancos in a civil war that proved that the regular army and new technologies were

too much for them—that if it had occurred it would have had any chance of victory. Besides those rumors, within both parties there was plenty of semiloyal and plainly disloyal behavior. Both the Blanco majority and a Colorado minority promoted voting abstention in the 1932 election to the National Council of Administration; those abstentions had often been a cautionary device designed to provide later a reasonable argument supporting insurrection. Needless to say, all of these real or supposed activities were based at least in part on a very real distrust from all those involved towards Terra and his behavior.

4. These occurred particularly during the initial period of the regime: press censorship, some persecutions by the police, and harassment of political parties.

5. The Senate was presided over by the vice president, and the most voted list of each *lema*, that is, the main fraction within each *lema*, got half of the Senate's seats. The system was scarcely viable for other reasons: it assumed a permanent agreement of those fractions on several matters which required special legislative majorities. Nevertheless, in the medium and long run the strengthening of the position of the main fractions alone would have certainly discouraged fractionalism.

6. The year 1968 is an important watershed: it marked the beginning of the truly political crisis leading to the 1973 coup. The GDP averages reported above were computed on the data presented in Instituto de Economía: *Uruguay: Estadísticas Básicas*, Montevideo, Universidad de la República, 1969.

7. In 1968 there were 19 industrial and 19 semi-industrial nations. In the ranking of those 38 most industrial countries of market-oriented economies Uruguay fell from the 21st place in 1953 to the 31st in 1973 (Obradovic 1984, pp. 21 and 31).

8. The romantic aura of the Tupamaros generated a relatively abundant and easily accessible literature of very disparate value, whereas almost nothing has been written on the bulk of the left.

9. I am indebted in this to Aguiar (1977, pp. 62–63). My point is not whether the Blanco failed policy would have been successful, but that it was not given time enough to see if it could bear fruit.

10. Such a situation was very exceptional. He was called a *radish*, because he was red (Colorado) outside but white (Blanco) inside. His nomination alone is a good example of the peculiar relationship Pacheco had with most of the Colorado elite and of his way of handling party matters.

11. As summarized, for example, in O'Donnell (1978).

12. 1958 and 1966 were just borderline cases, however.

13. That is, the actual parliamentary representation of electoral parties. In Uruguay they are about the same, but this is a consequence of PR; for that reason I underscored "parliamentary."

14. The responsibility of a president towards the legislature is often called *politico-criminal* precisely to distinguish it from the normal political responsibility of prime ministers and their cabinets.

15. As it has been noted, from 1918 through the 1973 coup there was always party government except during the authoritarian situation of the years 1934–1942 and during the year preceding the 1973 coup. During the 1934–1942 authoritarian situation there was a peculiar coalition between a governing Colorado fraction led

by President Terra and the Blanco majority led by Herrera; in 1972 there was a pact between the Colorado majority and the Blanco minority.

16. Before the 1971 election the democratic Colorados could hope to win, and the relative weight of the conservative Blancos within their party was still unknown. This was an important point, for to moderate Colorados the conservative Blanco surely looked far worse than Pacheco. After the election Bordaberry had to be tested, then the Tupamaro offensive further complicated things during the rest of the year 1972, and in 1973 events happened in quick succession until the coup took place in June.

17. Fragmentation refers to the number of relevant parties of the system and/or to that number somehow "weighted" according to the size of the parties. There are several well-known measures of fragmentation based on these approaches; according to all of them the fragmentations the party system exhibited in the last three elections (1971, 1984, and 1989) were the highest of Uruguayan political history. In comparative terms, however, Uruguay is not a highly fragmented polity.

18. Although it is obviously true that small countries in particular are always obliged to react and constantly adapt to changes in the external environments they do not control. This means that external shocks are unavoidable; as a result, political structures that complicate those adjustments will lead, sooner or later, to political crises.

19. The DSV device produced perverse results in this regard as well. Bordaberry won the 1971 election, but in two-person races he would have almost surely lost to the main Blanco candidate (Ferreira) and probably even to the Colorado runner-up (Batlle).

20. Contemporary "solutions" in Latin America opted for a restricted franchise (Chile), fraud (Argentina), or both (most of the other countries).

21. The logic of the argument is that of Tocqueville's—and later Lipset's—view on religious tolerance in the United States: "Tocqueville pointed out that all American denominations were minorities and hence had an interest in liberty and a weak state . . . [thus] . . . deeply religious men in government [argued] strongly that the rights of the irreligious and of Jews must be the same as those of Christians." (Lipset 1968, p. 54).

22. During the 1971 electoral campaign most fractions of the two traditional parties stated more or less vaguely the need of reforming the internal structure of the parties. It seems to me that it was more than mere propaganda and that most politicians did feel this was a real problem. De Sierra et al. (1972, passim) provide a good sample of those worries.

23. Franco (1986b) summarizes a wide spectrum of opinions on this matter presented and discussed after the 1985 democratic restoration. I will return to this in Chapter 8.

24. Critics could be found in unexpected quarters. Besides the views from the intelligentsia—and from the left—mentioned in chapter 2, after the 1973 coup the military argued that electoral law had to be changed and, in particular, that parties could be allowed only one presidential candidate each. Facing political defeat, however, they later changed their views.

4. The 1984 Election: Restoration

1. Michelini wrote these views in early 1976, in a report on the Uruguayan situation later published in *Cuadernos de Marcha* 1:1 (1985).

2. *Búsqueda*, July 17, 1985.

3. Though this does not mean that direct fraud was necessary for them to win; in 1978 it was probably not necessary; as for 1980, probably we will never know. I attempted elsewhere a preliminary comparison between the Chilean and Uruguayan plebiscites (González 1985b). My views on the Uruguayan plebiscite and in particular on the behavior of the military may be seen in González (1983).

4. The military regime applied to the parties two sets of double standards. On the one hand, whereas the parties and groups of the left were banned, the traditional parties were "suspended." This was consistent with the military's view on the role of the left as intellectual mentors—at the very least—of the guerrillas. The differences were not merely legal: on the whole, the military were far more tolerant towards the opposition from the traditional parties. Though by no means free to do what they wanted, in practice there were certain grey zones on what was and was not permitted to Blanco and Colorado opposition leaders, particularly towards the end of the authoritarian regime. In those final stages the "grey zone" was a moving frontier; politicians were continually testing and expanding its limits. The double standard was more notorious with regard to the repression of real or supposed transgressions. On the other hand, to this double standard in dealing with the left and dealing with the traditional parties, the regime added another double standard: it dealt with Blancos and Colorados themselves in different ways—which is the point made below.

5. The "plebiscitarian" Brazilian elections since 1974 pointed in the same direction, however, though with far more limited scope and consequences.

6. The single most useful source on this period is perhaps a three-volume compilation by Charles G. Gillespie et al. (1984–1985). The ideas I summarize here were presented in a paper in that compilation (González 1985a). The most detailed discussion of the final stages of the transition towards democratic restoration is that of Gillespie's (1987).

7. In 1984, however, the small Unión Cívica (the conservative wing of Catholic activism) won 2.5 percent of the popular vote.

8. The classic statement of the "freezing" hypothesis with regard to Western Europe is Lipset and Rokkan's (1967). Later developments in those party systems are examined in Maguire (1983). Leaving aside the details of the discussion concerning to what extent Lipset and Rokkan's original argument has to be adjusted in the light of later evidence, the implications of all of this literature for the Uruguayan case are clear. Even in Spain, after forty years of Franquismo, there were important continuities with the pre-Franco party system (Linz 1980).

9. Pedersen's index has its drawbacks, as any summarizing index, but it is simple, it has a straightforward and politically relevant meaning, and it enables quick comparisons with other democratic party systems. Furthermore, it has been found that *net* volatility is empirically related to *gross* volatility—i.e., the total amount of individual switching between parties and to and from abstention (Denver 1985, p. 405). Gross volatility may occur without net volatility if voters' movements cancel

each other. Thus, net volatility necessarily implies gross volatility, but not vice-versa. Because of that, the empirical relationship between net and gross volatility lends additional attraction to the first, for gross volatility needs panel studies or recall questions in regular surveys—known to be inaccurate—to be estimated.

10. The surprises were in the specific results. Many thought that the Frente Amplio could win Montevideo; some did not expect a Colorado victory, much less the size of the lead they obtained nationally over the Blancos. But I think that most expected a result on the whole comparable to the 1971 election. Two years before the election, concluding an analysis of the vote in the plebiscite of 1980 I wrote: "the potential voters of the left probably did not increase significantly. If this is so, the vote for the traditional parties did not diminish either, and the recomposition of the electorate is a process developing within their boundaries . . . [thus] . . . the authoritarian order did not destroy; it froze. The term *restoration* appears then extremely significant. If it were necessary to summarize in one image the conclusions of this discussion . . . perhaps it could be said that this [restoration] is the 'most probable scenario' for the next quinquennium" (González 1984, pp. 29, 31; this is an expanded Spanish version of a paper presented at the 1982 Meeting of the Latin American Studies Association later published in the *Latin American Research Review* in 1983).

11. Bordaberry later exposed his views in a notable document (Bordaberry 1980). Zubillaga (1985) provides a brief but excellent history of the discussions about the role of political parties within the regime.

12. Needless to say, this was true for the traditional parties and eventually other minor, non-Marxist parties. The Marxist parties—both those avowedly Marxists and some small groups which were considered Marxist according to the military's own definition—had been outlawed since 1973.

13. Besides, after the Institutional Act #4 was issued, individual politicians could appeal the decision, and some more or less friendly to the regime actually did so. The proscription of several allies of the military was directly revoked without their appealing.

14. In this and the following discussion turnover will refer to previous parliamentary experience, no matter in which chamber. This is a more inclusive definition than the one usually accepted in the literature on legislatures in two different senses: first, it refers to both chambers, and second, it refers to previous parliamentary experience, not just in the immediately precedent legislature. With regard to the first aspect, this definition seems reasonable in the light of the relatively small size of the Uruguayan legislature (129 members) and particularly of its upper chamber (30 members). These are not small numbers with regard to Uruguay's population size or by comparison with other small Latin American countries, but they are indeed small by comparison with most democracies (Blondel 1973, Appendix A). With regard to the second aspect, the present definition also seems reasonable both because of the coup that interrupted the precedent legislature and the eleven years that elapsed till the 1984 general election, and because it allows the use of the scarce data available on the Uruguayan legislature for comparison.

15. Guidobono (1986), pp. 158–159. Guidobono's pioneer essay uses the definition for turnover explained above: he simply considers presence or absence of parliamentary experience.

16. The terms of all national authorities were four years according to the 1952 Constitution; the present (1966) Constitution added one year to all terms.

17. Within the Frente Amplio there were no *elecciones internas*, for the members of the left coalition were explicitly or tacitly outlawed. Its top leadership did not experience changes comparable to the other parties'.

18. This is an estimate somewhat laboriously computed on the basis of Butler and Kavanagh (1984, pp. 219 and 233) and Rush (1979, p. 81) data. Butler and Kavanagh do not present separately the number of MPs first entering Parliament in the 1970, February, 1974, and October, 1974, general elections. To compare with the Uruguayan data, however, it is necessary to isolate the figure corresponding to the 1970 election. I estimated that figure with the help of Rush's turnover data and of Butler and Kavanagh data on MPs who actually first entered Parliament in 1970–74. Once this estimation was made, it was easy to compute the number of 1983 MPs who had first entered Parliament on or before the 1970 general election. This time span is equal to Uruguay's (1971–84). As an additional check, it may be added that this "thirteen-years turnover" estimated for the British 1983 election (60 percent) is close to the percentage of MPs who served thirteen or more years among MPs who left Parliament from 1900 through 1974, 55 percent. This percentage is an entirely independent estimate based on Rush's data on length of parliamentary service (1979, p. 91).

19. Linz 1972, p. 386. His case on the discontinuity between the Spanish political elites before and after Primo de Rivera is based on comparisons with the Weimar republic—as summarized above—and with post-World War II Italy. Analyzing several different indicators he showed that there was more continuity between pre- and postfascism Italian political elites—in spite of the longer interval and the war—than in Spain between the constitutional monarchy and the second republic.

20. According to Guidobono's data, this turnover is slightly higher, 72 percent. Guidobono does not report this figure; he presents three separate series of turnovers, 1950–84: for the Senate, representatives from Montevideo, and representatives from the rest of the country. The global numbers discussed here are easily computed using the appropriate weights (Guidobono 1986, pp. 158–159). Rial also reports separate turnover data for the 1984 election for the Senate and the lower chamber. According to his data the global 1984 turnover was 64 percent (Rial 1985, pp. 28–29). Thus, the turnover from Table 4.2 (66 percent) falls in between these independent results. The mean of all the estimates is 67 percent. Neither Guidobono nor Rial report the sources of their data.

21. Both Guidobono (1986, p. 159) and Rial (1985, p. 28) report an even lower turnover—33 percent—for the Senate.

22. At the sub-lema level the proauthoritarian Blancos fell from 18 percent of the party vote in 1971 to 3 percent in 1984, when they were unable to elect a representative, much less a senator. Within the Colorados the proauthoritarian strength fell from 56 percent of the party vote to 24 percent (Fabregat 1972, pp. 36–39; Rial 1985, p. 65).

23. This legislature was the *Consejo de Estado*, a rather rubber-stamp body with very rare moments of relative independence. One of its members, a conservative Colorado, became representative in the 1984 election. This discontinuity is equal to that observed by Linz between the political elites of Primo de Rivera's *Asamblea* (1927) and the first legislature of the second republic (1931): just 1 percent of the members returned to their seats (Linz 1987, p. 572).

24. In Uruguayan political jargon "leader" is a strong word. Most of the senators are leaders, but probably most parliamentarians would agree that many representatives, perhaps no less than a half of the chamber, are not. I have already argued that the legislature includes the upper stratum of the political elite. Thus, simply doubling the size of the legislature gives room enough to include many influential politicians who did not run this time or failed to get elected. The number of top leaders who do not run for parliament is very small (e.g., Líber Seregni, the leader of the Frente Amplio). Because of that 500 is indeed a very safe maximum estimate: twice the legislature is just 258 politicians. The number of military officers is the official figure, not an estimate. Finally, the number of civilian collaborators of the military is an estimate based upon the number of positions available, the number of years elapsed, and a relatively low (estimated) turnover.

5. The 1984 Election: Changes

1. It might be argued that a better indicator for the proauthoritarian regime vote within the Colorados in the 1971 election is the vote for the (failed) project of constitutional reform aiming to allow presidential reelection. Pacheco sought a reelection not allowed by the Constitution. He brought a constitutional reform to a plebiscite but did not obtain the votes needed to pass. The reform, however, obtained more votes than Bordaberry. These votes, which were not necessarily Colorados, amounted to 72 percent of the Colorado vote. Thus, Bordaberry's voters were the hard-core Pachequistas willing to vote the candidate their leader had endorsed, and the 56 percent mentioned above is a conservative estimate of the Colorado support for proauthoritarian leaders in 1971.

2. The most useful data compilations for the 1971, 1982, and 1984 elections are Fabregat (1972), Venturini (1984), and Rial (1985) respectively. These are the data sources used in this section.

3. The error in the estimates of the electoral strength of Blanco proauthoritarian fractions is opposite to the equivalent error for the Colorados. These are not conservative estimates, but too generous. Important backers of Aguerrondo's candidacy were against the coup since its first day. Even though less clearly, the error goes in the same direction in the *elecciones internas*. For analytical purposes, however, it is important to compare pro- and antiauthoritarian fractions defined on the same basis in both general elections (1971 and 1984) and within both traditional parties. The only way of doing so—short of a specific research—is defining broad fractions on the basis of presidential candidates.

4. Agreeing with this view Rial (1985) subtitled his essay on the 1984 election "A triumph of the center."

5. As so many important details of this history, this point cannot be discussed here as carefully as it deserves. Most observers, however, agree with this contention. To quote only one of them: "even though the political perspective and strategy of the Frente Amplio and the Tupamaros [the guerrilla movement] opposed each other, we never made a clear distinction among them. The Frente Amplio's leadership is responsible for that" (Bruschera 1986, p. 79). Bruschera is a particularly well-qualified witness and direct participant in the events: he was elected as Frentista representative in 1971; he was one of the Frente's founders.

6. This criticism includes my own previous work, e.g., González (1983).

7. The scale was a standard ten-point version. The question on self-placement was followed by a set of questions asking for the placement of all the parties which won parliamentary representation and all the fractions within each of the three main *lemas* which obtained more than five percent of their *lema*'s vote. This meant seventeen questions: one for each of the four *lemas*, four Colorado fractions, four Blanco fractions, and the five Frentista groups. The same card was used in these questions.

8. This is a strict definition of overlapping. With other, more inclusive definitions there is some overlap, albeit very small, even between Colorados and Frentistas. But it is a significant fact that comparing averages for all of the methods above does show overlap between the traditional parties and not between them and the Frente.

9. On purely geometrical terms, if two distributions have equal shape but one of the areas doubles the other, then a linear relationship as the distance between left and right wings varies according to the factor 1.4 (the square root of 2).

10. For example, the French data presented by Cayrol, Parodi, and Ysmal (1973, p. 84) shows that the dispersion of gaullistes and républicaines indépendants was relatively similar to that of Colorados and Blancos. The comparison is imperfect, though, because they present their results using a seven-point scale.

11. Cayrol et al. (1973, p. 84). They studied the French representatives elected in June 1968, just after the events of May. This makes their data even more impressive, because their interviewees were elected in the conservative backlash that followed May 1968.

12. Converse and Pierce (1986); they interviewed a sample of candidates in 1967, many of whom were elected, and small samples of voters from the same constituencies. They did follow up interviews in 1968 and 1969. This is one of the very few studies which compares data on these matters both at the elite and mass-public levels.

13. It is interesting to note that this centrifugal countertendency is not present in the Blanco right wing.

14. Aberbach, Putnam, and Rockman (1981, pp. 116–117). More systematic references to the relevant literature may be found in Lijphart (1981, pp. 30–33). Sartori also provides a concise review (1982, pp. 254–256).

15. Gamma -.68; the sign is negative because the two variables are ordered in opposite directions.

16. Both in terms of attitudes and historical record.

17. The difference between the self-placement means corresponding to the sixth and seventh categories is in the wrong direction, even though it amounts to just

one percentile of the scale. The same is true for the first and second categories as well; however, not only is the difference also small (two percentiles), but the first mean is computed on just two respondents.

18. Gamma .41.

19. The equation regressed self-placement on the role of the state in the economy and egalitarianism. R squared was .50 (and the multiple R .71). The correlation coefficients are equal to the Gammas reported above (-.68 with role of the state and .40 with egalitarianism). The unstandardized coefficients show the far more important effect of the role of the state (-.76) than of egalitarianism (.19).

20. The dispersion of the judgments on each party's position could be an indicator. Recent or still in progress displacements along the scale would make sound judgments more difficult, increasing the frequence of disagreements. Thus, higher standard deviations for each party's average position would suggest more displacement along the scale. The data shows that the standard deviation of the judgments on the position of the Colorados is slightly higher: 1.64 vs. 1.42 for the Blancos, suggesting that the Colorados changed more than the Blancos. But this seems to be a result of rather consistently different judgments within each party on the position of the Colorados: when analyzing separately the judgments of each party's legislators on the positions of Blancos and Colorados, the standard deviations of the judgments on the Blancos are higher than for the Colorados. The standard deviations of Frentista opinions are .72 for the Colorados and 1.15 for the Blancos; the standard deviations of Colorado opinions are .75 on themselves and 1.17 on the Blancos, and the standard deviations of the Blanco opinions are 1.13 on the Colorados and 1.13 on themselves as well. Thus, within each party the opinions are more dispersed on the Blancos than on the Colorados, except within the Blancos, where they are equally dispersed. This would suggest that the Blancos changed more than the Colorados.

21. It is not by chance, then, that the election with the lowest turnover since 1950 was precisely 1971 (Guidobono 1986, p. 159), even though this election witnessed the birth of the Frente Amplio and the Blanco displacement towards the center of the political spectrum. The 1971 Senate turnover, in particular, was astonishingly low: just 3 percent.

22. All of this needed the cement of strong party identifications, of course, but this has been indeed the case in Uruguay, as noted above.

6. A Polarized and More Fragmented Party System

1. Between 1985 and 1990 about one hundred surveys conducted in Montevideo by Equipos Consultores Asociados have always found that about 85 percent of interviewees do self-position themselves in the left-right scale. Other independent research has also found similar results on this point and, more generally, on the profiles of the answers studied here: CELADU (1988), on an urban national survey conducted in June, 1987, with the technical support of the U.S.-based National Democratic Institute and NRIAA, and Filgueira et al. (1989), on the basis of a Montevidean survey conducted in November, 1987.

2. Many studies conducted after the present survey (March, 1985) have consistently shown that the level of answers obtained in the whole of the urban country are the same as those reported here. In particular, a survey conducted four-and-a-half years after this one—in November, 1989, very close to the second national elections of the democratic restoration—found exactly the same level of answers as 1985 (86 percent) in both Montevideo and the rest of the urban national population; the main results of that survey are summarized in Chapter 9 below. Since that sample covered about 75 percent of all voters, truly national figures cannot be far from those reported above. The CELADU survey quoted in the preceding footnote leads to the same conclusion. In fact, the answers of the rural population to this and other political questions are probably similar to those of urban residents in the Interior of the country.

3. At least this is what recent data suggest. Latin American publics are heterogeneous in this regard. Even within the relatively affluent Southern Cone nations there are large differences: Chileans are about as well acquainted with the left-right dimension as Uruguayans (Huneeus 1987, p. 163), but Argentinians (Catterberg and Braun 1989) and Brazilians (according to IDESP/Datafolha data; personal communication from Judith Muszynski) are even less familiar with it than U.S. citizens.

4. Putnam (1976, pp. 115–121). Elites are called consensual when the inter-party distances at the elite level are smaller than those at the middle elite's, and these, in turn, are smaller than at the mass-public level. Elites are called coalescent when inter-party distances at the elite level are smaller than at any of the other two levels and when those at the mass-public level are also smaller than at the middle elite's.

5. Moreover, this is also true considering the fractions presented in Table 6.1, not merely the wings. The dispersion of self-placements of all Blanco voters is smaller than the dispersion of all other fractions and *lemas* except for the relatively small Flores Silva's fraction, which has the smallest standard deviation of all the reported fractions, 1.07, and the even smaller Democracia Cristiana, 1.29.

6. In this sense the Colorado and Frentista wings look quite similar. The Colorado total is larger than the Frente's because the Colorado wings have more separation between them than the Frentes'.

7. Ortiz's voters seem farther to the right, as Table 6.1 shows, even though the reported average is based on six voters; but in Montevideo they simply do not count—Ortiz obtained just a 5.9 per thousand of the Montevidean vote. In Montevideo the Blanco right wing is Lacalle. In the Interior both leaders had the same strength.

8. I suspect that some of the legislators would argue that the present data simply show that Lacalle himself and his voters are far apart on the left-right scale, and that their answers concerned Lacalle, not his voters. But this, I think, misses the central point: what matters is the signals he sends to his voters, not his "true" position in the scale, whatever it may be. His voters respond to those signals. Another objection to my remark could be that the legislators' judgments were national, not restricted to Montevideo, and as a consequence they reflected the situation in the Interior as well. But this objection could be correct for Ortiz, who obtained enough votes in the Interior to become Senator, and almost none in Montevideo. Lacalle's electoral strength in Montevideo—in relative terms—was comparable to Pacheco's

or Sanguinetti's among the Colorados, and about the same as the Blanco majority. Why, then, does the error appear restricted to just his case?

9. Converse and Pierce (1986, p. 132). Discussing tentative explanations for this pattern, they recalled "the classic McClosky . . . findings that the issue positions of party elites turn out to be more extreme than is characteristic of their own party's rank and file. From this point of view, the centrist preference observed in the self-locations of the French rank and file may well reflect no more than a simple recognition by the party sympathizer that this is true. The adherent finds the left-right Coloration of his particular party to be quite palatable, but he is also aware that his party leaders are more vociferous in their policy positions than it would occur to him to be. Therefore he codes them as a shade more extreme than he feels he himself is" (ibid., pp. 132–133). This reasoning does not apply in the Uruguayan case because elites are always to the left (not more extreme, to the left and to the right) of the mass public. McClosky's findings do not apply in Uruguay either, for they describe a competitive elite, whereas the Uruguayan elite is coalescent—or even consensual. On the other hand, this kind of explanation seems to me a step forward in the correct direction, because it does not rely on specific aspects of French political culture and history alone, as their discussion of the leftist bias of elites did. Needless to say, I am not suggesting that specific aspects of French history have nothing to do in the explanation of those patterns. The point is that there are more general, nonspecifically French aspects in them. This does not preclude the possibility for French history to have a large share in the shaping of these very "nonspecifically French" aspects. After all, the French Revolution had many consequences that certainly are not specifically French.

10. The less cautious view on the other parties may well reflect a more adversarial spirit. This is the meaning, after all, of pushing other parties towards the extremes of the scale whereas one's own is seen more to the center than the position the voters of other parties assign to it.

11. There is one exception: the small Izquierda Democrática Independiente, which elected only one representative. But the IDI is a recent coalition of tiny groups.

12. The differences in the percentages of no answers are related neither to the size nor to the position in the scale of the evaluated fractions. Among the Blancos the fractions the position of which was most visible were Ferreira's and Ortiz's, i.e., the leftmost (and biggest) and the rightmost (and smallest) of Blanco fractions. Among the Frentistas they were the small Democracia Cristiana, Democracia Avanzada, and Batalla's fraction.

13. This point was already present in the discussion following the comparison of the three indicators at the elite's level. I think it is true at the mass-public level as well. The "centrist preference" found at the voters' level through these comparisons is no less relevant than the leftist bias of the elites tapped through the same procedure.

14. The U.S., Switzerland, West Germany, Austria, Belgium, United Kingdom, The Netherlands, Spain, France, Italy, and Finland. The data were collected in the mid-1970s except for Spain; the Spanish survey was conducted in 1979. On average, then, I will compare the Uruguayan results with data ten years older. Nevertheless, all the available evidence suggests that these profiles change little in the

short and medium run. Sartori (1982, p. 297) presents Italian data covering a seven-year period that show little change—and practically no change at all for the larger parties.

15. The third measure they used, ordinal similarity, refers to "the extent to which the distribution of any two groups of partisans across the left-right dimension differs ordinally"; it is "equal to the proportion of pairs of partisans (of any two groups) that are 'tied' or in the 'wrong' order" (Sani and Sartori 1983, p. 321). It may be easily seen that given two distributions A and B the similarity of A with respect to B is not equal to the similarity of B with respect to A. This is an undesirable characteristic for the present purpose; besides, the measure did not add any particular insight of its own to Sani and Sartori's study other than a further corroboration of what the other measures could establish by themselves. Because of that the present analysis is based on the other two measures. In fact, in a later version of the same paper (even though published in Italian before the English original) Sartori himself dropped the similarity measure.

16. Not every definition of *closeness* satisfies (i) above; the definition of "ordinal similarity" quoted in the preceding footnote provides a good example of this. Regarding (ii) above, if A is close to B and B to C, whether A is close to C or not is an empirical matter, as will be seen below. We might well have a "starred" configuration in which parties X, Y, and Z are "close" to a central party C but not to each other—thus not forming a family. If A is indeed close to C, then A, B, and C do form a family, or are part of a larger family.

17. But not exactly in the same sense as in The Netherlands. Sartori analyzes the results of a standard feelings thermometer towards clergymen; this discriminates between lay and religious-oriented persons, not between different denominations. In The Netherlands both distinctions—between lay and religious persons and between different denominations—are involved, because there is a lay party and three other parties associated to different denominations, whereas in Finland only the first matters. With regard to these two countries the discussion above follows Sartori's (1982, pp. 274–276) in his comparative analysis of the religious dimension.

18. Lijphart (1980, p. 299). Inglehart and Sigjanski (1976) argue that Swiss politics must be understood in the framework of a three-dimensional space. Two of them are the left-right and religious-secular dimensions; the third is a cosmopolitan-traditional dimension: the Farmers are "traditional" and the Radicals "cosmopolitan." This is, then, an alternative explanation that leads to the same conclusion in the present matter. Sani and Sartori's view would seem to mildly support, if any, the region-language view: to them Switzerland appears "characterized by very little in competition or unique [on] sui generis grounds: namely, its thoroughgoing decentralization and, indeed, *dispersion at the cantonal level*." (Sani and Sartori 1983, p. 333; emphasis added).

19. The labels are left (positions 1 and 2 of the scale), center-left (3 and 4), center (5 and 6), center-right (7 and 8), and right (9 and 10). In this labelling Italian Neo-Fascists are a center-right party, and there does not exist any party of the right among their data. This seems a counterintuitive result. The alternative labelling—

extreme left, left, center, right and extreme right—also has its shortcomings, however. Here Sani and Sartori's original practice is followed.

20. The Finnish KES, of the second family, is close to both the Finnish and Italian Liberals and to the Swiss PAB, of the first family. Neither the Italian DC nor the Spanish UCD (of the second family) are close to any of the parties of the other family. The two families are thus linked by the Colorados and the KES.

21. Religion is important to Republicans in the U.S., but to the same extent as to Democrats; this importance, then, reflects a trait of American society common to both parties, not a characteristic that distinguishes between them.

22. With regard to British Liberals and religion the same remark as that on U.S. Republicans may be made.

23. Strictly speaking, since 1962 there is no way of counting separately the Communist votes, because they appear mixed in "coalitions," the Fidel first and then Democracia Avanzada since 1984. In practice, however, all available data suggest that the voters of such coalitions are basically Communist voters. In spite of their names, then, the "coalitions" would not differ from the practice of Italian Communists of inviting distinguished independents, close to but not members of the party, to run for office within the Communist slates.

24. The means are similar (distances of .05 or less in all cases), but the profiles are different: none of the overlaps satisfy the requisites of the definition above. The Italian Communists are the most akin to the Spaniards by both counts: a distance of merely .02, but an overlap of .82 that falls short of the minimum level (.85) required for "closeness."

25. Were we to stiffen the requisites for "closeness" these conclusions would remain. If we define closeness as a distance of .03 or less and an overlap of .90 or more, the following results would be found: (i) the Colorado families boil down to just one that includes the Italian Liberals and the Finnish KES; (ii) the Blanco family is likewise limited to the British Liberals and the Swiss Independents; (iii) the "strong" socialist family—including the PSOE and excluding the PSI—remains intact, and (iv) the Communist family disappears as such, the PCI alone remaining close to the Frente Amplio left wing. The global picture would still be the same: the Colorados and Blancos as the two wings of European liberalism, and so on.

26. Sartori (1976, pp. 121–122). The Unión Cívica obtained 2.5 percent of the national vote, and its two diputados were too few to have any decisional weight given the relative size of the other parties.

27. That is, the argument holds because the distant wing is to the right of the party; the left wing could not play this "captive" role. The exceptional character of Colorado fractionalization most probably involves special risks for the party: its perceived lack of consistency makes it more vulnerable to desertions, both at voter and leader levels, than the remaining parties of the system. According to this argument desertions would be more likely at its noncaptive end, i.e., from its left wing. This conclusion agrees with the facts, as will be seen below.

28. At any rate the point is essentially irrelevant for, were we to leave the PS outside any of these families, then it would become a nonrelevant party—we should have to drop it from the analysis. The PS obtained just 3.2 percent of the national vote

in 1984. Within the Frente's left wing, DA and IDI alone—without the PS—obtained 7.4 percent of the national vote in that election, most of it (6.0 percent) DA votes.

29. It might still be asked why Batalla and the Christian Democrats were "close" but separate organizations, and the same question holds for DA and IDI. With regard to the first question, the difference lies in religion. Though it is true that religion has never been a really important factor in Uruguayan politics, the Democracia Cristiana is the party of most of the Catholic left, whereas Batalla's party inherited the masonic, anti-clerical traditions of the Colorados—specifically from the batllista sector of the Colorado Party. This is more than enough to explain their separate coexistence. Regarding Democracia Avanzada (the Communists and their associates) and the IDI, the latter was a transitional coalition of small groups (it disappeared before the 1989 election), a microcosmos which somehow managed to reproduce in a very small space many of the conflicts of the old left.

30. Though probably neither part would accept its respective label. On the one hand, the term "social democrat" was usually despised within the Uruguayan left, following the revolutionary traditions of the socialist movement, even by those who for all practical purposes were indeed social democrats. On the other hand, the Communists have been proud of their name so far. They also accept their more general socialist inheritance, but their own identity is "Communists." Main leaders of the party strongly disagreed publicly with the recent change of name of the Italian—now ex-Communists.

31. Though no longer so at least from 1989 onwards, as will be seen below.

32. As it is well known, the left-right dimension is also commonly called "ideological dimension" in the literature. Maybe it is not a perfect labelling, but it is difficult to find a better term for the contents of the left-right dimension.

33. Sani and Sartori (1983) showed that democratic stability is not directly linked to the fragmentation of party systems (i.e., to the number of relevant parties), but to their polarization instead. There are other cases of central questions whose explanation in the past was couched in terms of purely structural characteristics that later were best understood in terms of both structural and ideological traits—as DeSwaan's (1973) demonstration (against earlier "minimal winning coalition" theories) that the formation of coalitions also depends on the ideological "connectedness" of the partners.

34. This is so because its usefulness as an information-processing device is greater in larger party systems. It should play "a relatively prominent role where there is a multiplicity of salient political alternatives [. . . and where this is not so] it will not play an important role. Nor is it needed much where there are only two alternatives: such a choice already is uni-dimensional, with no need for further abstraction" (Inglehart and Klingemann 1976, p. 246).

7. Voters and the Changing Party System

1. Aguiar (1984) presented an original and elaborate version of this argument according to which class and sectoral cleavages are indeed important between elections. In his view, the most important source of instability in the Uruguayan political

system is precisely the lack of congruence between the factors deciding election outcomes and those at work the rest of the time.

2. Ures 1972, pp. 9 and ff. His work was based on a pre-election survey conducted in November, 1971.

3. He did not mention, however, the differences between Biles's and Graceras's analyses.

4. "Perfil del votante montevideano según partido," *Búsqueda*, November 14, 1984. The analysis was based on a Gallup poll conducted in October, 1984.

5. Real de Azúa wrote illuminating pages on the reasons for these traits of Uruguayan elites (Real de Azúa 1961; 1984, especially pp. 41–43 and 90–91).

6. Perón could have not been Uruguayan, not merely because of the relative size of the working class in the two countries in the early 1940s. From the perspective of Lipset's ideas on American "exceptionalism" I think that an even more fruitful comparison is that between the party systems of Chile and Uruguay. I sketched some preliminary ideas on this elsewhere (González 1985b).

7. Besides those general considerations, the fractionalization of Uruguayan major parties further contributed to their catch-all character.

8. Biles 1972, pp. 220–221. Although I think that Biles's data on this point is rather preliminary and unconclusive because of some methodological problems.

9. It also suggests that at least in this regard it is not a drawback to study a solely Montevidean sample but the quickest way to assess the changes.

10. Since the mean of percent differences (without taking absolute values) is always zero.

11. The average of absolute values of percent differences with respect to the total sample distribution by sex for each of the four relevant parties were 6, 1, 3 and 12 (Colorados, Blancos, and the Frentes' right and left wings respectively).

12. Young voters are eleven points overrepresented in the FA right wing and not at all in the PSOE (that means an 11-point gap following the trend), and old voters are ten points more underrepresented in the FA right wing than in the PSOE—also following the trend. The comparisons are based on the findings of Chapter 5 concerning political families. The Spanish data are those reported by Linz (1980, p. 156).

13. The 1979 Spanish data shows a faint trace of such a relationship, with the signs of the percent differences corresponding to the UCD and PCE distributions being the same that those of the Colorados and FA left wing. But the differences themselves vary between two and three points, whereas their average in Uruguay is eleven points. The signs of the percent differences corresponding to the PSOE do not agree with those of the FA right wing, but with the Blancos instead.

14. The average percent differences (absolute values) are 1.7 for each of the traditional parties, and 4.4 for each of the FA wings.

15. Gallup Uruguay, *Indice Gallup de Opinión Pública* 349 (November 1984); "Perfil del votante montevideano según Partido," *Búsqueda*, November 14, 1984, based on Gallup data as well, and an interview with César Aguiar, "Las elecciones vistas por un sociólogo," *Las Bases*, December 9, 1984, in which Aguiar discusses pre-election data from surveys conducted by Equipos Consultores.

16. Relatively small sample sizes often contributed to this, as well as other misleading manners of analyzing the data.

17. "Comparación de las encuestas con el resultado real," *Búsqueda*, November 29, 1984.

18. That is, I am referring to generations in Mannheim's sense. Graceras (1977) centered his work in age-related differences, but not in this sense, and his conclusions are also different to those presented here.

19. Putnam (1973, pp. 64–65) analyzes the methodological problems involved in this discussion in a concise manner. Differences "across age cohorts in data gathered at a single point in time are, of course, notoriously ambiguous," because they may result from different processes. Life-cycle models assume "that the differences in the dependent variable are a function of age . . . [as people] become older and more experienced, their attitudes and perspective change." Generational models are those that link cohort differences to their different collective experiences—normally referring to a particular, forming period within their life span (Lipset 1983a, pp. 279–280). Natural-selection models, finally, are those according to which persons having a particular trait tend "disproportionately to leave the population early," and accordingly older cohorts show a lower frequency of that trait.

20. Consider the voters of the three main *lemas* alone, and let us assume first that the net volatility between the 1971 and 1984 elections among those who voted in both elections is zero—i.e., changes at the individual level cancel each other. If we consider the voters in the 1984 election who were over 30 years old, discarding younger voters, then we should find that the distribution of the remaining voters in the sample is that of the 1971 election. These assumptions simplify too much: it is likely that one "natural selection" process—death—affects the Colorados more than the Blancos, and the Blancos more than the Frentistas; the effect of international migrations is most probably exactly the opposite. Internal migrations add another problem. Whatever the case, the results of the exercise are as follows: the transformed 1984 sample is 28 percent Frentista (less than the 30 percent of 1971), 30 percent Blanco (the actual 1971 figure) and 42 percent Colorado (more than the 40 percent of 1971). If we are willing to assume that the error sources mentioned above "cancel each other," then about 7 percent of the Frentista voters in 1971 deserted to their right in 1984, the Blancos broke even (they won as many voters as they lost), and the Colorados were the net winners. In other words, this would suggest that the life-cycle effect would favor the conservatives, though the differences are small.

21. In 1942 the students in their first year of secondary education amounted to 11 percent of those who had been born twelve years before, in 1930. In 1961 the same indicator had risen to 43 percent. Data from Ministerio de Instrucción Pública y Previsión Social, *Informe sobre el estado de la educación en el Uruguay*, Montevideo, 1965.

22. Filgueira (1973, 1970) discusses the point and provides interesting data. According to Heintz (1970), in the 1960s Uruguay had reached the top level in his scale of structural imbalance between formal education and per capita income.

23. That state of affairs began to change after the 1985 democratic restoration, though it is too early to assess the consequences of those changes.

24. The literature on Uruguayan unions is extremely scarce. The most useful recent description is Rial's (1986a).

25. Gargiulo (1986, pp. 19–20) presents one of the most recent versions of this view. Errandonea and Costábile (1969) argued that the Uruguayan labor movement was "dualist," for rank and file saw the unions as an instrument for protecting their interests vis-à-vis employers, while their leaders regarded the unions essentially as a political tool. The "dualist" and "divided political personality" theses are not identical, but the first may be seen as an explanation of the second.

26. The party experienced an internal crisis in 1955; in that year it changed leadership and strategy—which has essentially been maintained since then. A very brief but interesting historical summary was published in *Búsqueda* (February 28, 1985): "La desproscripción del PCU: Una historia de 64 aõs y medio."

27. González (1986). The survey included about 800 interviews conducted in Montevideo by Equipos Consultores Asociados. "Unionized" workers were those whose working place was unionized, irrespective of whether they were members of the union or not. A more strict definition ("members of the union") produced similar results, though more favorable for the left.

28. In spite of its importance, however, these facts have not yet been fully recognized. As in the discussion presented in Section 7.1 on the class composition of the left vote, there has been a slow evolution in the scarce writings on this point. Cosse (1985, p. 106) pointed in the correct direction, though falling short of the actual extent of the changes, and his view has remained rather isolated.

29. The additive character of these effects also explains why educated workers vote the FA more than their less educated peers. In all the Scandinavian countries, for example, the opposite is true, but in Scandinavia the traditional political behavior of the workers is to support the left.

8. Political Elites and Democratic Stability

1. Sixteen percent of legislators disagreed with the statement that "democracy allows the present problems of Uruguay to be solved." The answers to this question exhibited important differences following party lines. Only 4 and 7 percent respectively of Colorado and Blanco legislators disagreed, but a full half of the legislators of each of the Frente Amplio wings did not agree with that statement. The traditional political elite shared an almost unanimous "don't rock the boat" attitude, whereas the left appeared sharply divided.

2. The indexes are formally similar: they may vary from 0 to 4, 0 and 1 being "low," 2 "middle," and 3 and 4 "high" values. The items of each dimension are moderately to strongly correlated to each other, as should be expected from different indicators of a single dimension.

3. On the grounds that such franchise was already in practice, though against the law, and that no harm had followed from that practice.

4. That is, what to do with the excesses of military and security personnel during the authoritarian regime. An amnesty law was passed after the completion of the field work of this research.

5. Legislators are moderately optimistic about the prospects of Uruguayan democracy. They were asked to rank the democratic stability of seven countries on a standard ten-point scale where 1 was the minimum and 10 the maximum; the question was repeated for each country separately. Uruguay ended in the middle of the group: its average score was 7.0, about as distant from Perú (4.6, the worst placed) as from West Germany (9.6, the best average). The other countries were Italy (8.7), Spain (8.6), Brazil (6.6), and Argentina (5.7).

6. Although the second ("non-traditional" two-partyism) was stated in neutral terms: it did not mention the identity of the parties which would exchange positions.

7. The reform which merely limits candidacies probably will not happen because it is too minor a change to obtain support outside the Colorados. In fact, given its rather scarce chances of success—which will be clear for politicians—most likely nobody will make the effort of seriously promoting such an idea.

8. Gamma is .85.

9. The closest is a construct defined on the basis of the four categories of Table 8.3 (Gamma is .64).

9. Political Structures and the Prospects for Democracy

1. Rama (1989) and Weschler (1990) provide differing views on the referendum on the amnesty for violators of human rights.

2. GNP per capita US$ 3,477 in 1980, US$ 3,863 in 1981, and just US$ 2,736 in 1989, though these figures overstate the point because of the undervaluation of the U.S. dollar against the Uruguayan peso until 1982. In billions of Uruguayan pesos of 1978, total GNP went down from 35.5 in 1981 to 29.8 in 1984, its lowest value during this period, and then climbed again to 34.7 in 1989. Real wages in 1989 were 7.4 percent below their 1981 level.

3. Both the vice president views and the economist's remarks in *Búsqueda*, November 26, 1987.

4. Since the mid-1950s investment and production grew in a significant manner only during the quinquennium 1976–80, that is, during the authoritarian regime. The military themselves, though, ended that bonanza in a crash whose consequences have not yet been cancelled out.

5. The evolution of the desencanto during Sanguinetti's five-year term is discussed in Canzani (1990); González and Rius (1989) probe some of its aspects.

6. González Risotto (1990), Mieres (1990), and Perelli and Rial (1990) examine the 1989 election results.

7. Though this does not imply that the number of lists will go on increasing indefinitely; the process must stop somewhere, and it has already reached fantastic levels. The link does imply that within the present electoral legislation we should not expect any significant, sustained decrease of party fractionalization. The data reported above are Vernazza's (1990), p. 37.

8. During a comparable period in Spain (1977–82) because of both its length and the surrounding political circumstances, the national average changed .7 units of the scale (from 5.5 to 4.8) towards the left (Montero and Torcal 1990, p. 123).

9. As a result of those changes, the two traditional parties appear now as parties of the center-right, the only party of the center is the New Space, and the Broad Front remains a party of the center-left. In the process all four actors swapped "political families," as defined in Chapter 6, to their right. In fact, each party in 1989 is "close," strictly speaking, to the position its nearest neighbor to the right occupied in 1985: the Frente 1989 to the Nuevo Espacio (i.e., its old right wing) 1985; the Nuevo Espacio 1989 to the Blancos 1985, and the Blancos 1989 to the Colorados 1985. The Colorados 1989 went out of the 1985 field. "Political families" changed accordingly.

10. Estimates based on data from the press and from Perelli and Rial (1990).

11. The first process, the anti-Colorado *desencanto* was discussed at the beginning of this section; González (1988) probes in greater detail the reasons of the Colorado weakening in the 1989 election. The second process—the weakening of both traditional parties, summarized in Tables 9.1 and 9.2—has been a recurrent theme throughout this book, particularly in Chapter 3, section 2, Chapter 5, section 4, and Chapter 7, section 3. The third process, the relative success of the former Frente's left wing within the left, is partly a result of its stronger social roots and a better mix of resources, as seen in Chapter 7, and partly a result of a very good campaign headed in Montevideo by a strong candidate, Tabaré Vázquez. The sources quoted in footnote 6 above agree on this view of the Frente's campaign.

12. Needless to say, those were the dominant currents which in the end shaped the net result of the displacement of all voters. The survey quoted above also asked about vote in 1984, and the cross-classification of voters according to vote in 1984 and intended vote in 1989 leads to the same conclusion. As for the new voters, most of them voted the left, maintaining the same pattern already seen in 1984.

13. Furthermore, it is difficult to see how the present level of ideological tension could be packed within a two-party format—it would require an extraordinarily big vacuum in the center.

14. Any further increase of the left's share of the vote, which is likely, would most probably increase fragmentation. This may be accompanied by a change towards a more catch-all condition. The situation described in Chapter 7 (the left as "the party of the working class," if any deserved that label) would have been thus a transitional stage resulting from the fact that the expansion of the electorate of the left at first is concentrated in certain social groups—those within which it has a certain "comparative advantage." Later, however, this must change for the parties of the left to succeed. Przeworski (1985) noted that even during the early history of European social democratic and socialists parties—with a far larger working class to recruit from—there was a trade-off between class "purity" and real chances of winning elections. More recently it has been noted that in 1985, after considerable growth, the electoral base of the Italian Communists was more catch-all than in the sixties (Mannheimer and Sani 1987, p. 69). Keck (1986, pp. 496 and ff.) underscored the same point when pondering the future prospects of the Brazilian Workers' Party.

In Uruguay, the displacement towards the right of the voters of the New Space and the Broad Front which accompanied the electoral growth of the left suggests that this process may be already underway.

15. Further discussions of ballotage are thus superfluous, but it seems clear to me that ballotage at the presidential level alone, leaving all the rest of the system as it is now, would simply increase the dangers for democracy. For exactly the same arguments would still be valid, but in addition the president might belong to the party that did not even win a plurality, and the pressures for delivery and presidential legitimacy itself would be higher than in the present system, since the president would be elected by an absolute majority. The potential for conflict is definitely higher under those conditions than in the present system.

16. It thus contributes to a growing body of literature focusing on the presidential institution and its eventual shortcomings. Some of the works that are directly linked to the present argument are: Linz (1990b) on the general terms of the problem; Mainwaring on Latin American presidentialism (1990a) and on Brazil (1990b) and Valenzuela on Chile (1990 and previous versions as well), which provides a particularly interesting term of comparison for the Uruguayan case. Linz and Valenzuela are editing a volume that will present theoretical papers and case studies.

17. Thus, the lack of "responsible party government" so often criticized as a major deficiency of the U.S. system becomes, from this perspective, a politico-structural factor contributing to democratic stability. The U.S. also has the "right" electoral system in this regard.